Poor Representation

Tens of millions of Americans live in poverty, but this book reveals that they receive very little representation in Congress. While a burgeoning literature examines the links between political and economic inequality, this book is the first to comprehensively examine the poor as a distinct constituency. Drawing on three decades of data on political speeches, party platforms, and congressional behavior, Miler first shows that, contrary to what many believe, the poor are highly visible to legislators. Yet, the poor are grossly underrepresented when it comes to legislative activity, both by Congress as a whole and by individual legislators, even those who represent high-poverty districts. To take up their issues in Congress, the poor must rely on a few surrogate champions who have little district connection to poverty but view themselves as broader advocates and often see poverty from a racial or gender-based perspective.

KRISTINA C. MILER'S research focuses on political representation in the US Congress, particularly how different constituents are represented in the policymaking process. Her previous book, *Constituency Representation in Congress: The View from Capitol Hill* (Cambridge, 2010), examined legislators' perceptions of their constituents, and won the Alan Rosenthal Prize from the American Political Science Association. Her research has been funded by the National Science Foundation, the Hewlett Foundation, the Democracy Fund, and the Dirksen Congressional Center. She holds a BA from the College of William and Mary and a PhD from the University of Michigan.

Poor Representation

Congress and the Politics of Poverty in the United States

KRISTINA C. MILER

University of Maryland

CAMBRIDGE
UNIVERSITY PRESS

CAMBRIDGE
UNIVERSITY PRESS

University Printing House, Cambridge CB2 8BS, United Kingdom

One Liberty Plaza, 20th Floor, New York, NY 10006, USA

477 Williamstown Road, Port Melbourne, VIC 3207, Australia

314–321, 3rd Floor, Plot 3, Splendor Forum, Jasola District Centre, New Delhi – 110025, India

79 Anson Road, #06–04/06, Singapore 079906

Cambridge University Press is part of the University of Cambridge.

It furthers the University's mission by disseminating knowledge in the pursuit of education, learning, and research at the highest international levels of excellence.

www.cambridge.org
Information on this title: www.cambridge.org/9781108473507
DOI: 10.1017/9781108562386

First published 2018

Printed in the United States of America by Sheridan Books, Inc.

A catalogue record for this publication is available from the British Library.

Library of Congress Cataloging-in-Publication Data
NAMES: Miler, Kristina C., 1974– author.
TITLE: Poor representation : Congress and the politics of poverty in the United States / Kristina C. Miler, University of Maryland.
DESCRIPTION: New York, NY : Cambridge University Press, [2018] | Includes bibliographical references and index.
IDENTIFIERS: LCCN 2018010100 | ISBN 9781108473507 (hardback) | ISBN 9781108461818 (pbk.)
SUBJECTS: LCSH: Poor–Government policy–United States. | Poor–Political activity–United States. | United States. Congress. | Representative government and representation–United States. | United States–Social policy.
CLASSIFICATION: LCC HV95 .M46 2018 | DDC 362.5/05610973–dc23
LC record available at https://lccn.loc.gov/2018010100

ISBN 978-1-108-47350-7 Hardback
ISBN 978-1-108-46181-8 Paperback

For my father

Contents

Figures

Tables

Acknowledgments

Over the course of researching and writing this book, I have been fortunate to enjoy the support of colleagues and friends at the University of Maryland. The early stages of the research were hastened by encouragement from Frances Lee and David Karol, as well as participation in the Congress and History Conference, which provided valuable early feedback. I thank Frances for her keen eye and perspective. I could always count on her for constructive comments, and the book is immeasurably better for her counsel. David and Ric Uslaner also graciously read and commented on the manuscript, and their insightful feedback has improved the book as well. I thank Jim Gimpel for his support and expertise on geographic analyses. Stella Rouse and the Center for American Politics and Citizenship at the University of Maryland provided much appreciated support through the undergraduate research program. I also thank Irwin Morris for his assistance and for engaging conversations about inequality. In addition, I appreciate the graduate students who helped with parts of this project: Joon Chang, Charlie Hunt, Nathan Lovin, and Katti McNally. My undergraduate research assistants, Arlynnell Dickson, Daryan Ver Ploeg, and Paige Padmore, provided much valued help as well.

I am also grateful for the helpful comments and support of Larry Evans, Mike Minta, Ellie Powell, Ron Rapoport, Eric Schickler, Wendy Schiller, Tracy Sulkin, and Sean Theriault. Their feedback on various parts of this project has strengthened the book and made writing it much more enjoyable. I also note my appreciation of the late Barbara Sinclair, who influenced my research and that of so many congressional scholars. A special debt of gratitude is due to Rick Hall. As both a mentor and friend, he is unflinchingly generous and supportive. His thoughtful and challenging comments undoubtedly made this book better. Moreover, I'm grateful for his encouragement to pursue big questions and to take the time to try to do them justice.

At Cambridge, I have had the pleasure of working with Sara Doskow. She has been everything one could hope for in an editor. From the beginning she championed the project, provided helpful guidance, and shepherded the manuscript through to completion. I am grateful for her support. I also thank the reviewers for their enthusiasm for the project. Their insights and suggestions have made the book better in numerous ways, and I appreciate their helpful comments.

The motivation for this book was sparked a long time ago, and was fostered by growing up in a house where politics and inequality were discussed. I thank my mother, Veronica, for her ongoing support and her example of compassion and perseverance. I also thank Gary and Norma Allee for being my second wellspring of support. Together my parents' and in-laws' belief in the proverbial underdog have shaped me and this project. As I spent the last few years thinking about the poor and their role in American politics, I am glad to have had their perspectives.

Most of all, I am grateful to my family for bearing with me through the late nights, early mornings, and constant presence of my laptop. I thank my daughters, Camille and Serena, who provided (mostly welcome) distractions and (always welcome) encouragement. Their patience is much appreciated, and I promise to keep better hours next time. I thank my husband, Todd, for his unflagging support for the project. He experienced with me all of the ups and downs of turning an idea for a book into an actual book. He endured countless conversations and read many drafts, and yet still managed to bring enthusiasm and a fresh eye to the project. Without his unwavering support, this book would not have been possible. There is simply no one I'd rather have by my side.

Lastly, this book is dedicated to the memory of my father, Josef. He is dearly missed.

What about the Poor?

Today's politicians all embrace an increasingly popular storyline of the super-rich against everyone else. In the 2016 US presidential election, for instance, Hillary Clinton spoke frequently about creating an economy that works for "everyone, not just those at the top" and she criticized Donald Trump as an enemy of "the Little Guy" (Applebaum 2016). Bernie Sanders also talked about "working people" throughout his campaign as he championed those who are not "millionaires and billionaires" (Frizell 2016). For his part, Donald Trump declared in his inaugural address that elites had not "thought about the millions and millions of American workers that were left behind," and that "the wealth of our middle class has been ripped from their homes."

Social scientists invoke similar themes of inequality in ways that also are resonating with the broader public. Most illustrative is the rise to the bestseller list of Piketty's (2014) 700-page economic tome on wealth and inequality, *Capital in the Twenty-First Century*. Recent books by prominent political scientists on the concentration of power in American politics (Bartels 2008; Gilens 2012; Hacker and Pierson 2010, 2016; Mettler 2011, 2014) have also garnered attention outside academia, including from media outlets, both traditional (e.g., *New York Times*, NBC) and nontraditional (e.g., *The Daily Show*).

The first half of the inequality equation, the super-rich or "1 percent," is well understood. We are presented with eye-popping statistics about them, such as the fact that the four hundred richest people in America have more wealth than the bottom three-fifths of Americans (Collins and Hoxie 2015). Another prominent fact is that the top 1 percent holds over

40 percent of the nation's wealth (Saez and Zucman 2016).[1] Additionally, we are told that "the gap between the 'haves' and 'have nots' is widening," and are reminded that, because "the wealthy earned more, someone else in America had to get less" (Long 2016).

It is often less clear who this "someone else" is. It has become fashionable to consider the rest of society, the "have nots," as everyone but the top 1 percent. This is reflected in the Occupy Wall Street movement, which entered the national conversation in the fall of 2011 and coined the specific phrase "We are the 99 percent." In fact, the 99 percent catchphrase has been described by one commentator as being "part of our folklore" (Gitlin, quoted in Sanchez 2016). The phrase may be catchy, but "the rest of us" are far from an undifferentiated mass.

This conflation of everyone else is problematic because it obscures important political and economic differences among the non-super-rich. A family with a household income of $100,000 is much different from a family living at the poverty level, which is less than $25,000 for a family of four.[2] The family living on the brink of poverty confronts matters of subsistence every day. They care more about policies that directly affect their basic needs, whether that is Medicaid, the Earned Income Tax Credit (EITC), unemployment insurance, or school lunch programs. By contrast, the policies that affect the economic interests of middle-class families are very different: the mortgage–interest tax deduction, college savings plans, or Social Security.

When the 99 percent are differentiated, the focus tends to be on the "middle class" or some notion of the "average American." The middle class is central to American political discourse, and, along with apple pie and baseball, it is a rhetorical safe bet for politicians looking to appeal to "real" Americans (Soergel 2016). Politicians from both parties regularly invoke the middle class, as illustrated by then-candidate George W. Bush's budget plan, entitled the "Blueprint for the Middle Class" (Bruni 2000) and President Barack Obama's emphasis on "middle-class economics" during his reelection campaign (Farrington 2012). Part of the political appeal of the middle class is that it is both vague and inclusive. Indeed, most Americans identify as middle class, regardless of their objective

---

[1] This estimate from Saez and Zucman (2016) was widely reported in the media. Politifact has evaluated and classified it as "mostly true," which reflects disagreements among some economists, who estimate the top 1 percent's share to be closer to 34 percent (Bricker et al., 2016).

[2] The official poverty level in 2016 was $24,300 for a family of four, according to the US Department of Health and Human Services.

standing (Pew 2012, 2014). This myopia toward the middle class is reinforced in political science by median voter theory (Downs 1957), which elevates the voter in the middle as being decisive in determining election outcomes. The central tendency bias in psychology also tells us that humans tend to gravitate to the middle category (Poulton 1989), which is based, in part, on the implicit assumption that the middle is the most representative option. Together, these dynamics combine to reinforce the middle class as the primary "non-rich" segment of society when talking about politics.

However, this focus on the rich and middle class neglects those at the very bottom, and their distinctive needs and interests. This is not a small oversight. There are forty-six million people living in poverty in the United States, along with nearly fifteen million "near poor" just above the poverty line (Hokayem and Heggeness 2014).[3] This means that, on average, there are approximately 140,000 people in every congressional district who live in poverty or uncomfortably close to it. Furthermore, the American public believes in helping them: two-thirds of all Americans say that government should play a "major role" in helping people get out of poverty (Pew Research Center 2017). This makes the lack of attention to the poor all the more striking.

Political scientists also tend to overlook the poor. Indeed, just over a decade ago, an American Political Science Association Task Force (Jacobs and Skocpol 2005) called attention to the fact that inequality in general is understudied by political scientists. Its report lamented the combination of professional "hyperspecialization" and the tendency to avoid "normative questions about the extent and nature of democratic governance" (see also Jacobs and Soss 2010).

Since the Task Force's report, scholars have increasingly examined inequality in American politics and the advantages enjoyed by the wealthy, especially from the vantage point of public opinion (e.g., Bartels 2008; Ellis 2013; Ellis and Faricy 2011; Enns and Wlezien 2011; Gilens 2009, 2012; McCall 2013; Page and Jacobs 2009). Still other approaches focus on inequality and party polarization (e.g., Faricy 2015; McCarty, Poole, and Rosenthal, 2006, 2013) or state-level politics (Butler 2014;

[3] There is no official definition for the "near poor," but the US Census Bureau uses 125 percent of the poverty line to delineate this group (see Hokayem and Heggeness 2014). In 2016, a family of four would be considered "near poor" if the family's annual income was less than $30,375.

Flavin 2012a, 2015; Kelly and Witko 2012; Rigby and Wright 2011).[4] This reinvigorated study of inequality is an important development in political science, but there remain significant gaps in our knowledge, most notably when it comes to the poor and their voice in the lawmaking process. Thus, to all of the aforementioned discussions, I pose a simple but important question: what about the poor?

In this book, I investigate the twin questions of whether the poor receive adequate representation in Congress and by what means that representation occurs. I first examine what Congress as a whole does to represent the poor (collective representation), whether by taking up relevant bills, holding hearings, or passing legislation, particularly when poverty intensifies or spreads into more districts. I next examine whether legislators from districts with greater poverty do more to represent the poor. That is, do the poor receive the same dyadic representation as other constituents? Across both ways of thinking about representation, I find little evidence of congressional activity on behalf of the poor. Congress spends only about 1–2 percent of its time on poverty-related issues, and this effort remains low, even during periods of greater need. Perhaps most sobering is that legislators from districts with high poverty are not particularly active on poverty-related issues.

I then highlight surrogate representation, or the representation of constituents outside one's district, as the primary way the poor receive some representation. Some sympathetic lawmakers, particularly women and African Americans, are likely to see overlap between issues of concern to female or black constituents and issues that affect the poor. I find that they, along with certain partisans, are much more likely to put poverty-related issues on the congressional agenda, suggesting that greater diversity in Congress could elevate the representation of the poor. Yet surrogate representation affords no electoral accountability and is insufficient for getting legislation passed, which underscores the need for dyadic representation where the poor can be represented by "their" legislator. The 2016 election year saw a heightened awareness of left-behind constituents, which creates some optimism that legislators may begin to focus on poor constituents in their districts that they previously neglected. However, there is not yet evidence of major changes in legislative activity on Capitol Hill, leaving doubts that the representation of the poor will improve.

---

[4] See Faricy 2016 for an excellent review.

THE IMPORTANCE OF REPRESENTING THE POOR

Representing all constituents equally, including disadvantaged groups like the poor, is a foundational principle of representative democracy. There is widespread agreement among political scientists on the normative desirability of this benchmark of representative government. In more colloquial terms, the American public expects government, including Congress, to fulfill the promise of "government by the people, for the people." That the practice of democracy often falls short of the ideal does not diminish the importance of the goal, it only underlines the importance of efforts to bring practice closer to the democratic ideal.

Indeed, there are multiple reasons why the representation of the poor deserves more attention as part of the growing scholarship on inequality. The first is that the poor themselves are negatively affected by unequal representation. If Congress fails to consider the interests of the poor, then solutions to poverty are unlikely to be discussed, and few programs will be created to address it. Also, to the extent that Congress does take action, the resulting policies may not reflect the interests or needs of the poor. Both of these scenarios have direct, negative impacts on the lives of the poor.

Second, a failure to represent the poor can result in an incomplete and biased policy agenda. As Lindblom and Woodhouse argue: "When some important problems are not forcefully called to attention, then all of us are deprived of the opportunity to deliberate about them, deprived of the opportunity to reappraise our own judgements of what issues most deserve scarce time, attention, and funding" (1993, 147–8).[5] Space on the congressional agenda is limited, and the failure to engage problems (including those facing the poor) by debating them, or even by recognizing them as questions of public policy, can be consequential not only for the individuals affected, but for society in general (e.g., Bachrach and Baratz 1962, 1963; Baumgartner and Jones 1993; Jones and Baumgartner 2005; Kingdon 1984).

A third concern is that, when members of Congress do make poverty policy, they will do so without understanding its full implications (e.g., Baumgartner and Jones 1993, 2015; Jones 2001; Jones and Baumgartner 2005; Tetlock 2005; Tversky and Kahneman 1982). If the poor are not represented, then Congress will develop programs for the poor without

---

[5] As quoted in Schlozman, Verba, and Brady 2012.

the perspective, experiences, and input of the millions of Americans who
have first-hand experience with poverty. Such information is uniquely
valuable in order to combat poverty, but relevant policy decisions are
unlikely to reflect the interests of constituents who do not have a seat at
the table (Miler 2010). As a result, Congress may continue to pursue
ineffective anti-poverty policies that reflect the "extreme allegiance to the
status quo" in congressional decision-making (Jones and Baumgartner
2005, 54). Moreover, Congress may miss opportunities to innovate and
improve how poverty is addressed in the United States.

Lastly, it is particularly important that members of Congress are active
on issues affecting the poor, because there are relatively few interest
groups advocating for them. Despite the explosive growth in the number
of interest groups in Washington, DC, groups focused on poverty policy
are a small fraction of the advocacy community (e.g., Baumgartner and
Leech 1998; Berry 1999; Schlozman 1984; Skocpol 2004). A recent study
estimates that, since the 1980s, social welfare interest groups have made
up less than 1 percent of all politically active organizations in Washington
(Schlozman 2010).[6] Thus, the famous upper-class accent in the interest
group community identified by Schattschneider (1960) persists today. In
short, while outside groups can help most constituents amplify their voice
and attract the attention of their elected representatives, this typically is
not a strategy available to the poor.

There also are strong normative reasons to care if the poor are represented in Congress. In Dahl's classic book *Polyarchy*, he argues that
"a key characteristic of a democracy is the continuing responsiveness of
the government to the preferences of its citizens, considered as political
equals" (1971, 1). The responsibility for putting this into action falls
to elected representatives, who must "make present" in government the
interests and needs of all of their constituents.[7] Young illustrates this
point when she emphasizes the importance of the inclusiveness of the
process: "The normative legitimacy of a democratic decision depends on
the degree to which those affected by it have been included in the decision-
making processes and have had the opportunity to influence the

---

[6] Schlozman examines more than 27,000 organizations in the 1981, 1991, 2001, and 2006
Washington Representatives directory, which is a comprehensive listing of organizations
actively involved in national politics.

[7] Pitkin (1967) likewise envisions legislators as representatives who "act for" constituents
by representing their interests in the legislative process.

outcomes" (2002, 2). When this does not happen, representative bodies like the US Congress fail to provide complete political representation.

The normative stakes are arguably higher when the potentially unrepresented group is economically disadvantaged. This is because economic and political inequality may reinforce one another. The tension between a free-market economy which produces economic inequality and a democratic government which guarantees political equality has long been a challenge in American politics. Initially, the upper class feared that popular government would allow the lower class to use majority rule to promote a tyranny of the poor. Indeed, the Federalist Papers and the US Constitution wrestled with how to reconcile support for the broad principles of democracy with elites' self-interest in preserving certain arrangements from which they benefited (see Williams 1998).

In modern American society, however, the fear of majority tyranny of the poor has been replaced by concerns that the poor are overlooked in the majoritarian political system. Cameron describes democracy in the United States as one in which "a political system grounded on a principle of equality coexists with an economic system that produces and perpetuates inequality" (1988, 219). Put differently, the United States has chosen an economic system that produces winners and losers, and we accept the resulting economic inequalities. However, we also have chosen a political system that emphasizes political equality. The concern, then, is that economic inequality will taint political equality. As Dahl argues, "I have long believed that the effect of socioeconomic inequalities in political systems, certainly in the United States, is to lead to political inequalities" (in Shapiro and Reeher 1988, 154). Williams expresses similar concerns over "the ways in which existing political processes, while facially neutral, function to reproduce existing patterns of social inequality along group lines" (1998, 78). The problem that Williams identifies is not that political practices explicitly codify economic inequalities by giving different rights or access to some citizens over others. Instead, the political inequalities become apparent when government is systematically more responsive to wealthier groups than poor groups within society and advances policies that promote their interests.

THE INTERSECTION OF POVERTY AND CONGRESS

There is a great deal of research in both the poverty and congressional literatures that informs this book, but connections across these studies are all too scarce. Research on poverty tends to leave the legislative process by which anti-poverty policies are developed in a "black box." In turn, studies of congressional representation seldom focus on the poor as a constituency. This book fills this gap by treating the poor as a distinctive, and potentially under-represented, constituency, and by unpacking the legislative process to examine the procedures, rules, and incentives that shape House members' decisions.

Research on Poverty

One of the fundamental insights gained from studies of poverty is that the context of poverty, or its place, matters a great deal. Where poverty is located affects how hard it is for the poor to access social services, to buy fresh food, or to commute to a job (e.g., Allard 2009; Reckhow and Weir 2011). The location of poverty also has implications for the congressional representation of the poor. Members of Congress are elected from geographically defined districts, which means that there is variation in poverty across congressional districts. Some districts will encompass neighborhoods with concentrated, high levels of poverty, while other districts may include more sparsely distributed or low rates of poverty. Therefore, we might expect legislators from these districts also to vary in their activity on poverty-related issues.

The context of poverty as either rural or urban also has played an important role in how poverty in America is portrayed and addressed. Numerous scholars from sociology, political science, and history focus on the particular concerns of rural poverty, including Gaventa's (1980) seminal work on political power in Appalachia (see also Cramer 2012; Duncan 1992, 1999; Sherman 2009). Rural poverty has been central to the politics of poverty. It was rural poverty in Appalachia that caught the attention of President John F. Kennedy during the 1960 campaign, and it was Appalachian poverty that President Lyndon B. Johnson saw in 1964 when he declared an "unconditional war on poverty." Today, rural poverty is increasingly likely to exist in districts represented by Republican members of Congress, and to occur in Southern states (Farrigan 2017).

Cities are the other geographic place typically associated with poverty in America. Poverty has long existed in urban areas, but several post-war trends in the United States heightened the concentration of urban poverty. These include the residential shift to the suburbs, the change in urban economies from manufacturing to services, and the changing racial composition of urban areas. Research by sociologists and political scientists alike chronicles the ways in which urban poverty affects economic environments, job opportunities, crime rates, educational opportunities, and cultural norms (e.g., Jargowsky 1997; Jennings 1994; Morgen and Maskovsky 2003; Wilson 1987, 1996). Traditionally, poor urban congressional districts have been more likely to include concentrations of minority poverty, particularly among African Americans, and to be represented by Democratic members of Congress.

Another key insight is that, despite the concentration of poverty in some communities, poverty is not an exclusively urban nor rural problem. Recently, a number of scholars have begun to examine the rise of the suburban poor (e.g., Allard 2017; Kneebone and Berube 2013; Kneebone and Garr 2010; Weir 2011). This trend partially reflects the resurgence (and gentrification) of many urban areas, which has forced low-income residents out of the cities and into the suburbs. The collapse of the housing market in the late 2000s and the Great Recession also contributed to the rising number of poor who live in the suburbs. As a result, poverty may be relevant to more congressional districts, including those that previously had relatively few poor residents. An outstanding question, then, is how quickly legislators from these newly poor, suburban districts adapt to the changes in their constituency?

Scholarship on poverty and race also provides an important foundation for the examination of the political representation of the poor in Congress. Specifically, the racial and ethnic distribution of poverty has implications for the types of congressional districts that are likely to experience higher rates of poverty. The reality is that poverty rates are higher among racial and ethnic minorities in America than among whites, even though more white Americans live in poverty in absolute terms. Recent data from the US Census Bureau reveals that poverty rates are approximately twice as high for Native Americans (27%), African Americans (26%), and Latinos (23%), as compared to whites (12%) (see Macartney, Bishaw, and Fontenot 2013). Rather than look at these numbers in isolation, poverty scholars consider them in light of patterns of residential segregation, which can create (and perpetuate) poor minority communities (e.g., Allard 2008; Cohen and Dawson 1993; Jargowsky 1997; Massey and Denton 1993; Pattillo 2007; Sharkey 2013; Stoll 2008; Wilson 1987, 1996). To this, public opinion scholars add a valuable, if at times contentious, debate about the extent to which race and poverty are linked in the public's mind, and whether the primary culprit is racial attitudes, beliefs about fairness, or the promise of upward mobility (e.g., Avery and Peffley 2003; Bobo and Smith 1994; DeSante 2013; Gilens

1999; 2003; Hochschild 1981, 1995; Kinder and Sanders 1996; Lin and Harris 2008; McCall 2013; Page and Jacobs 2009; Sniderman and Piazza 1993). Focusing on political institutions, congressional scholars consider the role of race-based redistricting and the creation of majority-minority districts, which may contribute to concentrated minority poverty (e.g., Cameron, Epstein, and O'Halloran 1996; Canon 1999; Lublin 1997a; Overby and Cosgrove 1996). A critical question for congressional representation of the poor, then, is whether minority legislators are more likely to represent high poverty districts, and, in turn, more likely to be active on poverty-related issues.

These studies raise another important question for the representation of the poor in Congress. Do legislators who are themselves members of a racial or ethnic minority have a unique perspective that shapes their behavior on poverty-related issues? Of particular interest is whether African American legislators pay greater attention to issues related to poverty, regardless of the level of poverty in their district. Minority legislators' sense of "linked fate" (Dawson 1995) may compel them to act as surrogate representatives for the poor (see also Dawson 2003; Fenno 2003; Gamble 2007; Mansbridge 1999; Minta 2009, 2011; Tate 2003). Moreover, racial and ethnic identity may be particularly important, because the poor lack descriptive representatives in Congress who would otherwise be expected to take up poverty-related issues. As Carnes (2013) shows, there is a scarcity of members of Congress who come from working class roots, and arguably even fewer members who have personal experience with poverty (see also Carnes and Sadin 2015; Grumbach 2015). As a constituency, then, the poor may be more dependent on legislators who identify with a community familiar with poverty issues, as compared to legislators who are poor themselves.

Moments of major legislative action also provide an important focal point for studies of poverty. Scholars provide rich and often historical examinations of national policy success, including major policies like the G.I. Bill, Medicare, Aid to Families with Dependent Children, Social Security, and public education (e.g., Campbell 2003; Katznelson 2006; Katznelson and Weir 1988; Mettler 1998, 2005; Skocpol 1992, 1995, 1997). They illustrate the political conditions under which Congress can advance the interests of the poor, and suggest that there may be times when Congress is systematically more likely to take up poverty-related issues. These high-profile successes, however, are notable because they are unusual. Major legislation often reflects years of work and previous legislative failures, as well as the good fortune of a perfect storm of political conditions. Additionally, moments of high profile legislative success illustrate one, but not the only, way that policy is made. Policy-making is also a long slog of small bills and adjustments to existing programs that do not make the front page, but, nevertheless, impact people's lives (Hacker, Mettler, and Soss 2007). In addition, policies can experience "drift" (Hacker 2004) if policy-makers do not maintain and update legislation.[8] Therefore, in addition to occasional peaks in policy-making, we might expect to see a fairly regular stream of legislative activity on poverty-related issues, as existing policies are revisited and new policies are considered.

Research on Congressional Representation

This book is also informed by the sizable literature on constituency representation in Congress, which provides insights into legislators' behavior and the ways that the institution shapes activity. Congressional scholars have long recognized that Congress plays the central role in political representation. As Sinclair notes, Congress' job "is to provide a forum in which the demands, interests, opinions, and needs of citizens find articulation" (1989, 2). In fact, members of Congress themselves believe that elected representatives have a responsibility to represent all the constituents in the district (e.g., Fenno 1978, 2000, 2003, 2013; Kingdon 1989; Miler 2010). Consequently, the primary goal of many studies is to evaluate the extent to which constituents are represented in the actions of individual legislators, as well as Congress as a whole. There are many ways to approach questions about constituency representation, and I briefly highlight here those approaches on which this book draws most heavily.[9]

When evaluating which constituents are represented, scholars note that whether a constituency group is salient to a legislator is critical to under-standing whether the legislator will act on its behalf (e.g., Fenno 1973, 2003, 2013; Kingdon 1989). If a legislator sees a constituent group in the district, he is much more likely to act for it than if he is unaware of their interest in a given issue (Miler 2007, 2010). In fact, this positive effect of visibility on legislative behavior is why many organized constituency groups engage in grassroots campaigns and why citizens contact

---

[8] See Enns et al. 2014 regarding drift and economic inequality.
[9] In subsequent chapters, I provide a more detailed discussion of existing work relevant to the different forms of representation examined.

their legislators on issues where they want their voice to be heard. When looking at the representation of the poor, then, one question is whether legislators are aware of the poor, and, thus, can reasonably be expected to be active on poverty issues. In Chapter 2, I establish the visibility of the poor to political elites, which generates a stronger expectation that the poor will be represented in Congress.

An extensive literature examines the ways in which legislators articulate the interests of a variety of constituents during the legislative process (e.g., Adler 2002; Arnold 1990; Bishin 2000, 2009; Hall 1987, 1996; Schiller 1995; Sulkin 2005). Of particular relevance here are studies that show that Congress often represents smaller constituencies and minority opinions, including politically disadvantaged groups such as racial and ethnic minorities (e.g., Canon 1999; Casellas 2011; Griffin and Newman 2008; Grose 2011; Minta 2009, 2011; Rocca, Sanchez, and Uscinski 2008; Tate 2003), women (e.g., Frederick 2009; Kathlene 1994; Reingold 1992; Swers 2002a, 2002b, 2013; Thomas 1994), and LGBT constituents (e.g., Bishin and Smith 2013; Haider-Markel 2010; Hansen and Truel 2015; Krimmel, Lax, and Phillips 2016). Although the congressional literature does not speak to the specific question of whether the poor are represented, the above studies provide reason to think that members of Congress also should represent the poor.

In addition to their primary focus on constituents in the district, congressional scholars often emphasize the institutions of Congress, particularly parties and committees, when examining constituency representation. One of the most well-established facts of legislative behavior is that majority party legislators have numerous procedural advantages in the legislative process. Thus, majority party legislators are better able to act on behalf of their constituents. Similarly, constituency representation also is affected by the committee system, in which legislators with district-driven interests often serve on a relevant committee (e.g., Adler 2002; Frisch and Kelly 2006; Shepsle 1978). Committee members, therefore, are seen as policy demanders who promote the interests of their constituents, arguably not always to the benefit of the full chamber (e.g., Carson, Finocchiaro, and Rohde 2002; Hall and Grofman 1990; Krehbiel 1990, 1991). This also means that legislators who serve on committees of relevance to their district are in a better position to advocate for their constituents in the policy-making process. An important question, then, is whether the party and committee systems facilitate or constrain the representation of the poor.

Still other congressional research focuses on evaluating constituency representation as the congruence between public opinion and policy outcomes. This approach has deep roots in the congressional literature, including Miller and Stokes' (1963) seminal article on dyadic representation, or the extent to which individual legislators vote consistent with district opinion. It also serves as the foundation for the literature on macro-representation, which examines the correspondence between national public opinion and government action (e.g., Erikson, MacKuen, and Stimson 2002; Shapiro and Page 1994; Soroka and Wlezien 2008; Stimson 1999, 2004; Wlezien 1995; Wlezien and Soroka 2011). Recent work on representation and economic inequality, which I discuss in greater detail in Chapters 4 and 5, follows in this tradition. In short, these studies examine how well policy outcomes correspond to public opinion, most often divided into the aggregate preferences of the upper, middle, and lower classes (e.g., Bartels 2008; Ellis 2012; Gilens 2009, 2011, 2012; Kelly 2009; Ura and Ellis 2008). The congruence between public opinion and policy outcomes is one important approach to evaluating representation and inequality, but it is not the only one. Nor is it without its limitations. As I discuss in the next section, there are a variety of concerns about the quality and measurement of public opinion, as well as broader, theoretical disagreements over whether preference congruence is the most appropriate standard for political representation.

IMPORTANT FEATURES OF THE BOOK

The first of three distinguishing features of my approach to studying the representation of the poor is that representation is based on constituents' interests. An interest-based approach is a hallmark of the congressional literature on representation, and commonly uses demographic or objective data to capture constituency interests (e.g., Adler 2000; Ensley, Tofias, and De Marchi 2009; Hall 1996; Lazarus 2013; Miler 2010, 2011). The theoretical distinction between representation of preferences and representation of interests draws on an important difference in how one conceives of the basis of political representation. In her classic work on democratic theory, Pitkin describes the interest-based notion of representation: "The member is to pursue the interest of his constituency rather than do its bidding ... (t)he representative owes the people 'devotion to their interest' rather than 'submission to their will'" (1967, 176). Theoretically, this distinction posits different ideas about the proper role of a representative and expectations for legislators' behavior. Critically, constituents' interests are seen as more stable than their preferences, and, hence, more appropriate as the foundation for representation (see Pitkin 1967, Ch. 7). Similarly, scholars raise concerns that citizens' political knowledge is insufficient to serve as the basis for representation (e.g., Converse 1964; Delli Carpini and Keeter 1997; Jacobs and Shapiro 2005). From a practical standpoint, focusing on constituents' interests allows scholars to examine representation even when survey data is not available, whether due to the shortage of district-level data or the absence of certain topics in surveys. The ability to overcome these survey-based limitations is especially valuable in the case of inequality and poverty, which are not frequent topics on surveys.

A second distinguishing feature of this book is that it examines a range of legislative behaviors. This contrasts with the existing literature on policy responsiveness and inequality, which is concerned solely with votes or outcomes. Expanding how we think about representational activities better reflects the current state of congressional research. Congressional scholars now focus beyond policy outcomes and roll-call votes to also examine bill introductions, co-sponsorship activity, committee participation, floor speeches, and public statements (e.g., Hall 1996; Highton and Rocca 2005; Koger 2003; Minta 2009, 2011; Sulkin 2005; Volden and Wiseman 2014). I argue that any assessment of how well Congress represents the poor likewise should take into account the different ways that legislators can act for their constituents. Additionally, broadening the notion of representation beyond policy outcomes is consistent with democratic theorists' understanding of representation as having a voice in government deliberations.

Third, in the tradition of previous congressional research, I consider multiple ways of thinking about representation: collective (or aggregate) representation, dyadic (or district-based) representation, and surrogate representation. Weissberg's (1978) influential article articulates the differences between collective and dyadic representation. He argues that collective representation is whether Congress as a whole reflects the full range of interests (or preferences) held by the public. As a result, collective representation does not have a geographic dimension, and does not evaluate individual members of Congress and their unique districts. This notion of collective representation underpins many existing studies of policy responsiveness to public opinion, which rely on national surveys and policy outcomes, and is a natural place to begin this examination of the representation of the poor. Accordingly, the first set of empirical tests, in Chapters 3 and 4, considers whether Congress provides collective representation of the poor.

In contrast, dyadic representation is the classical notion of representation, in which a single legislator behaves in a way that reflects the constituents in his district. This type of representation is rooted in elections, which allow constituents to hold their legislator electorally accountable. When one talks about congressional representation, this is frequently what is assumed. Moreover, the legislator–district relationship serves as the foundation of much of the classic literature on congressional representation (e.g., Fenno 1978; Kingdon 1973; Miller and Stokes 1963), as well as congressional elections (e.g., Cain, Ferejohn, and Fiorina 1987; Jacobson 1987; Mayhew 1974). Scholars also note a key challenge of dyadic representation, which is that a minority interest within a district may not be represented by its designated legislator (see Mansbridge 1999, 2003; Pitkin 1967). Therefore, beginning in Chapter 5, I focus on the possible dyadic representation of the poor, and continue to examine this relationship in Chapters 6 and 7.

Furthermore, surrogate representation is another form of representation that receives less attention in the literature, but which I argue is central to the representation of the poor. Mansbridge defines surrogate representation as "representation by a representative with whom one has no electoral relationship – that is, a representative in another district" (2003, 522). A legislator acting on behalf of constituents to whom he is not electorally obligated addresses the previously noted concern that minorities within a district may go unrepresented in dyadic representation. Burke's (1949) notion of "virtual representation" is in many ways a precursor to Mansbridge's concept of surrogate representation. Virtual representation is described by Pitkin as the representation of "particular disenfranchised groups or localities. They do not send a member to Parliament, yet they are represented by some members from some other constituency. Thus some disenfranchised groups are virtually represented and others are not ..." (1967, 174). I argue that surrogate representation is the primary way that the poor are represented in Congress, and reveal in Chapter 6 the types of legislators who serve as such surrogates.

Surrogate representation is not without its limitations, however, which raises concerns if the poor are heavily dependent on this one form of representation. Mansbridge recognizes the tenuous nature of surrogate representation and calls it "a noninstitutional, informal, and chance arrangement" (2003, 523) that lacks any formal accountability.

Yet, she also argues (Mansbridge 2003, 2011) that surrogate representation ultimately serves to advance collective representation; that is, legislators acting as surrogates can increase the degree to which Congress as a whole represents a constituency – a point which I return to in Chapter 8.

PLAN FOR THE BOOK

The remaining chapters evolve in two general ways. First, the manner in which representation is conceptualized moves from collective representation of the poor (Chapters 3 and 4) to dyadic representation of the poor (Chapters 5 and 7), as well as surrogate representation (Chapter 6). Put differently, the initial emphasis is on whether Congress as a whole represents the interests of the poor, but then this shifts to whether individual members, and which ones, represent the poor. Second, the meaning of "poor representation" transforms during the study. The book starts out somewhat hopefully in Chapters 1 and 2, with an expectation that the poor can and should be represented. But then pessimism sets in with findings of underrepresentation of the poor in Chapters 3–5. Yet Chapter 6 reveals a silver lining by highlighting the surrogate representatives who champion the poor, and Chapter 7 examines who is best able to successfully pass poverty-related legislation. Finally, Chapter 8 takes on a cautiously optimistic note when considering the future representation of the poor.

In Chapter 2, I address and dispel the twin notions that the poor are invisible politically and unimportant electorally. The political visibility of the poor is demonstrated by text-analyzing the content of all State of the Union addresses and political party platforms since 1960, which constitute the policy agenda of the president and both major parties, respectively. Poverty is frequently and consistently emphasized in both venues, by both Democrats and Republicans, and the poor are evoked more often than the middle class or other politically established groups such as seniors and veterans. I also reject the misconception that it is rational for election-oriented legislators to ignore the poor. The poor constitute a sizable percentage of many constituencies and vote at notable rates, and failure to address poverty in one's district can have undesirable spillover effects for legislators. Chapter 2, therefore, provides an important foundation for the rest of the book, since it establishes that it is reasonable to expect Congress to represent the interests of the poor.

The following two chapters evaluate the record of Congress as a whole in representing the poor – and the findings are disappointing. Chapter 3 discusses the wide range of policies that are relevant to the poor and establishes a thorough coding scheme for identifying poverty-relevant legislation that reflects different ideological and partisan angles. The consistent finding in Chapter 3 is that, despite the political visibility of the poor, Congress in the aggregate does little to represent them. Since 1960, Congress has passed on average three poverty-related bills each year – about 1 percent of all legislative output – and findings for the relative percentage of poverty-related hearings and bill introductions are only marginally higher.

Chapter 4 considers whether we might witness greater congressional effort when the national poverty rate increases or when moderate-to-high poverty spreads into more congressional districts, an expectation bolstered by scholarship on both legislative responsiveness and political geography. However, a series of empirical analyses uncover no evidence that Congress extends any more effort to address poverty – in terms of new legislation, hearings, or laws passed – in periods when poverty has intensified or spread. Thus, Chapters 3 and 4 reveal poor collective responsiveness to the poor by Congress.

Chapter 5 is the first of three chapters that considers the representative links between individual members and poor constituents. It reveals that the poor do not receive the dyadic representation that other constituents typically do. Even if overall congressional activity is low, individual members who represent sizable numbers of poor constituents should be active on poverty issues. However, across multiple analyses there is little evidence that this is the case, aside from a handful of legislators from extremely poor districts. Some lawmakers appear to advocate for poverty-related issues, even though they have few poor constituents in their districts, yet the lack of dyadic representation of the poor in Chapter 5 presents a serious challenge to our ideals of representative democracy.

Chapter 6 identifies and discusses the legislators who emerge as the "champions of the poor," and advances the concept of surrogate representation as the primary way that the poor receive some representation. I identify the thirty-five members that have exerted the greatest and most sustained effort throughout their careers to put poverty-related issues on the agenda, nearly all of whom are surrogates from districts without high poverty. Four groups of such "consistent champions" emerge: Old-School Democrats, Democratic Women, Urban Black Democrats, and Indigo Republicans. I discuss in detail the members of each group and the types of legislation they propose, which often reflects the unique features of the group and their role as surrogates. Absent from this select group are

Latino legislators, many of whom are nevertheless "occasional champions" for the poor, and the "missing" rural Republicans from high-poverty districts, who fail to provide dyadic representation for their many poor constituents.

Chapter 7 examines the passage of poverty legislation, and asks whether the legislative champions who are responsible for putting poverty bills on the agenda also are successful in passing them. I find that legislators who call attention to the poor by actively proposing legislation hit an institutional wall and are not likely to shepherd their bills through to passage. Rather, the legislators most likely to pass poverty-related legislation are those in positions of institutional power, such as party leaders, members of key committees, and majority party legislators (of either party). An important conclusion from Chapter 7, then, is that those most committed to addressing poverty, namely African American, female, and Democratic champions, are often unable to do so, while those less engaged with poverty-related issues are the ones best-positioned for legislative success.

Chapter 8 outlines three reasons why representation of the poor in Congress falls short, and discusses how each might be improved. First, the poor have relatively few organized groups to advance their interests. Furthermore, it is not clear who the friends of the poor are, which makes it difficult for the limited number of groups who do lobby on behalf of the poor to know which legislators to target. Thus, insights about surrogate champions can help groups focus their limited resources on the most receptive legislators. A second concern is the lack of diversity in Congress, since legislative advocates for the poor are disproportionately women and African Americans. As Congress continues to become more diverse, it raises the prospect of greater representation of the poor in the future. However, the lack of diversity among congressional leaders suggests that poverty-related issues still might not be a priority. A final challenge is the striking lack of representation of the poor by Republicans, particularly among rural members from high-poverty districts. The current wave of economic populism and attention to previously-ignored voters, however, suggests that some of these heretofore inactive members may begin to take the interests of the poor more seriously, or else may face repercussions.

2

The Political Visibility of the Poor

Cynics often dismiss the poor as being unimportant politically due to their lack of visibility and their lack of electoral significance. I reject this view, and instead argue that the poor are quite visible, and that members have electoral reasons to be attentive to them. Consequently, we should expect elected legislators to treat the poor as they do other constituents. Any failure to do so reflects a deliberate decision not to represent the poor, instead of mere oversight, and any political discussions should be based on this reality.

This chapter debunks two common myths about the politics of poverty that perpetuate the unjustified expectation that Congress is unlikely to represent the poor. The first and most central misconception is that the poor are not politically visible. We often treat the poor as simply forgotten, which makes any failure to represent them the result of benign neglect. The unspoken assumption of this myth of the invisible poor is that, if our elected representatives could only see the poor, they would do more to help them. However, the evidence presented in this chapter directly contradicts this view, and demonstrates clearly that politicians are well aware of the poor. The poor are mentioned consistently and repeatedly in the president's most important policy speech to Congress, the State of the Union address, as well as in the official policy platforms of the two major political parties. Moreover, they receive more attention in these agenda-setting venues than other politically salient constituents. Quite simply, the poor are not politically invisible.

This leads to the second common myth, which is that it is reasonable for legislators to neglect the poor due to their lower rate of political participation. Bartels neatly characterizes this type of response:

"Of course the poor don't get represented; they don't vote!" (2008, 275). This perspective is based on the misleading premise that there is little electoral risk in failing to represent the interests of the poor. Even if we set aside normative concerns about whether politicians have a moral responsibility to represent the poor – which is a major leap for many – the rational argument is still dubious. Although the poor do vote at a lower rate than those of higher economic status, they still vote in sufficient numbers such that strategic, risk-averse legislators should not ignore them, especially those who represent high-poverty districts. Moreover, election-minded legislators should anticipate the possibility that poor constituents in their district could be mobilized to vote in the next election, as well as that some non-poor voters might care about their commitment to representing the entire district. Consequently, a legislator has multiple, reelection-driven reasons to represent the poor.

In the remainder of this chapter, I establish the political visibility of the poor using two distinct sources: the president's State of the Union address, and the official platforms of the Democratic and Republican parties. Using two approaches to text-based analyses – lexical frequency and policy content – I show that the poor are not only visible, but more frequently invoked than groups such as the middle class, seniors, veterans, or farmers. I then discuss the electoral risks associated with ignoring poor constituents, and establish the rationality of representing the poor.

ARE THE POOR POLITICALLY VISIBLE?

The belief that the poor are invisible is rooted in popular and journalistic accounts of poverty in America. Indeed, the phrase the "invisible poor" dates back at least to an essay by MacDonald published in *The New Yorker* in January 1963. In this extensive discussion about the state of poverty in the United States, MacDonald refers to the invisibility of the poor in society, and the fact that increasing prosperity for many Americans at the time had masked the persistent poverty of some. As MacDonald writes, "That mass poverty can persist despite this rise to affluence is hard to believe, or see, especially if one is among those who have risen" (1963).

MacDonald draws on Harrington's (1962) book, *The Other America: Poverty in the United States*, to highlight the ways in which the non-poor are increasingly able to avoid the poor in their daily lives. Reflecting the housing dynamics of the time, MacDonald points to the residential isolation of the poor as the well-to-do increasingly populate the new suburbs. However, MacDonald also notes the separation in workplaces, the disparities in education, and the link between poverty and racial segregation that allow for the poor to slip "out of the very experience and consciousness of the nation."[1] Consequently, he argues, politics does not focus attention on the poor. The widespread impression that the New Deal ended poverty, MacDonald argues, also allowed for the false sense that the problem of poverty had been "solved."

MacDonald's essay has been very influential, both in its own time and in the decades since it was published. "Our Invisible Poor" was one of the most read pieces published in the *New Yorker* that year (Lepore 2012). Some historical accounts report that President John F. Kennedy also read MacDonald's essay (Dreier 2012; Keefe 2010). It brought such attention to Harrington's book that 70,000 copies of it were sold in the year after MacDonald's essay (Lepore 2012).

Although coined over fifty years ago, the phrase "the invisible poor," and the dynamics it captures, remain relevant today. The *New York Review of Magazines* (Schwarzer 2012) included "Our Invisible Poor" on its list of the ten most influential magazine articles of the twentieth-century. The phrase "the invisible poor" has been invoked many times in the years since MacDonald's essay, including by academics, journalists, and government officials (e.g., Glickman 2013; Gurley 2016; Younge 2008). Writing for the *New York Times* about the prevalence of poverty, despite considerable national wealth, Fallows argues that there exists a "simple invisibility, because of increasing geographic, occupational and social barriers that block one group from the other's view" (2000). Fallows likens the resulting disconnect between most Americans and the poor to our relationship with the poor in developing countries: "We feel bad for them, but they live someplace else." Overall, the widespread belief that the poor are not prominent in the public consciousness persists.

The key question, then, is whether "invisible" is an accurate description of the poor in national politics? This question is critical, because it shapes what is reasonable to expect of elected officials when it comes to the representation of the poor. Legislators are more likely to act for the constituents they see in their districts (e.g., Dexter 1957; Fenno 1978; Kingdon 1989; Miler 2010). If the poor are politically invisible, then they are unlikely to be part of the political discourse in Washington. In that

---

[1] Harrington (1962), *The Other America: Poverty in the United States*, as quoted by MacDonald 1963.

case, members of Congress might be excused for not acting on behalf of the poor. Any shortcomings in their representation would be a natural, albeit regrettable, consequence of political elites' lack of awareness of the poor. Underlying this scenario is an assumption that politicians are not deliberately neglecting the poor, but instead are benignly unaware of their interests. The logical implication is that increasing the political visibility of the poor in Washington would result in improved representation.

However, I argue that there is more political awareness of the poor than the popular phrase "the invisible poor" might imply. Even if the poor are not seen by many individual Americans, they should be more visible to political elites. One initial reason that the poor are likely to be seen by those in and around government is that class-based distinctions are a routine part of public policy. Whether in debates over means-testing benefits, or analyzing the impact of proposed changes to the tax code, political elites are well-versed in the general language of class. In addition, political elites regularly consider reports and data from federal agencies, congressional committees, think tanks, and interest groups that may delineate policy impacts by income groups. In short, thinking of politics in terms of low-, middle-, and high-income groups is much more common among politicians and policymakers than among average citizens.

The Poor on the President's Agenda

The legislative agenda of the president, as captured in his State of the Union address, is an important barometer of the political visibility of the poor in national politics. The State of the Union is the single most important policy speech that the president gives to Congress, as well as to the public. This address is made annually, is televised by the major networks, and is watched widely. Most importantly for my purposes, it takes place in the Capitol, with nearly all members of Congress in attendance. More than any other presidential address, the State of the Union is widely considered to be an indicator of the president's policy agenda (Campbell and Jamieson 2000; Cohen 1995; Edwards and Wood 1999; Hoffman and Howard 2006; Lovett, Bevan, and Baumgartner 2014). It is an essential way for the president to signal the issues that he would like to see Congress address. The political spotlight of the State of the Union is bright, and to have a president call attention to the poor in this venue makes it difficult to argue that Congress is unaware of the poor due to their invisibility.

In order to assess the political visibility of the poor, I conduct text analyses of the content of every State of the Union address from President John F. Kennedy's first address in 1961 through President Barack Obama's final address in 2016.[2] This provides me with fifty-five years of data, and includes the addresses of ten presidents – five Republicans and five Democrats. The text of the State of the Union speeches are taken from official records, accessed through the American Presidency Project at the University of California at Santa Barbara.[3]

I first perform a succession of keyword searches to identify all language in the speeches that refers to poverty as an issue and the poor as a constituency group (before later doing the same for other economic and non-economic groups). The initial step is to search for all discrete mentions of "the poor" and "poverty" in the addresses. Next I pinpoint the relevant synonyms for both terms, and conduct additional searches for all of those keywords. After identifying all possible references to the poor and poverty (including synonyms), I then use a series of coding rules to omit inappropriate references and ensure that only relevant references are being counted.[4] Specifically, the word "poverty" is only included when it is specified in a domestic (as compared to global) context, and when it applies to economic conditions. For references to the poor as a constituent group, in addition to the term "the poor," I only include synonyms when their use is in clear reference to people, as in the case of the following terms: poor Americans, poor families, Americans in poverty, low-income Americans, and low-income families. Instances in which "poor" describes something other than individuals (e.g., poor neighborhoods, poor economy, poor performance) are excluded. Also omitted are terms that have vague or broader connotations, such as "needy," as well as mentions of "welfare."

The totals returned from this systematic examination of presidential addresses reveal that the poor are far from invisible politically. Table 2.1 identifies the State of the Union speeches that include references to the poor and/or poverty, as well as those that do not. Overall, forty-nine of

---

[2] Richard Nixon did not give a traditional State of the Union address in 1973, so it is not included in the analyses and totals provided. See: www.presidency.ucsb.edu/ws/?pid=3996.

[3] www.presidency.ucsb.edu/sou.php

[4] The references to these terms (and all terms for other constituency groups) are coded by the author and another trained coder. Coding of the text was conducted independently and resulted in nearly 95 percent intercoder reliability. In the case of any difference in coding, the text was reexamined in its context, and a final coding decision was made by the author.

TABLE 2.1 *Visibility of the poor in State of the Union addresses, 1961–2016*

Mentions the poor or poverty	No mention of the poor or poverty
Kennedy 1961, 1962, 1963	Nixon 1971
Johnson 1964, 1965, 1966, 1967, 1968, 1969	Ford 1977
Nixon 1970, 1972, 1974	Carter 1980
Ford 1975, 1976	Bush 1990, 1991
Carter 1978, 1979	Obama 2011
Reagan 1981, 1982, 1983, 1984, 1985, 1986, 1987, 1988	
Bush 1989, 1992	
Clinton 1993, 1994, 1995, 1996, 1997, 1998, 1999, 2000	
Bush 2001, 2002, 2003, 2004, 2005, 2006, 2007, 2008	
Obama 2009, 2010, 2012, 2013, 2014, 2015, 2016	
TOTAL: 49	TOTAL: 6

Source: *The American Presidency Project* (Woolley and Peters 2017)

fifty-five speeches analyzed contain such references, including twenty-six given by Democratic presidents and twenty-three given by Republican ones (see Table 2.1). In turn, the few addresses in which neither is mentioned are split between the two parties (two Democratic presidents and three Republican ones), and scattered across the decades examined. The inclusion of the poor and poverty in 90 percent of speeches is particularly notable, given that State of the Union addresses can be brief and narrowly focused, with some speeches lasting less than a half an hour, and six presidents saying fewer than 4,000 words in one or more of their speeches.[5] This illustrates that not all issues can be mentioned in an address, and makes the consistent inclusion of the poor particularly noteworthy.

Moreover, more than two-thirds (thirty-three of forty-nine) of the State of the Union addresses that engage the poor and poverty do so multiple times. This suggests a regular, heightened emphasis on the poor. Well over half of these multiple-reference speeches contain four or more such references. In absolute terms, then, the poor are a repeated presence in the president's annual articulation of his legislative

---

[5] See the American Presidency Project, www.presidency.ucsb.edu/sou_minutes.php and www.presidency.ucsb.edu/sou_words.php

agenda – and, by extension, are visible to Congress, who is the audience for these addresses. Although noteworthy, this consistent and frequent emphasis on the poor in State of the Union addresses needs to be assessed in a comparative context. Given the book's focus on the visibility of the poor and representation of them as a constituency, the logical way to do so is to compare the emphasis on the poor in State of the Union speeches to that placed on other notable constituent groups, both economic and non-economic.

The logical starting point is to examine the poor compared to other economic classes, particularly the politically-ubiquitous "middle class."[6] One might expect the middle class to be mentioned particularly frequently by the president, because it is a political cliché (e.g., Shenkar-Osorio 2013; Soergel 2016). Additionally, more Americans consider themselves to be middle class than any other label, which provides a large audience for rhetorical appeals to the middle class (Pew Research Center 2015). As before, mentions of the middle class as a constituency group take multiple forms and include various synonyms. Therefore, I include not just the term "middle class," which refers to the group as a noun, but also the adjectives "middle-class" and "middle-income," when placed before nouns such as "Americans," "individuals," and "families."

The clear and surprising take-away from Figures 2.1 and 2.2, which compare the number and consistency of references to the poor and middle class, respectively, is that the poor are much more visible. By any metric, the poor have had double the presence of the middle class in presidential addresses to Congress since 1960. In terms of raw totals, there are almost twice as many references to the poor (ninety-nine) as there are to the middle class (fifty-three), as shown in Figure 2.1. If references to poverty are included, there are 167 mentions of the poor and poverty, which is more than three times as many as the middle class.

The poor are also evoked much more consistently across the decades, at a rate more than twice that for the middle class. Figure 2.2 illustrates that nearly 80 percent of State of the Union addresses, or forty-three of fifty-five, emphasize the poor to at least some degree, and this climbs to forty-nine addresses (90 percent) if the term poverty is included,

---

[6] I also included the wealthy (including related words "upper class," "the rich, "wealthy *noun*," and "upper income") in the text searches, but they appear infrequently and in inconsistent contexts and, thus, are not included in any systematic comparisons. The wealthy are mentioned in one-quarter of addresses and only twenty-one times total.

Poor Representation

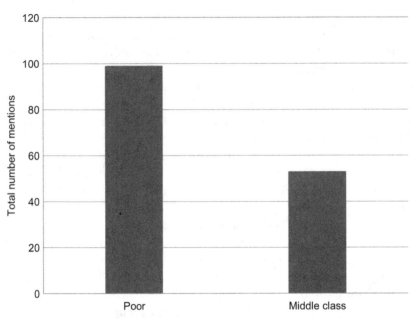

FIGURE 2.1 Visibility of economic constituency groups in State of the Union addresses, 1960–2016

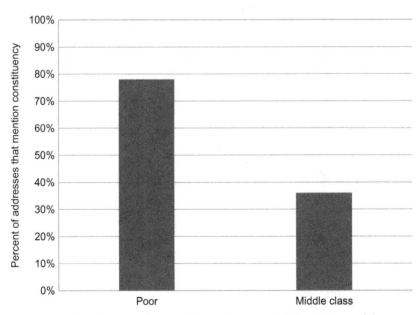

FIGURE 2.2 Consistency of economic constituency visibility in State of the Union addresses, 1960–2016

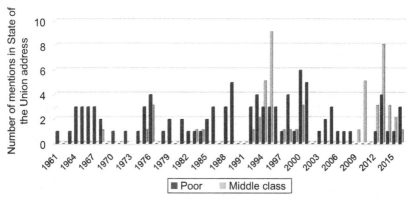

FIGURE 2.3 Annual mentions of economic constituency groups in State of the Union addresses, 1960–2016

as noted earlier. By contrast, only 36 percent of State of the Union speeches, or twenty of fifty-five, evoke the middle class in some way, which includes the range of middle class synonyms. Figure 2.3 breaks down the mentions of the poor and middle class by year, and shows that there are only eight years in which mentions of the middle class exceeded mentions of the poor, and six of those years occurred during the Great Recession and its aftermath. In sum, contrary to what one might expect, the poor are emphasized far more than the middle class when the president conveys his legislative agenda to Congress, suggesting further that the poor are pre-eminently visible to lawmakers among the economic classes.

However, do the poor figure as prominently in State of the Union addresses when compared to prominent non-economic groups? This time I focus on three important constituency groups: seniors, farmers, and veterans. All three share two important characteristics, which provide for meaningful comparisons to the poor. First, members of these constituencies are readily identifiable as a constituency group. Just as there are objective indicators of who is poor and who is not, seniors, farmers, and veterans can all be clearly identified as well. Second, these three constituencies are widely considered to be important and well-represented in American politics, which means that we would expect elected officials to attend to their interests. Indeed, the conventional expectation is that seniors, farmers, and veterans would be mentioned more often than the poor when the president is declaring his legislative priorities before Congress. To facilitate these parallel comparisons,

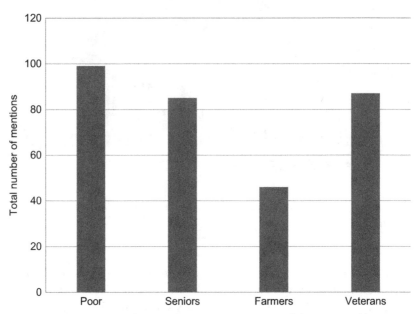

FIGURE 2.4 Mentions of constituency groups in State of the Union addresses, 1960–2016

references to these three politically-important groups are coded in the same way as before, using both the terms and notable synonyms.[7]

Perhaps surprisingly, Figures 2.4 and 2.5 once again confirm the elevated visibility of the poor in State of the Union addresses, even when compared to other prominent constituencies. References to the poor continue to outpace references to popular and powerful groups such as seniors, veterans, and farmers. Figure 2.4 depicts a gap of at least fifteen references between the poor and the next-most mentioned groups on the presidential agenda: seniors and veterans. Farmers are mentioned even less frequently – less than half as often as the poor. The regularity with which the poor are evoked over time continues to be unmatched too. Their rate of inclusion in nearly 80 percent of State of the Union addresses easily eclipses that for seniors (67%), veterans (62%), and farmers (47%). On the whole, then, the keyword-based data presented in these first four figures tell a powerful story about the visibility of the poor in an important congressional setting.

---

[7] Mentions of "seniors" also include references to "retirees," "the elderly," and "senior citizens." Similarly, the count of mentions of "veterans" also includes "servicemen" and "*noun* in the military," as in "men and women in the military."

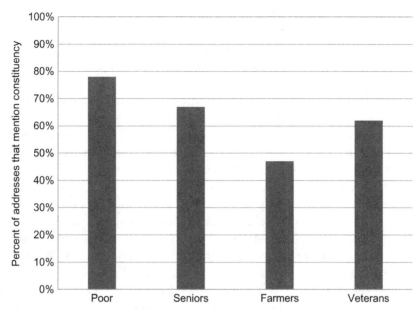

FIGURE 2.5 Relative visibility of constituency groups in State of the Union addresses, 1960–2016

The Visibility of the Poor in Party Platforms

A second way to assess the political visibility of the poor is to examine the extent to which they are included in the official policy platforms of the Republican and Democratic parties. Party platforms are "the most important document that a political party produces" (Maisel 1993, 671). These platforms lay out the priorities and agenda of each party, as well as their positions on major public policy issues (e.g., Azari and Engel 2007; Gerring 2001; Karol 2009). Members of Congress, because they are prominent members of the party and may contribute to the drafting of the platforms, therefore, have a good understanding of the priorities reflected in the platform. In addition to making clear what the party stands for, platforms are also a means of accountability. Going back to the 1950 report by the American Political Science Association's Committee on Political Parties, scholars have argued that the articulation of policy positions in party platforms makes it possible for voters to hold parties and politicians accountable for what they do and fail to do (see also Fiorina 1981; Karol 2009; Key 1966; Ranney 1954). For the purpose of determining further the political visibility of the poor, then, their prominence in the two major party platforms is a second logical place to look.

Party platforms are written and approved every four years at each party's national convention, coinciding with the presidential election. Here, I examine all party platforms for both parties, beginning in 1960 and ending with the 2016 platforms. These analyses are based on the complete text of a total of thirty platforms (fifteen from each party), which also come from the American Presidency Project at the University of California at Santa Barbara.[8] I employ the same keyword-based coding scheme I used to evaluate the State of the Union addresses, meaning that I focus on the term "the poor" and close variants, and directly compare these to reference to the "middle class" (and synonyms), as well as non-economic groups such as seniors, farmers, and veterans.

Once again, the visibility of the poor in this second political forum is strikingly high, in both absolute terms and when compared to other high-profile economic and non-economic groups. The poor are mentioned 408 times overall, which averages nearly fourteen times in each platform. If we include references to poverty, the number climbs to 606, which pushes the average above twenty-two references per party platform. These references are consistent, too, as statements about the poor are seen in every platform for both parties over the more than five decades analyzed.

Moreover, the poor are also emphasized almost equally by both parties (see Figure 2.6). Democrats make 218 references to the poor as a group in their platforms, while Republicans make 190 references to them. This partisan balance contrasts sharply with references to the middle class, discussed below, which are very rare in Republican platforms, and for which the data are skewed fourfold toward the Democrats.[9] In general, this frequent, consistent, and balanced emphasis on the poor in party platforms suggests that lawmakers from both parties are aware of issues related to the poor and poverty.

This conclusion is bolstered further upon comparing the poor to other important constituency groups in the platforms. As in the State of the Union addresses, the poor receive much more attention than the middle class. In fact, the poor are mentioned nearly three times as frequently in the platforms as the middle class (including synonyms like "middle-class Americans" or "middle-income families"), who are mentioned only

---

[8] See www.presidency.ucsb.edu/platforms.php

[9] Democrats make 114 references to the middle class, whereas Republicans make only twenty-eight.

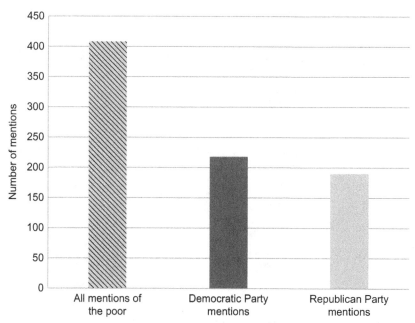

FIGURE 2.6 Visibility of the poor in Democratic party and Republican party platforms, 1960–2016

142 times (see Figure 2.7).[10] Additionally, the poor are once again evoked more regularly than important non-economic groups such as farmers, seniors, and veterans (see Figure 2.8). These other groups are emphasized regularly in their own right, with 283, 299, and 304 mentions, respectively. Yet their tallies fall more than 100 shy of those for the poor (and more than 300 shy if poverty is included with the poor), adding further to the emerging sense that the poor are easily visible to lawmakers.

An Alternate Metric for Assessing the Visibility of the Poor

Another way to gauge the political visibility of the poor is to use a policy-based metric, as compared to a word-based one. Next, I re-analyze the same two agenda-setting venues, State of the Union addresses and party platforms, but with an eye toward how much of their policy content

---

[10] Once again, the wealthy are mentioned even less frequently than the middle class. The "wealthy" are mentioned only twenty-four times in total across all thirty platforms. If one includes synonyms such as rich and upper-income, there are a total of sixty-eight mentions across all the party platforms.

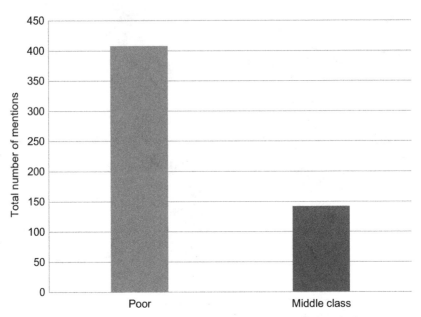

FIGURE 2.7 Visibility of economic constituency groups in party platforms, 1960–2016

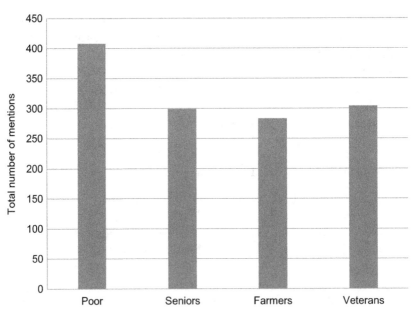

FIGURE 2.8 Mentions of constituency groups in party platforms, 1960–2016

centers on the poor. The Policy Agendas Project facilitates these comparisons because it codes a variety of political texts, including the two I am investigating, according to the substantive policy areas they address. It applies an overarching classification of twenty-one policies (major topics) and more than 220 sub-codes (minor topics) to code each "quasi-statement," or phrase, in a document based on the substantive policy issue each engages.[11]

In order to examine the political visibility of the poor using this alternate, policy-based approach, I identify poverty-related issues using the Policy Agendas Project's more granular minor-topic codes. Poverty-focused issues are not limited to traditional welfare policy, but instead exist across a number of substantive policy areas (e.g., Gilens 2009, 2011; Sargent Shriver National Center on Poverty Law). As a result, I carefully survey the 220 sub-codes to identify the handful of them that specifically affect the poor, including relevant issues such as housing, homelessness, education, food assistance, job training, and safety net programs. Since these types of policies tend toward more liberal or Democratic-leaning approaches to reducing poverty, I also include more conservative or Republican-leaning policies that address poverty by increasing employment and promoting economic growth. The result is a comprehensive scheme that identifies eleven sub-topic codes as being poverty-related, in a manner that is consistent with previous scholarship (Gilens 2009; 2012) and specific enough to avoid upward bias in the determination of poverty-related content. Chapter 3 provides a full and detailed discussion of each of the eleven minor-topic issue areas I single out, including their impact on the poor, and examples of specific policies within each of the policy areas included. Since the Policy Agendas Project codes all phrases in each speech or party platform, a major benefit is that I can express the frequency of poverty-focused statements as a percentage of all the issues that are addressed in the documents. This provides for a consistent, standardized measure of the percentage of the agenda that is focused on poverty-related issues.

Using this alternate evaluative approach, the first important finding is that the poor remain heavily emphasized in State of the Union

---

[11] The Policy Agendas Project data is based on the work of multiple investigators, including Frank Baumgartner and Bryan Jones (State of the Union data), as well as Christina Wolbrecht (party platform data). For more details see www.comparativeagendas.net/.

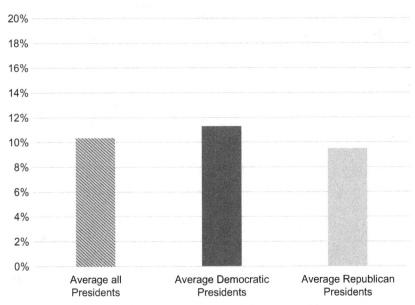

FIGURE 2.9 Poverty policy content in State of the Union addresses, 1961–2016

addresses.[12] Figure 2.9 shows that a notable 10.5 percent of all phrases across all speeches are poverty-focused in nature. This is striking when one stops to think that the State of the Union is the president's primary opportunity to present his legislative agenda to both Congress and the American people, and that dozens of other issues, reflected in more than 200 other possible sub-codes, could be integrated into these speeches. In addition to this high baseline percentage of greater than 10 percent, we see speeches in each of the six decades studied, in which 15 percent or more of the emphasis is on poverty issues. The numbers are roughly similar across presidents from both parties, too (see Figure 2.9). Although the percentage for Democrats is slightly higher, the average percentage in Republican addresses is a still-notable 9.4 percent.

The emphasis on poverty in these presidential addresses is consistent across the period from President Kennedy to President Obama. Figure 2.10 depicts the average percentage of poverty-focused rhetoric in these annual presidential addresses to Congress by decade, based on the content codings. Most obvious is the consistency of the emphasis on

---

[12] See The Policy Agendas Project at the University of Texas at Austin, www.comparativea gendas.net.

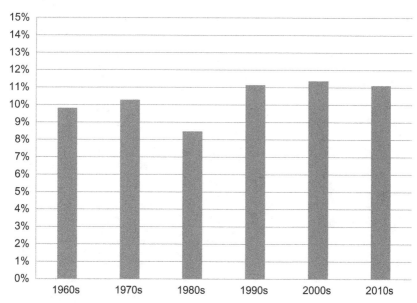

FIGURE 2.10 Average poverty policy content in State of the Union addresses by decade

the poor, as evidenced in Figure 2.10. Furthermore, in three of the decades it eclipses 11 percent, on average, and in only one decade does it drop below 9.8 percent. One can also compare across presidents, and Figure 2.11 reveals that presidents of both parties are remarkably consistent in their attention to poverty policy. The presidential averages vary from a low of 7.5 percent (for President Jimmy Carter), to a high under President Barack Obama of 12.9 percent.

Applying the same methodology to party platforms also returns sizeable percentages that reach and often eclipse 10 percent, which adds a fourth and final piece of evidence to illustrate the visibility of the poor on the political agenda.[13] Figure 2.12 reveals that, across all thirty party platforms since 1960, about 8 percent of the statements in them are focused on poverty-related issues. The averages are somewhat higher for Democrats (just over 9 percent) than Republicans (nearly 7 percent), although the latter figure is still sizeable. These percentages are once again

---

[13] See Christina Wolbrecht, *American Political Party Platforms: 1948–2008*. These data are made possible in part by support from the Institute for Scholarship in the Liberal Arts, College of Arts and Letters, University of Notre Dame. Neither ISLA nor the original collectors of the data bear any responsibility for the analysis reported here.

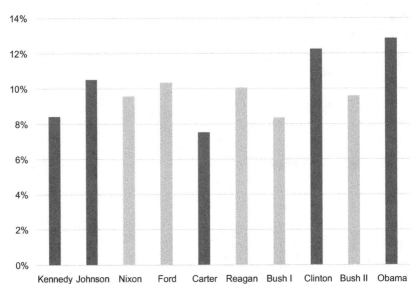

FIGURE 2.11 Average poverty policy content in State of the Union addresses by president

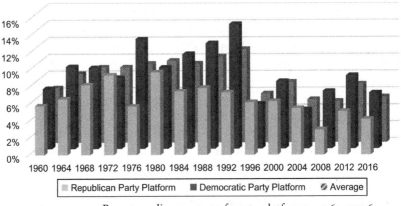

FIGURE 2.12 Poverty policy content of party platforms, 1960–2016

fairly consistent over the duration of the study. In only one platform (out of thirty) does the percentage dip just below 4 percent, and in about one-third of the platforms the percentage is greater than 10 percent. These figures must also be put into context: each political party includes a vast coalition of interests and has dozens of issues on their respective policy agendas (e.g., Bawn et al. 2012; Karol 2009). The fact that both consistently have elevated the issue of poverty in their platforms, to such levels, for so many years, is nothing short of remarkable.

Overall, there is an abundance of evidence that the poor are far from invisible in agenda-setting discourse among political elites. Whether examining the president's State of the Union addresses or the political parties' platforms, looking at the parties separately or combined, or using constituency word counts or policy topics to evaluate the texts, the conclusion is the same: the poor are politically visible. In fact, the multi-part evidence presented above suggests that the poor are among the more visible groups on the political agenda. In the context of economic-based constituencies, references to the poor are overwhelmingly more frequent than mentions of the middle class, which is noteworthy. The conventional wisdom is that politicians talk a lot about the middle class, and, while this may still be true in other venues (e.g., campaigns), the data clearly show that, when it comes to the policy agenda, the poor are more visible. Additionally, the poor are more politically visible than groups that are widely considered to be well-represented, such as seniors, farmers, and veterans. The favorable comparison to seniors is especially notable, because seniors are a large, non-partisan, and politically active constituency. In light of the totality of evidence, then, it is reasonable to expect that Congress should be addressing poverty-related issues.

THE RATIONALITY OF REPRESENTING THE POOR

The second common misconception about the politics of poverty is that it is rational for strategic, election-minded legislators to ignore the poor. This assertion is based on the idea that there is minimal benefit to representing the poor, and little electoral risk in failing to do so. Although this may sound like a reasonable logic, upon closer consideration there is little basis to believe that strategic legislators should write off the poor. Instead, I argue that there are multiple reasons to expect – and considerable evidence to suggest – that legislators should be responsive to poor constituents.

First, although the poor do vote at a lower rate than wealthier income groups, they still vote in significant numbers. This makes it irrational for an electorally-minded legislator to ignore them. Looking at the income breakdown of who votes, a series of exit polls conducted from 1998 to 2012 reveals that low-income Americans (making less than $30,000), and those making between $30,000 and $49,999, comprise a near equal portion of the House electorate, never differing by more than two percentage points. Notably, this is not an artifact of a single election, but is true across the past seven election cycles. Together these two income groups account for approximately 40 percent of the voters who participate in House elections (*New York Times* 2014).

Furthermore, while low-income individuals turnout at lower rates than other Americans, the US Census Bureau reports that those making less than $30,000 tend to vote at a rate of only 12 percentage points below the national turnout rate (File 2015). In the 2014 midterm election, for instance, even the lowest income (<$30,000) citizens turned out at a rate of approximately 30 percent, as compared to national turnout rates of 42 percent. In the 2012 presidential election, low-income citizens turned out at rates of around 50 percent, as compared to national turnout of 62 percent (ibid). For risk-averse legislators who are running scared, as is commonly assumed in studies of legislative behavior, the poor still constitute a sizeable number of potential votes (e.g., Jacobson 1987; Mayhew 1974). Moreover, in districts with higher poverty rates, poor voters make up a significant portion of the constituency (up to one-quarter or even one-third of district residents), so a legislator risks an even larger loss of votes if he chooses to ignore their interests. Put differently, all votes are important to members of Congress, even those from poor voters, who are only slightly less reliable.

Those who study the responsiveness of government to different economic groups also challenge this misconception. Bartels (2008) directly addresses the question of whether higher levels of political engagement (defined primarily by voting) explain the patterns he finds in senators' responsiveness to the preferences of low-income, middle-income, and high-income constituents. He concludes that the magnitude of difference in turnout by income groups is dwarfed by the magnitude of differences in responsiveness: "income-related disparities in turnout simply do not seem large enough to provide a plausible explanation for the income-related disparities in responsiveness documented here" (Bartels 2008, 275). Similarly, Gilens (2012) highlights this issue at the national level. He notes that voter turnout by income group does not resemble the patterns of representational inequality he finds, concluding that "the disproportionate responsiveness to the preferences of the affluent cannot be attributed to their higher turnout rates or their greater involvement with political campaigns" (Gilens 2012, 10).

Further evidence that we should not expect legislators to dismiss poor constituents comes from Griffin and Newman (2013), who examine different constituents' "voting power." The notion of voting power combines a group's likelihood of voting, their tendency to favor one party, and their size in the constituency (see Bartels 1998). They find evidence that the average voting power of low income constituents is nearly comparable to that of other groups (Griffin and Newman 2013, 58). They also assert that turnout does not impact the likelihood of representation of the low-income group (Griffin and Newman 2013, 59), such that legislators are equally responsive to low-income voters and low-income non-voters. Offering further evidence that inequality in politics is not caused by lower rates of voting and participation among the poor, Butler (2014) argues that bias would persist, even if voting and forms of participation (e.g., donating money, contacting officials) occurred at equal rates. Given the weight of the scholarship, then, it is far more reasonable to expect legislators to make some effort to represent the poor than to argue that they should do nothing on their behalf.

In addition to these arguments about the relatively small impact of disparities in voter turnout, Arnold (1990) famously argues that election-oriented legislators engage in rational anticipation, whereby they consider who could be mobilized to vote in the future by a potential opponent, interest group, or social movement, even if such constituents are not currently active participants. Consequently, Arnold argues that strategic politicians will represent inactive constituents "enough" to reduce the risk of such a challenge. Engaging in some limited amount of relatively low-cost activity on behalf of the poor has the potential to inoculate a member against the potential accusation that he does not represent the poor (or the totality of his constituents), with little cost or risk. This logic is extended by Evans (2001), who argues that legislators will address issues in order to neutralize them, and Sulkin (2005), who posits an "inoculation hypothesis" in her work on how incumbent legislators pursue policies to guard against potential challengers. Ainsworth and Hall (2010) make a similar argument when discussing how legislators take limited legislative actions to protect themselves from political challenges, even on the controversial issue of abortion.

If we see this type of anticipatory behavior on an issue like abortion, which generally is not thought of as having much room for politicians to navigate, then it seems exceedingly likely that legislators would engage in similar calculations and take relatively small actions on poverty-related issues to inoculate against charges of ignoring the poor. In fact, Ura and Ellis (2008, 791) argue that poorer constituents may actually "require the most attention" from politicians, because they are politically "malleable." Introducing a bill or two to demonstrate attentiveness to the needs of the poor is the type of action that we should expect to see from legislators who have a significant number of poor constituents in the district. Therefore, a legislator's electoral self-interest should result in at least some actions being taken on poverty-related issues.

Members of Congress may also be responsive to the poor based on how other voters would react to a failure to do so. Put simply, there may be audience costs to ignoring the poor in one's district. A member's failure to address issues relevant to poverty in the community may hurt their image among non-poor voters, either because it conveys inattentiveness, or because of the spillover effects in the district associated with high poverty (e.g., crime, unemployment, etc.). As a result, legislators have electoral incentives to act on behalf of the poor, not only to appeal to poor constituents, but also to appeal to a broader portion of the constituency. For this logic to hold, one only needs to assume that *some* non-poor constituents would like to see this type of responsiveness from their Member of Congress.

The above type of audience effect has its roots in the literature on sociotropic voting and the evidence that people judge officials' performance based in part on collective economic conditions, separate of their own personal economic experience (Kinder and Kiewiet 1979, 1981).[14] In a notable application of this literature to the context of income inequality, Ellis (2013) finds that the poor are less disadvantaged vis-à-vis wealthy constituents in districts that have what I term "high audience costs." Ellis finds smaller gaps in representation of the rich and poor when the non-poor constituents are more favorable towards representational equity, and when legislators have greater electoral incentives to be responsive to their constituents. His conclusion, that gaps in the ideological representation of the rich and poor are smaller when the political environment makes the poor more relevant, reflects a logic similar to that put forward here.

In short, both previous scholarship and the empirical evidence fails to support the conventional wisdom that members of Congress should not represent the poor because the poor do not vote. For rational, election-minded legislators there are potential votes to be gained from low-income voters, and also electoral risks for failing to represent them. Therefore,

---

[14] The debate over how personal and collective assessments affect individuals' vote choice is unresolved, with some research suggesting that these two considerations are both important determinants, and that there may be interplay between the two (e.g., Arceneaux 2003; Erikson 1990; Fiorina 1978; Killian, Schoen, and Dusso 2008; Mutz and Mondak 1997).

taking action on behalf of Americans who live in poverty should not be dismissed out of hand as illogical, especially for those legislators with many poor citizens in their districts.

BUT ARE THE POOR REPRESENTED?

Having established both the political visibility of the poor and the rationality of representing their interests, the focus now turns to the question of whether Congress actually represents the poor. The evidence presented in this chapter creates a new set of expectations, based on the political visibility of the poor and the strategic benefits of activity on their behalf. With the two myths dispelled, legislators have little excuse for failing to represent the poor. Legislators are expected to take some action on poverty-related issues because the poor are on the policy agendas of all presidents and both political parties. Similarly, legislators should engage in poverty issues because they are concerned about their electoral prospects and recognize that neglectful choices have the potential to cost them votes. This is critical because, if members of Congress still do not act on behalf of the poor, despite their visibility, this would suggest that legislators are opting not to represent the poor.

In the forthcoming chapters, I evaluate thoroughly the record of congressional action on issues related to poverty. I assess representation of the poor from the traditional vantage points of representation: collective representation, or how Congress as a whole represents the poor (Chapters 3 and 4), and dyadic representation, or how individual legislators represent the poor in their respective districts (Chapters 5 and 7). I then examine surrogate representation, or whether legislators without district ties to poverty nevertheless represent the poor (Chapter 6).

3

Congressional Inaction for the Poor

This chapter begins with a clearer view of the political salience of the poor, and turns to the question of what Congress does on their behalf. Since the poor are routinely evoked in prominent and meaningful political settings, I argue that we should expect Congress should take some actions to address issues that affect the poor. However, in order to examine whether Congress as a whole represents the interests of poor Americans across the country, poverty-relevant legislation has to be defined and congressional actions identified.

Here, I establish an inclusive conceptualization of poverty-related issues that encompasses traditional social welfare issues, but also reaches beyond this traditional definition to incorporate other issues that target the poor in areas such as employment, tax policy, education, and housing. Detailed discussions of these policy areas illustrate their impact on the lives of the poor, and address how the issues are measured in order to provide a wide-ranging, substantively meaningful definition of poverty-related public policy. I then examine what Congress has actually done on these poverty issues over more than fifty years. This includes the laws passed, which directly affect the poor, as well as earlier stages in the legislative process, such as holding congressional hearings to gather information and build support for policy issues. A final measure of congressional activity on poverty-related issues is the composition of the congressional agenda, or the collection of bills that legislators proposed for consideration, regardless of their ultimate success or failure.

Together, these legislative actions provide the empirical and theoretical foundation for evaluating whether – and to what extent – Congress as a whole has addressed poverty-relevant issues over more than five decades.

Despite the broad definition of poverty-related issues and the multiple ways in which Congress could take them up, my examination of the data reveals that Congress as a whole has done remarkably little to address poverty-focused issues or help the poor. This finding suggests that the political visibility evident in the previous chapter does not translate into political attention in the US Congress.

DEFINING POVERTY ISSUES

A key feature of this book is that it examines the representation of interests, not preferences. In this way, it breaks with recent studies that evaluate the "goodness of fit" between public opinion and policy outcomes, and instead looks at whether Congress works on issues that directly affect the lives of poor Americans. Focusing on the policy interests of the poor also helps to identify what could be done on their behalf, even if Congress is not currently doing so. For instance, if a substantive policy area such as low-income housing assistance is classified as poverty-related, but Congress takes no actions in that area in a given year, the absence of activity can still be captured. This is critically important, because it provides a way to measure both action and inaction in Congress and, therefore, to develop a richer understanding of congressional representation of the poor.

I identify the set of issues that uniquely impact the lives of the poor in a way that expands the definition of poverty issues beyond social welfare programs to include issues across a range of policy areas. It also concentrates on issues that explicitly target the poor, in order to understand whether Congress is responsive to their particular needs. This approach also means that I do not examine universal programs such as Social Security, which helps older Americans who happen to be poor, but also helps many more Americans who are middle-class and even wealthy. There is some debate as to whether it is more politically advantageous to pursue universalistic programs that expand social programs for the non-poor as well as the poor, as compared to programs that target the poor (see Skocpol 1991; Wilson 1987). However, my primary interest is the extent to which Congress and its members represent poor Americans, and the ability to evaluate such relationships is greatly diminished when looking at universalistic programs. To return to the example of Social Security, when Congress increases Social Security benefits, it cannot reasonably be argued that this is evidence of acting specifically for the poor. Indeed, it is possible that such actions are taken on behalf of middle-income (and even wealthy) older constituents. In contrast, if Congress takes up a proposal to increase low-income housing, it is clearer to interpret such action as reflecting the interests of the poor as compared to other constituents.

My approach to defining these issues begins with traditional welfare and safety-net policies, and then builds out to an inclusive and non-partisan definition of the policy areas relevant to poverty. Such a wide-ranging definition increases the likelihood of finding evidence that Congress is active on issues relevant to the poor, although it also means that not finding significant activity would be especially striking. Social welfare policy is the natural starting point for defining issues related to poverty, and includes public assistance programs and social services. Since the New Deal policies of the 1930s, the federal government has enacted certain social policies designed to address poverty or to redistribute wealth in some way. Studies of economic inequality or poverty tend to focus on these issues, and scholars have found that the poor are more supportive of government spending on welfare programs than are the wealthy (e.g., Gilens 2005, 2009; Soroka and Wlezien 2008). Gilens (2009) also shows that the poor have different policy preferences when it comes to traditional welfare policy beyond the level of government spending. Additionally, there is evidence that the policy priorities of the poor are most distinct from those of wealthier citizens when it comes to issues of social welfare (Miler and McNally 2016).[1] As a result, social welfare issues are the starting point for how I define poverty-relevant issues, and a full discussion of the specific issues included in this category follows later in the chapter.

However, social welfare policies alone are not sufficient to capture the issues relevant to the poor. In his important book on affluence in politics, Gilens (2009) examines more than 1,700 survey questions that ask whether respondents support or oppose a specific policy or proposed policy. He finds a significant difference of close to 18 percentage points in the policy opinions of low-income and high-income individuals across a wide range of policies. Notably, his findings are robust to the inclusion (or exclusion) of welfare policy. Thus, the evidence presented by Gilens (2009) reveals that the poor have a distinctive perspective on issues far beyond welfare. Looking outside academia to the policy community

---

[1] Specifically, low-income Americans are consistently much more likely than wealthier Americans to say that these issues are the most important problem facing the country, and the government should address them.

reveals a similarly inclusive approach to defining the issues that affect the poor. The Sargent Shriver National Center on Poverty Law, a non-profit, charitable organization focused on legal and political advocacy for the poor, highlights "basic assistance, work supports, skill building, educational, and employment opportunities," as well as more traditional income support programs like cash assistance and food and nutrition benefits, as policy areas that directly affect the poor.

In keeping with these articulated policy priorities, I argue that poverty-focused issues go beyond "welfare," to include other policies that specifically impact low-income Americans. In order to provide an operational definition that allows for the empirical analysis of what Congress does for the poor, I turn to the substantive classification system established by the Policy Agendas Project (2017).[2] As discussed in Chapter 2, the Policy Agendas Project provides a comprehensive classification of all congressional activity by policy topic. I begin with relevant social welfare issues, including housing, homelessness, education, food assistance, jobs training, and safety net programs such as "welfare" and disability insurance. Each of these issue areas corresponds with a Policy Agendas Project subtopic that allows for the identification of related congressional activity (see Table 3.1).

This initial set of policy areas related to poverty could be seen as tending towards more liberal or Democratic-leaning policy solutions to poverty. Therefore, I also want to capture anti-poverty efforts that focus on economic growth and job growth, as well as tax-based tools like the Earned Income Tax Credit (EITC), all of which are typically considered to be more conservative or Republican-leaning approaches to poverty. A recent example of this approach to addressing poverty is Republican House Speaker Paul Ryan's June 2016 policy paper entitled "A Better Way: Poverty, Opportunity and Upward Mobility," that advocates promoting employment and tying benefits to work requirements. The potential concern would be that, if these types of economic-based proposals are not counted as poverty-relevant, then subsequent analyses of congressional activity may underestimate activity on behalf of the poor, especially by Republican legislators.

---

[2] These data were originally collected by Frank R. Baumgartner and Bryan D. Jones, with the support of National Science Foundation grant number SPR 9320922, and were made available through the Policy Agendas website and the Department of Government at the University of Texas at Austin. Neither NSF nor the original collectors of the data bear any responsibility for the analyses conducted here.

TABLE 3.1 *Poverty-related issues*

Policy topic and subtopic	Policy agendas project code
Macroeconomics; General Domestic Macroeconomic Issues	100
Examples: economic conditions and issues, long-term economic needs, general economic policy, promote economic recovery and full employment, distribution of income, assuring opportunity for employment	
Macroeconomics; Unemployment Rate	103
Examples: economic and social impact of unemployment, national employment priorities, employment and labor market development	
Labor and Employment; Employment Training and Workforce Development	502
Examples: job training partnership acts, job opportunities and basic skills training, federal aid for job retraining, DOL bonuses to states for training and employment of long-term welfare recipients, work incentive programs, public service jobs for unemployed, Comprehensive Employment and Training Act	
Education; Education of Underprivileged Students	603
Examples: Head Start programs, teaching disadvantaged students, Department of Education grants to improve skills of economically disadvantaged students, bilingual education needs, adult literacy programs, education for children from low income homes, rural education initiatives	
Social Welfare; General	1300
Examples: HHS and HEW appropriations, administration's welfare reform proposals, effectiveness of state and federal public welfare programs, social services proposals, public assistance programs	
Social Welfare; Food Stamps, Food Assistance, and Nutrition Monitoring	1301
Examples: USDA grants for women, infants, and children (WIC) supplemental food program, childhood hunger relief, child nutrition programs, food stamp abuse and fraud, approach to the United States hunger problem, USDA school breakfast/lunch program, food assistance for low income families, food stamp reductions, special milk program eligibility for public schools	
Social Welfare; Poverty and Assistance for Low-Income Families & Individuals	1302

Policy topic and subtopic	Policy agendas project code
Examples: Economic Opportunity Act antipoverty programs, programs to alleviate long-term welfare dependence, example proposals to reform Aid to Families with Dependent Children (AFDC) program, needs of disadvantaged children from low-income families, mandatory work and training programs for welfare recipients, promotion of economic self-sufficiency for single mothers on AFDC, HHS low-income energy assistance programs	
Social Welfare; Social Services and Volunteer Associations	1305
Examples: domestic volunteer service programs, youth volunteer programs, national meals-on-wheels programs, state social services programs, boys and girls clubs	
Social Welfare; Other	1399
Community Development and Housing Issues; Low and Middle Income Housing Programs and Needs	1406
Examples: housing affordability problems of low and moderate income families, federal housing assistance programs, low-income housing shortages, rent control, deficiencies in public housing projects, tenant-management initiatives in public housing projects, HUD management of multi-family programs, slum clearance and related problems, housing affordability and availability	
Community Development and Housing Issues; Housing Assistance for Homeless and Homeless Issues	1409
Examples: permanent housing for the homeless; federal aid for the homeless; Homeless Outreach Act, assistance for homeless veterans, lack of housing for homeless and low-income groups; extent and causes of homelessness in the United States	

Source: Policy Agendas Project (2017) Topics Codebook;
DOL, US Department of Labor; HHS, US Department of Health and Human Services;
HEW, US Department of Health, Education, and Welfare; USDA, US Department of Agriculture

As a result, to create a broad measure of poverty-relevant legislation that encompasses a range of approaches, I also include legislation identified by the Policy Agendas Project (2017) as addressing unemployment and economic growth, alongside the social welfare policies in my definition of poverty-relevant issues (see Table 3.1). All of these policies are targeted to low-income individuals, which is important in evaluating whether legislators are representing the poor through their legislative actions.

Having established this set of poverty-related issues, I next consider whether there may be variation among these bills, based on whether they are intended to expand assistance to the poor or to restrict support to the poor. Both types of legislation would be considered to address poverty-related issues, but they have rather different aims. To determine whether there is such variation in the intent of the poverty-relevant bills identified through the Policy Agendas Project, I conduct a check on a subset of the full data. For the subset, I chose the four congresses that immediately followed the new Census (1983–1984, 1993–1994, 2003–2004, and 2013–2014). Based on the bill title and official bill summary written by the Congressional Research Service, I carefully analyze the content of the 625 poverty-related bills in this sample, and classify each as positive, neutral, or negative.[3] Every bill in the subset selected for investigation was also coded by two independent coders, which resulted in a high level of intercoder reliability (88 percent) and any differences were resolved by the author reading the original bill text.

I find that 94 percent of the poverty-relevant legislation examined is partially or fully supportive in its proposed approach to address poverty. These are bills that propose pilot studies, renew funding for established programs, and amend existing policies. This in-depth examination of the content of poverty-related legislation reveals that there is little evidence that legislators are offering legislation that would reduce support for the poor. This in itself is interesting, since the rhetoric of dismantling the inefficient welfare state might lead one to expect that legislators would offer proposals to undercut or eliminate existing programs. However, actual legislative efforts to do so are exceedingly rare. Additionally, given the very small number of negative bills, the empirical analyses are robust to their inclusion or omission.[4]

---

[3] Positive bills were those that unequivocally supported the establishment or expansion of programs to help the poor, neutral/mixed bills were those whose impact was neutral (largely in cases of administrative changes) or could be characterized as both expanding a program while also providing some restrictions, and negative bills were those that imposed new restrictions on eligibility or benefits, or reduced the scope or scale of programs.

[4] The main empirical analyses were replicated for the sample congresses only. The results concerning congressional responsiveness to poverty are robust to the inclusion or exclusion of negatively-coded bills.

HOW POVERTY POLICY IMPACTS THE POOR

It is instructive to provide greater detail on the types of legislative proposals that are included in the data, which reveals the numerous and
varied ways that government policy directly affects the poor. I begin by
taking a closer look at housing policies. Housing is a major concern for
Americans living in poverty because it consumes an outsized percentage
of their resources. The Pew Charitable Trust reports that low-income
households (those in the bottom third) spend 40 percent of their income
on housing, as compared to 25 percent for middle-income households and
17 percent for upper-income households (Pew Research Center 2016).
The same report also finds that the costs of housing grew by more than
50 percent for low-income households from 1996 to 2014. These statistics convey the reality that housing costs relative to resources are exceedingly burdensome for low-income individuals, which not only makes
meeting other basic needs more difficult, but also leaves the poor more
vulnerable to losing their housing.

Reflecting these needs, several policy tools exist to address the twin
problems of affordability and availability. Public housing is a common
policy issue, as is rent control and other price-support policies. Also
relevant are efforts to encourage the creation of affordable housing
through favorable lending and tax incentives to owners and local housing
authorities. Proposals regarding public safety and discrimination in public
housing also occur with some regularity. Poverty-relevant housing issues
also include specific programs intended to help keep people in safe
housing, like the Low-Income Home Energy Assistance program, that
provides assistance with utilities during cold weather months as well as
financial incentives for weatherization of properties. There are also
numerous efforts to amend the tax code to help low-income individuals
through tax deductions for rent, assistance in home ownership, and a
range of other tax-based incentives.

Another subset of housing issues that are relevant to the poor are policies
addressing homelessness. These policies tend to focus on the causes of
homelessness, programs to reduce the number of people who become
homeless, and providing services for those who are homeless. There are
also efforts to connect existing social welfare programs to the homeless,
including food assistance and health services (including mental health
services). Of particular concern is federal funding for emergency shelters,
partnerships with local governments and charitable organizations, and the
protection of particularly vulnerable groups like homeless children.

Policies addressing education of underprivileged children, including the millions of children living in poverty, also are relevant. Both access and quality of education are important to poor families. Official government statistics show that children from low-income families consistently have a significantly higher drop-out rate than other children (US Department of Education 2016), and numerous academic studies highlight the growing education achievement gap between wealthy and poor students (see Tavernise 2012). Education policy relevant to poor families, therefore, tends to highlight efforts to increase early childhood education, such as through support and funding of the Head Start program. Other aspects of education policy affecting the poor revolve around equal access to educational services, including ensuring access in rural communities, in bilingual communities, and for children with special needs. For older students, relevant policies focus on mentorship, internships, and after-school programs intended to help students stay in school. In addition, education policy also explicitly targets lower-income children through a number of grants and programs administered to state and local governments.

Another issue area with direct relevance to the poor is employment and job training. Almost by definition, poor Americans are more likely to be unemployed, underemployed, or work in low-wage industries, which means that policies to create jobs and give individuals job-ready skills are of critical importance to the poor. As a special Federal Reserve report on unemployment notes, "getting to the root causes of the labor market issues facing low-income communities is far from easy, however, and even the best intentioned policies have faced difficulties in tackling the complicated and inter-woven barriers that keep lower-skilled adults from accessing living wage jobs" (Reid 2009, 5). The types of policies to address these challenges include efforts to provide public service employment, encourage private sector employers to promote job training through tax incentives, and provide bilingual training programs. Also relevant are job training programs for certain types of workers, including young people, former homemakers, miners, railroad employees, and workers affected by increasing trade. A well-known example of this type of legislation is the Job Training Partnership Act, which was enacted in 1982 to provide job training assistance to low-income youth and adults.

As discussed earlier, a strong job market and a growing economy are also seen by some (especially those on the political right) as market-based solutions to poverty that do not require government-run social programs. This approach to fighting poverty focuses on policies that stimulate economic growth through tax and monetary policy. Some proposals call for improving the economy by increasing jobs – either through federal investment or tax incentives – in certain sectors like public works, infrastructure and energy production. Certain policies call for tax incentives for businesses opening in economically depressed areas. Another approach involves programs to create new jobs through government incentives to the private sector, such as tax credits to businesses for hiring the long-term unemployed. There are also calls for government to provide financial assurances during times of economic recession, through loans, tax forgiveness, and direct assistance that would prevent businesses from failing and, thereby, increasing local unemployment levels. These types of policies are relevant to poverty, because they promise a work-based path to self-sufficiency, but also because low-income workers are disproportionately negatively affected by economic downturns, and have more difficulty recovering after a downturn (Edmiston 2013).

Lastly, social welfare issues are those most frequently associated with poverty, because they include programs explicitly designed to provide services and direct assistance to the poor, and provide a "safety net." For instance, there is considerable attention to issues related to child care for low-income families that reflects both the high costs of child care and the need for child care if parents are to participate in the work force. Relevant initiatives include grants to states to develop new policies, tax deductions for childcare expenses, and tax incentives for employers to assist employees' child care needs. Social welfare policy also includes the development of new anti-poverty programs, as well as reviews, reauthorization, and reforms to established programs like Temporary Assistance for Needy Families (TANF, also commonly referred to as "welfare"), food assistance, and school lunch programs. More broadly, government involvement in poverty-related social welfare programs includes the development of pilot programs, program studies, block grants to the states, and the use of tax policy to incentivize desired actions. Social welfare policy also includes support of a variety of volunteer programs and charitable organizations.

Altogether, these policy categories encompass a broad, but clearly defined, set of issues that are directly relevant to the poor. The inclusion of more traditionally left and right approaches to addressing poverty should make it easier to find evidence of congressional representation of the poor, since it offers a range of ways in which proposed legislation could advance the interests of the poor. It is noteworthy, however, that the substantive conclusions drawn throughout the book are robust to the use of this wide-ranging definition of poverty-relevant issues, as well as the use of a more traditional definition focused on social welfare issues. At the macro-level, this means that the addition of market-oriented policies does not dramatically increase the amount of poverty-focused activity by Congress. At the individual legislator-level (discussed in Chapters 5 and 6), this means that the legislators who propose market-based solutions to poverty are not vastly different from the types of legislators who propose more traditional government-based programs to address poverty.[5]

CONGRESSIONAL LAWMAKING

Having defined poverty-relevant issues, attention now turns to what Congress does on these issues. The most obvious measure of congressional action is to look at the number of poverty-related laws passed by Congress. These are legislative proposals that a majority of legislators in both the House and the Senate voted to support, and reflect the fact that the two chambers were able to reconcile any differences that might have existed between them. These successful bills then moved to the president's desk, and were enacted into law, where they have the potential to impact the tens of millions of Americans living in poverty. Accordingly, looking at laws passed by Congress every year from 1960 to 2014 best approximates congressional policy "outcomes."

Even an initial consideration of the data on poverty-related laws passed quickly reveals that Congress does not pass many laws related to poverty, even when defining poverty-relevance broadly (see Figure 3.1). After tallying the total number of bills passed in each of the policy categories, an average of only three bills addressing issues relevant to poverty become law in a given year, which is 1.2 percent of public laws passed by Congress. In more than three-quarters of the years from 1960 to 2014, Congress passed four or fewer poverty-focused bills. It never passed more than nine bills annually addressing the collection of issues identified here as relevant to poverty, and twenty-three times it passed two or fewer poverty-related bills. Therefore, whether looking at the absolute number of laws or the percentage of laws passed, there is no way around the conclusion that Congress passes very few laws on behalf of the poor.

---

[5] Democrats and Republicans introduced a near equal number of these market-oriented bills, and the overall partisan balance of poverty-related legislation shifts by only one percentage point when using this broadly defined measure.

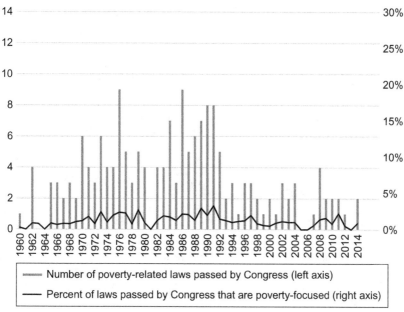

FIGURE 3.1 Poverty-related laws passed, 1960–2014

The low level of congressional activity is even more striking when one considers that this number is not necessarily a count of major or entirely new legislation to address poverty. Rather, it includes legislation that makes administrative and technical corrections to existing legislation, creates studies or pilot programs, and declares commemorative events. Consequently, the figure of 1.2 percent of laws devoted to poverty-related issues counts even small or symbolic legislation like National Meals on Wheels week as a form of congressional action. If one were to require that bills passed by Congress have a substantively significant impact on the poor, the proportion of relevant bills passed each congress would fall even lower.

In order to put congressional activity on poverty-related issues further into context, Figure 3.2 shows the number of poverty-focused laws passed annually, as compared to the number of successful laws in a range of other policy areas.[6] As the figure illustrates, Congress passes fewer laws addressing poverty issues than nearly every other issue, and this is true

[6] These other policy areas are based on the "major topics" used in the Policy Agendas Project.

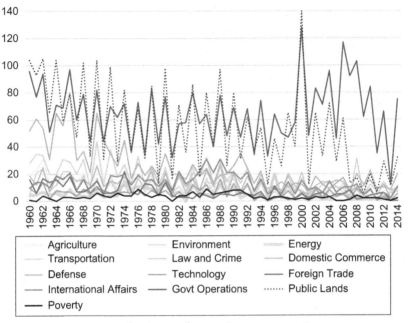

FIGURE 3.2 Laws passed across issue areas, 1960–2014

almost every year from 1960 to 2014. In all fifty-four years examined, there were fewer laws passed addressing poverty-relevant issues like unemployment, affordable child care, and housing assistance than there were laws dedicated to public lands. Furthermore, comparing poverty-focused policy to agriculture policy reveals that, on average, three times more agriculture bills pass each year.[7]

For a closer look at the few laws Congress makes on issues related to poverty, I examine the high point of passage of legislation addressing poverty issues, which came during the 101st Congress, 1989–1990. However, the majority of the fifteen laws that passed during this two-year congress were commemorative. Without these eight laws calling attention to relevant issues like Ending Hunger Month, National Jobs Skills Week, and the twenty-fifth Anniversary of Head Start, Congress did even less than it appears. In short, as the first answer to the question of whether Congress represents the poor, the small number of poverty-relevant laws passed by Congress conveys a resounding no.

---

[7] On average, 9.8 agriculture bills pass each year, compared with 3.3 poverty bills.

CONGRESSIONAL HEARINGS

Given that successful poverty-focused laws are rare, I next examine two complementary measures that provide a broader look at what Congress does: holding committee hearings and putting bills on the legislative agenda. As a measure of congressional activity, committee hearings offer a look at an important midway point in the legislative process. After a bill is introduced, it is frequently – but not always – referred to one or more congressional committees, based on the issue addressed in the bill and the substantive policy jurisdiction of the committee(s). Once a bill is referred to the committee, the committee chairperson has discretion as to whether or not to take further action. Committee hearings are one of the key actions that can occur at this stage. These hearings are called by the committee chairperson, in consultation with the ranking minority member of the committee, and offer a public forum in which chosen witnesses testify before the committee, and legislators who serve on the committee have the opportunity to ask questions. These hearings serve multiple functions, including providing information to members of the committee, providing opportunities for legislators to make public pronouncements, and giving organized interests and invited groups a visible seat at the policymaking table (e.g., Carpenter, Esterling, and Lazer 2004; Esterling 2007). Committees are also opportunities for Congress to advance policy solutions, oversee policy implementation, and actively engage in policymaking (e.g., Adler and Wilkerson 2012; MacDonald and McGrath 2016). If a bill receives a congressional hearing, it is a sign that the leaders of the committee to which the bill was referred are invested in moving the bill through the process. However, a congressional hearing is not a guarantee of a bill's success.

As a result, committee hearings represent an important stage in the legislative process that is more exclusive than bill introductions, but less restrictive than looking at either roll-call votes or successfully-passed laws. Put differently, hearings can be thought of as a measure of bills that Congress is taking seriously. Whereas one might be concerned that a bill can be introduced without expectation of following-through, hearings are an indicator that Congress is engaging the issue and spending its limited time and resources on it. In their extensive research on the progression of legislation through the U.S. House of Representatives, Volden and Wiseman (2014) find that approximately 13 percent of all bills introduced in the chamber receive "action in committee," as compared to only 4 percent of bills that become law.[8] Consequently, holding hearings related to poverty is more common than passing laws, but this is still a meaningful indication of congressional attention, and is not afforded to all proposals.

When it comes to congressional action for the poor, then, the question is whether Congress spends notable time and resources to hold hearings on issues identified as relevant to poverty. In light of the evidence that the poor are politically visible in other venues (see Chapter 2), I argue that it is reasonable to expect Congress to also devote public hearings to issues relevant to the poor, even if an underwhelming amount of poverty-related legislation becomes law. Such hearings do not require Congress to reach a majority agreement on a policy solution and how to pay for it (as is the case with passing new laws), but only to agree to call attention to the problem of poverty and discuss possible approaches for alleviating poverty.

As one illustration, during the 105th Congress (1997–1998), the House Ways and Means Committee's Subcommittee on Oversight held hearings on low-income housing tax credits.[9] In addition to government officials from relevant administrative agencies, there were more than thirty individuals and organizations who testified before members of the committee. These participants represent a range of perspectives and include members of the business and construction communities, affordable housing groups, local community organizations, and national advocacy groups. Specifically, witnesses from groups as varied as the Affordable Housing Group, US Chamber of Commerce, National Association of Home Builders, National Council of State Housing Agencies, Rural Rental Housing Association of Texas, Connecticut Housing Financing Authority, and the Lake Havasu City Apartment Owners Association offered their perspectives on the efficacy of the tax credit for low-income housing and answered questions from legislators.

Even though hearings can reflect a range of perspectives and do not require reaching a consensus, Figure 3.3 illustrates that, in general, Congress holds remarkably few hearings on issues relevant to the poor. Between 1960 and 2014, there were an average of forty committee and subcommittee hearings held each year on poverty-relevant policies like

---

[8] Volden and Wiseman 2014 define "action in committee" as including committee hearings, committee markup, and/or receiving a committee vote.

[9] See US Government Printing Office Serial 105–82, Hearings before the Subcommittee on Oversight of the Committee on Ways and Means, House of Representatives, April 23 and May 1, 1997.

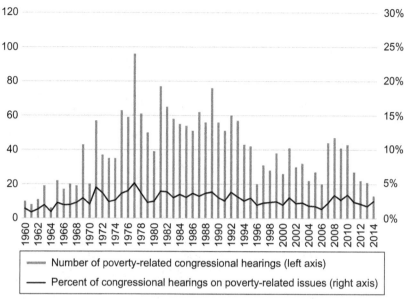

FIGURE 3.3 Poverty-related hearings held, 1960–2014

low-income housing, Head Start, job skills training, and welfare programs. Moreover, this figure reflects hearings held by all House committees, since poverty-related issues do not fall under a single committee jurisdiction.

Forty hearings may sound like a significant amount of congressional activity, until it is put into the context of the more than 1,450 committee hearings typically held each year. The reality is that, on average, only 2.6 percent of committee hearings in Congress are held on poverty-focused issues. In fact, the percentage of hearings devoted to issues related to the poor has never exceeded 5 percent in over forty years. These low rates hold true even for the years since the economic recession in 2009, an issue I take up in detail in Chapter 4. Put bluntly, despite the largest economic collapse in generations, which sent millions of low-income families into poverty, Congress still only spent 2.3 percent of hearings held from 2010 to 2014 discussing the types of social programs and economic policies that could help those most affected by the economic downturn. Moreover, Congress almost always holds fewer hearings addressing poverty-related issues than hearings addressing other issues such as public lands, foreign trade, or agriculture (see Figure 3.4). Overall, while the proportion of hearings on poverty issues (2.6%) is slightly greater than

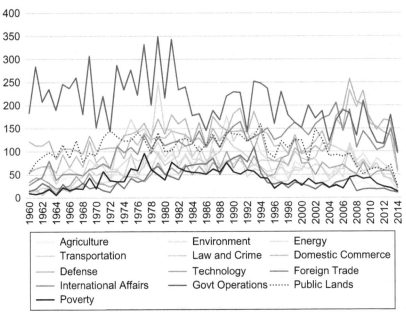

400
350
300
250
200
150
100
50
0

1960 1962 1964 1966 1968 1970 1972 1974 1976 1978 1980 1982 1984 1986 1988 1990 1992 1994 1996 1998 2000 2002 2004 2006 2008 2010 2012 2014

Agriculture	Environment	Energy
Transportation	Law and Crime	Domestic Commerce
Defense	Technology	Foreign Trade
International Affairs	Govt Operations	Public Lands
Poverty		

FIGURE 3.4 Congressional hearings across issue areas, 1960–2014

the proportion of laws passed that address poverty-relevant issues (1.2%), it is still a very small fraction of Congress' time and attention.

A closer look at 1977, the year in which Congress held the most hearings on poverty-related issues (5%) reveals that, even when Congress is relatively active in holding hearings, there are still many poverty-related issues that are not addressed. Of the ninety-six relevant hearings held in 1977, nearly two-thirds of them were on issues of macroeconomics or social welfare, including twenty-eight hearings on the subject of the Carter administration's welfare reform proposal. Another dozen committee hearings were held on affordable housing, including housing assistance programs, HUD (Department of Housing and Urban Development) loan guarantees, housing subsidies, and rent-control programs. However, even at the peak of congressional attention to poverty-related issues, there were no hearings held specifically on food assistance, welfare, tax credits for low-income families, child care for low income families, or policies to address homelessness.

Thus, the data reveal substantively meaningful holes in Congress' attention to issues that affect the lives of the poor. For instance, in twenty-seven of the fifty-five years examined, there was not a single congressional hearing on issues of child care or parental leave. Another example is that, between 2004 and 2014, Congress did not hold a hearing on education for underprivileged students, including rural education, bilingual education, and literacy programs. This absence of congressional attention means that real issues that matter deeply to poor communities are not being discussed, let alone being enacted into law.

CONGRESSIONAL AGENDA

Lastly, I turn to a third measure of congressional activity on poverty-related issues – the collection of bills introduced in Congress. The number of bills introduced provides the most inclusive look at the collection of policy issues on the congressional agenda. As Gilens (2009) notes, bill introductions are an important measure of congressional activity because they reveal what could have been, not just the policy proposals that make it to a vote. Only members of the chamber can introduce legislation (i.e., only House members can introduce bills in the House, and only Senators can offer legislation in the Senate), and the introduction of a bill is a necessary first step if Congress is to take any further action. Simply put, without a bill being introduced, nothing else can happen.

The set of proposed legislation makes up the range of issues "on the table" – or the congressional agenda – during a congressional session (e.g., Baumgartner and Jones 1993; Kingdon 1984). These are the issues that Congress collectively has decided to highlight as being worthy of political attention and potential legislative action. There is no expectation, however, that a member has worked through the hard political and economic choices inherent in policymaking when he introduces a bill. Rather, the set of poverty-relevant bills introduced in Congress reflects a range of approaches that is both broader than the set of bills that become law and also narrower that the spectrum of all possible ideas for addressing poverty. Given that bill introductions need only reflect the interest of a single legislator, I contend that the bill sponsorship is the least costly – and most likely – stage in the lawmaking process at which to find evidence of congressional attention to issues that affect the poor. In addition, this collection of proposed legislation serves an important purpose of getting policymakers discussing the issues on the agenda. This process of "softening up" and slowly building support for proposals is essential to understanding how Congress creates new policies or otherwise breaks with the status quo (Kingdon 1984).

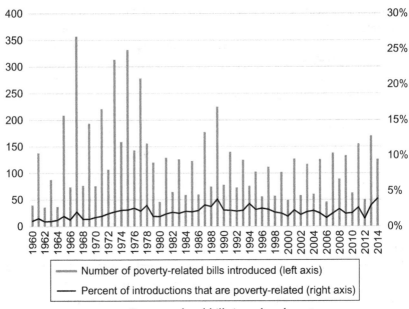

FIGURE 3.5 Poverty-related bills introduced, 1960–2014

Yet, as Figure 3.5 illustrates, Congress does little to even bring political attention to issues relevant to the poor. During the post-war period, poverty-related issues, on average, make up 2.8 percent of the legislative agenda. In contrast, during this same period, agriculture policy is an average of 3.4 percent of the agenda, and public land bills are nearly 9 percent of the agenda.[10] Especially striking is the fact that, during the most recent economic downtown of the late 2000s, bills focusing on poverty-related issues made up just 2.8 percent of the House agenda.

Although Congress consistently devotes only a small portion – never more than 4.5 percent – of its agenda to issues affecting the poor, Figure 3.5 also shows that the raw number of relevant bills introduced does fluctuate. Congress considered the fewest bills on poverty in 1962, when only forty-five pieces of legislation were proposed. In sharp contrast, just a few years later, in 1967, there were 463 poverty-related bills proposed in Congress. This high point in congressional attention to issues of poverty reflects President Lyndon Johnson's Great Society agenda,

[10] These figures are based on data from the Comparative Policy Agendas Project website, www.comparativeagendas.net.

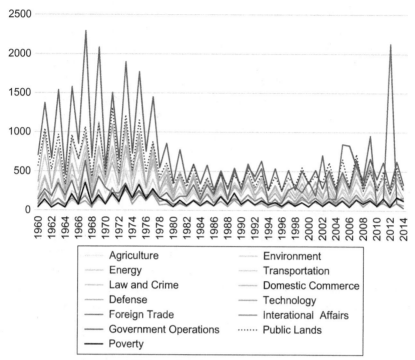

FIGURE 3.6 Bills introduced across issue areas, 1960–2014

which created major new social programs, including the Food Stamp Act (1964), the creation of Head Start (1965), and the creation of Social Security (1965). Additionally, some of this overall variation may reflect the cyclical nature of the two-year congress, because there are generally more bills introduced in the first session of a congress (i.e., the odd numbered years) as compared to the second year, during which members of Congress are running for reelection. Nevertheless, the relative amount of congressional attention to poverty-related issues is consistently low when compared to other major policy areas. As Figure 3.6 illustrates, issues related to the interests of the poor consistently occupy less congressional agenda space than issues related to transportation, technology, or even government operations.[11]

---

[11] Again, these comparison issue areas represent "major topics" according to the Policy Agendas Project.

It is useful to take a closer look at some of the issues addressed in the relatively small percentage of bills that are introduced. For purposes of illustration, I highlight the poverty-focused bills introduced in 2005, which is a relatively recent year in which a near-average number of bills were proposed (126, compared to the annual average of 121). In 2005, legislation addressing just three areas – job training, education, and housing – made up more than half of all poverty-focused proposals in Congress. Within these categories, however, there is variation in the specific focus of the proposed legislation. Among the job training bills are proposals calling for expanded vocational training and apprenticeship programs, as well as training targeting specified fields like healthcare and technology. In the area of education, bills were proposed to expand programs like Head Start, as well as support for programs to train and retain teachers in disadvantaged schools. Similarly, legislative proposals on the topic of housing include reforms to the Section 8 voucher program, calls for tax credits for developing affordable housing, and support for drug elimination programs in public housing. Additionally, some legislators offered more technical proposals, such as reducing administrative requirements or granting waivers to states for compliance with certain social welfare provisions. Thus, even though the number of bills proposed is quite low, a range of topics was introduced to the congressional agenda. I examine this variation in further detail in Chapter 6, which focuses on the actions of the few legislators who champion the interests of the poor.

CONCLUSION

This chapter began with the assertion that representative bodies like the US Congress are aware of the poor and should act in ways to reflect their interests. Using a multifaceted and inclusive definition of issues relevant to poverty, I examine the laws passed by Congress, the hearings held, and the bills offered for consideration. Figure 3.7 illustrates the consistently low-levels of congressional activity on poverty across these three stages in the legislative process. There are some slight differences in activity levels between measures, notably the slightly lower rate of poverty-related laws, which reflects the general difficulty of bill passage (e.g., Krutz 2005; Volden and Wiseman 2014). Figure 3.7 also shows that there are fluctuations over time in congressional activity; in some years Congress does a little more (or a little less) than in other years. In Chapter 4, I focus on these variations, and examine whether they occur in response to changes

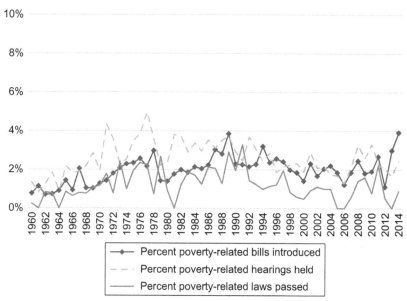

FIGURE 3.7 Poverty-related congressional activity, 1960–2014

in poverty. Overall, however, in the more than fifty years from 1960 to 2014, not once did Congress devote more than 5 percent of its energies to issues relevant to the poor.

The pattern of successful legislation, hearings, and bill introductions leaves two impressions – one more pessimistic and one more hopeful. First, when measured as a percentage of bills introduced, hearings held, or laws passed across all issues, Congress does very little for the poor. Second, however, is that, when one considers the raw numbers, especially of proposals and hearings, it is clear that Congress is doing something. Importantly, these actions provide opportunities for individual legislators to act on behalf of the poor, which is a dynamic I examine later in Chapters 5–7.

In Chapter 4, however, I continue to examine congressional activity, both on its own and as a proportion of Congress' overall activity, and turn to the question of how congressional activity on poverty-focused issues relates to actual levels of poverty in the United States. Specifically, I examine whether the ebb and flow in congressional activity on issues relevant to the poor reflects increases and decreases in the poverty rate. It is possible that, despite the low levels of activity uncovered in this chapter, Congress is, nevertheless, responsive to changes in the number of poor nationwide.

4

Congressional Unresponsiveness to the Poor

The previous chapter shows that Congress, as a whole, does little when it comes to poverty-related issues. Yet, it also reveals some evidence that congressional attention to these issues fluctuates over time. This variation raises the question of whether Congress is responsive to changes in poverty, even if the overall level of activity is rather low. That is, when poverty increases, does Congress do more in order to address the greater societal need? If so, this responsiveness would provide some consolation in the face of the underwhelming absolute levels of congressional activity.

Much of the recent scholarship on class and economic inequality draws heavily on the theory of macro-level responsiveness, which contends that representation can be assessed by measuring the congruence between the public's collective opinion and national policy outcomes. It concludes that Congress, as a whole, does in fact respond to shifts in public opinion (e.g., Erikson, MacKuen, and Stimson 2002; Stimson 1999; Wlezien 1995). In this chapter, I follow in that tradition in order to establish whether Congress, as a whole, is responsive to the needs of the poor. However, unlike previous scholarship, I focus specifically on responsiveness to shifts in actual poverty levels (rather than public opinion), and examine this relationship with an eye to multiple stages in the policy process, rather than only policy outcomes. Additionally, I look at congressional responsiveness in two different ways: first, to changing poverty over time and, second, to changes in the distribution of poverty across congressional districts.

The key question is whether congressional activity on poverty-related issues reflects changing levels and dynamics of poverty in the United States? If an institution like the US Congress is to reflect the interests of its constituents, then its actions should ebb and flow with the needs of the people. The broader macro-responsiveness literature suggests that Congress should do more on poverty-related issues when there are more people living in poverty. Similarly, when poverty rates fall, Congress should scale back its activity to focus on other issues. I argue that, even if the base level of congressional activity on poverty issues is low (as shown in Chapter 3), Congress may still be responsive to poor constituents if the ups and downs of congressional activity reflects changes in poverty. Furthermore, political economy theories suggest that the distribution of poverty across congressional districts also should affect how much Congress does to address poverty. When a sizeable degree of poverty extends to enough districts, such that legislators cannot overlook it, and there are enough districts affected to build a significant coalition, then we should expect to see more congressional activity on poverty-focused issues.

I start with an overview of poverty levels in the United States since 1960, and show that the number of poor in America fluctuates considerably over time. Consistent with Chapter 3, I then compare poverty levels with congressional activity at three stages in the legislative process: bill introductions, hearings, and bills passed. To evaluate congressional responsiveness to the poor, I use a series of initial, bivariate tests, followed by multivariate analyses that take into account the potential impact of economic and political context on congressional activity on poverty-related issues. The primary finding is that, across all three measures of congressional action, variation in the number of poor in the United States does not affect how much Congress does on poverty-related issues.

In light of the lack of responsiveness to changing nationwide poverty, I then ask whether national poverty levels may be masking important district-level variation. In the second half of the chapter, then, I examine the distribution of poverty across congressional districts, which political economy scholars highlight as a critical reason as to why some groups are better represented than others. The basic logic is that the dispersion (or concentration) of an interest affects the number of elected officials with incentives to take up the industry's needs, which in turn affects the likelihood that a winning political coalition can be created to advance policy. Therefore, I expect that, when more members of Congress represent districts with high levels of poverty, it will facilitate legislative cooperation that, in turn, will make congressional action on poverty legislation more likely. Contrary to the above logic, I find no evidence that the widespread distribution of the poor affects the passage of legislation or the holding of congressional hearings. There is suggestive evidence, however, that the distribution of the poor by congressional district is positively related to the number of poverty-related bills on the congressional agenda. An important implication of this finding is that individual members of Congress may do more to respond to the poor in their districts than is evident at the macro-level, an issue I examine in Chapters 5–7.

MACRO-LEVEL RESPONSIVENESS

A rich literature examines congressional representation in terms of the correspondence of aggregate-level changes in public sentiment and government action. Stimson's (1999, 2004) work alone, and with colleagues (Erikson et al. 2002, 2006; Stimson, MacKuen, and Erikson 1995), makes the case that government is responsive to the "public mood," which reflects the public's preference for more liberal or conservative policies. In a series of influential publications, these scholars find that the government responds to swings in the public mood: as the public prefers more liberal (conservative) policies, Congress produces more liberal (conservative) laws. Therefore, these studies conclude that Congress is responsive to the public, and argues that much of the hand-wringing about congressional representation is unfounded.

Related research on the thermostatic model of representation (Wlezien 1995) puts macro-responsiveness at its theoretical and empirical heart. In this model, responsiveness is the mechanism for a "dialogue" between the public and government over preferred outcomes. First, the public expresses preferences for more or less spending, and the government responds to these preferences. Then the public updates their preferences in response to the new policy by moving in the opposite direction, and the government responds again by reducing (or increasing) spending (see Erikson et al. 2002; Soroka and Wlezien 2010; Wlezien 1995). These studies are particularly notable, because they posit that responsiveness not only occurs, but that it is a regular feature of the political system.

Numerous other scholars also conceive of congressional representation as the congruence between majority public opinion and the enactment of policies (e.g., Jacobs and Page 2005; Page and Shapiro 1982, 1983, 1992; Shapiro and Page 1994, as well as Shapiro 2011 for an extensive review). Some of these studies break with previous work on macro-level responsiveness by focusing on responsiveness to public preferences on a specific issue, as compared to general policy "mood" or broad measures of liberal/conservative preferences. For instance, there is evidence of responsiveness to the public on issues like defense spending (Bartels 1991), mass incarceration (Enns 2014), and the death penalty (Baumgartner, DeBoeuf, and Boydstun 2008).

As applied to the study of economic inequality, the macro-level approach evaluates the extent to which policy outcomes reflect class-level public opinion (e.g., Kelly 2009; Wlezien 1995). In these studies, the question is whether Congress is equally responsive to the mood (or sometimes policy-specific preferences) of rich, middle-income, and low-income individuals.[1] A few scholars conclude that Congress is not more responsive to the wealthy, primarily because they find that economic groups have similar public moods and preferences, so there are no differences to reflect (e.g., Soroka and Wlezien 2008; Wlezien and Soroka 2011).[2] Ura and Ellis (2008) conceptualize responsiveness in terms of preferences over government spending, and also conclude that there is no evidence that Congress is more responsive to the wealthy. In discussing why Congress is equally responsive to the preferences of all incomes, the authors are agnostic as to whether it is because there are no significant differences between the preferences of richer and poorer Americans, or because re-election oriented politicians have incentives to be responsive to the preferences of all Americans.

Yet other scholars take issue with the argument that the rich and poor have common preferences, and offer evidence that class-based differences in public preferences exist, and that Congress is most responsive to the wealthy (Bartels 2008; Ellis 2012, 2013; Gilens 2005, 2009, 2012; Gilens and Page 2014). Bartels (2008) finds evidence of differences in public preferences by class when looking at ideological self-placement along the liberal to conservative continuum. When he examines to whom government policy is responsive, Bartels finds that policy is responsive to elite opinion rather than mass opinion (see also Jacobs and Page 2005). Moreover, when it is responsive to public opinion, government policies

---

[1] Some scholars also examine whether the policies created by differential responsiveness result in economic outcomes that have a differential impact on the wealthy and the poor and, thus, perpetuate income inequality (see especially Bartels 2008 and Kelly 2009).

[2] Soroka and Wlezien 2008 and Wlezien and Soroka 2011 note that government spending on welfare is an exception where preferences differ by income group, but they argue that the preferences of high, medium, and low-income groups are parallel, which they interpret as a sign of the underlying homogeneity across class.

reflect the preferences of the upper class and middle class, not the preferences of the lower class.

Gilens (2012) reaches similar conclusions, but via a different path. He argues that looking at individuals' liberal (or conservative) leanings can hide competing policy preferences, which could make assessments of responsiveness less accurate. Instead, Gilens (2009, 2012) focuses on responses to survey questions on a range of specific policy issues. Notwithstanding this different measure of public opinion, Gilens also finds evidence of differences along class lines such that government is more responsive to the preferences of the affluent.[3] The one exception is certain social welfare issues where there is a "happy coincidence" of the preferences of the poor overlapping with the preferences of well-resourced interest groups (see Gilens 2009). In these situations, however, it would be misleading to claim that government is responsive to the poor. As Gilens (2009, 2012) argues, the government may be responsive to the organized interests, and the poor just "get lucky."

Despite the different conclusions reached, an important similarity across macro-level studies of responsiveness to inequality is the use of policy outcomes as the dominant measure of government behavior.[4] Government action is conceptualized as either the enactment of public policy by government, what Gilens (2012, 41) calls "actual policy" (see also Shapiro 2011), or sometimes government spending (Soroka and Wlezien 2008; Ura and Ellis 2008; Wlezien and Soroka 2011). As shown in Chapter 3, however, this is not the only way to think about what Congress does. Passage of legislation is certainly an important metric for evaluating responsiveness, but an emphasis on the end stage of policymaking misses much of the behavior that comprises lawmaking and representation. Therefore, I argue that a yet-to-be examined element of collective congressional responsiveness to the poor is what Congress does at other stages in the lawmaking process. In the rest of this chapter, then, I extend the macro-responsiveness approach and examine whether Congress is responsive, in a variety of ways, to differences in poverty levels over time and across the country.

---

[3] Gilens uses the term "affluent" to describe Americans whose income puts them in the top 10 percent.
[4] See Erikson 2015 for a discussion of inequality in light of the broader findings of responsiveness to public opinion.

CONGRESSIONAL UNRESPONSIVENESS OVER TIME

In order to examine whether Congress is responsive to the poor, it is necessary to first define who the poor are. To do so, I use the official federal poverty level, as established by the Office of Management and Budget, which is particularly well-suited to examination over time, and is widely considered to be a somewhat conservative estimate of poverty. This poverty measure has been employed by the Census Bureau since the 1960s, and is based on pre-tax income in a given year. The threshold also takes into account family size, and is updated annually to adjust for inflation.[5] As an illustration, the official poverty threshold in 2014 was $11,670 for an individual and $23,850 for a family of four. Using this definition, there were approximately forty-six million people living in poverty in 2014, or approximately 15 percent of the United States population (US Census).

As Figure 4.1 illustrates, the poverty rate in the United States has fluctuated over the last six decades. Drawing on Census records, the highest rates of poverty occurred in 1960, when 22.2 percent of Americans lived below the poverty lines. This number dropped significantly in the early 1960s, and, since 1966, the poverty rate has fluctuated between 11 and 15 percent (see Figure 4.1). The high levels of poverty early in this period predate the creation of many federal antipoverty programs, including much of President Johnson's Great Society and War on Poverty. These policies account in large part for the sharp decline in poverty in the early 1960s. However, even since then, levels of poverty continue to fluctuate from year to year, sometimes increasing and sometimes decreasing. If Congress is responsive to the poor, we should expect to see congressional activity change in a parallel manner.

During the last fifty years (1966–2015), the country experienced its lowest poverty rate in the early 1970s (1973–1974), when just over 11 percent of Americans lived in poverty. Not surprisingly, the highest levels of poverty – when poverty rates were 15 percent or higher – occurred during economic downturns. The first occurred in the early

---

[5] Since the late 1990s, several experimental calculations of poverty have been developed to address issues such as child care costs, benefits and services received, and regional variation. These experimental poverty measures overwhelmingly track the established poverty rate by the US Census, with some measures producing slightly higher estimates and some producing slightly lower estimates (see Iceland 2006). For more information on the calculation of the poverty rate, see www.census.gov/hhes/www/poverty/data/threshold/index.html.

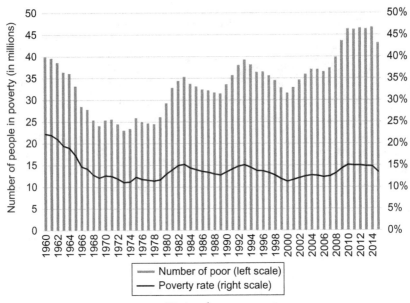

FIGURE 4.1 National poverty, 1960–2014

1980s, and was marked by increases in the consumer price index, coupled with cuts in domestic programs that impacted low-income Americans.[6] Poverty rates then fell for the remainder of the decade, before picking back up in the early 1990s, briefly reaching the 15 percent mark in 1993. A similar pattern of declining poverty followed for approximately fifteen years, capped by rising poverty rates and an increase during the Great Recession from 2010 to 2012, when poverty rates again exceeded 15 percent. The contracting economy and increasing unemployment, combined with the collapse of the housing market and high rates of foreclosures, continue to impact many Americans, especially low-income Americans (Mian and Sufi 2015; Sard 2009).

Additionally, Figure 4.1 illustrates a fluctuation in the number of people living in poverty. The variation in the number of poor Americans from 1960 to 2014 is due to a combination of changes in the national poverty rate across years, as well as the growing population. For instance, although the poverty rate was 12.7 percent in both 1998 and 2004, the rising US population means that, in 2004 there were 2.5 million more Americans living in poverty, despite the same poverty rate.

[6] See Reed 2014 for discussion of the Consumer Price Index over time.

A critical question is whether fluctuations in congressional activity on poverty-related issues correspond to variation in the number of poor Americans over time. During times when there is more poverty, such as during the recession that began in 2009, it is reasonable to expect that legislators would offer more proposals addressing the needs of the poor. Normatively, this type of responsiveness is desirable, as Congress should mirror changes in the needs and interests of the people that it represents.

Related past studies suggest competing expectations, however. On the one hand, there is ample evidence from the broader literature on macroresponsiveness that Congress, as a whole, is responsive to the public, which suggests that Congress will also be responsive to the poor (e.g., Adler and Lapinski 2006; Erikson, MacKuen, and Stimson 2002; Soroka and Wlezien 2010; Stimson 1999). On the other hand, there is also evidence from the studies of inequality discussed previously that policy outcomes are more likely to reflect the preferences and interests of the wealthy (e.g., Bartels 2008; Gilens 2009, 2012; Gilens and Page 2014), which suggests that we should not expect congressional activity to change with fluctuations in the level of poverty. Additionally, the fact that responsiveness is measured differently here than in previous studies (i.e., not only based on policy output, but also the congressional agenda and congressional hearings) makes it difficult to predict the relationship between poverty and congressional activity.

Towards this goal, Figure 4.2 provides an illustration of how poverty rates and Congressional legislative outcomes (i.e., laws passed) change relative to one another. In evaluating these patterns, I compare congressional activity to the previous year's poverty rate to allow for a reasonable lag in Congress' response. However, I also examine concurrent relationships and lags of two years and three years to account for the possibility that perhaps Congress reacts more quickly or more slowly.

Put simply, I fail to find a positive relationship between the amount of poverty-related legislation passed and the national poverty rate in the preceding year. In fact, the lagged national poverty rate and the percentage of laws passed by Congress that focus on poverty are negatively correlated, at −0.34, which is robust to alternate lagged timing.[7] Therefore, the bivariate relationships indicate that, when poverty rates increase, Congress

---

[7] The correlation between congressional activity and a concurrent measure of the poverty rate is −0.32. If the default one year lag applied to the poverty rate is extended to two years or three years, the correlation between poverty and congressional activity is −0.37 in both cases.

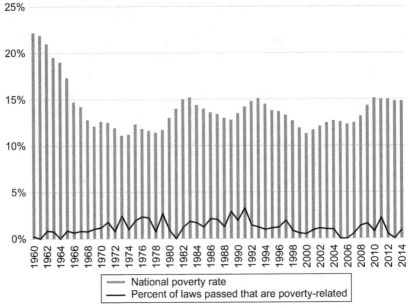

FIGURE 4.2 Congressional responsiveness to the poor: laws passed, 1960–2014

actually passes fewer new laws addressing issues that directly affect poor Americans. This may be, in part, due to the fact that some pre-existing policies are designed to accommodate fluctuations in the number of poor, including need-based programs like unemployment benefits. However, existing programs are exceedingly unlikely to meet all the needs of increasing numbers of poor Americans. As a result, one would still expect to see new legislation addressing other poverty-related issues, as well as an increase in the passage of laws that renew or revise existing poverty-focused programs. In a similar fashion, other federal programs that automatically expand to meet increased demand, such as more middle-class families claiming a mortgage tax deduction, do not preclude Congress from passing additional legislation targeting middle-class Americans. Altogether, the lack of a positive relationship between poverty and the laws Congress enacts is striking for a representative democratic institution.

Nevertheless, I also consider whether there is heightened activity during the earlier stages in the lawmaking process, when it may be easier to find evidence of responsiveness to the poor. I first examine whether Congress holds more hearings across the range of issues related to poverty when there are more people living in poverty. One reason to expect

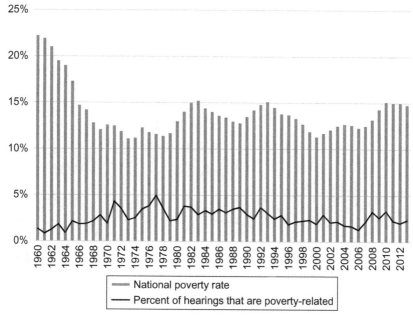

FIGURE 4.3 Congressional responsiveness to the poor: hearings held, 1960–2014

greater responsiveness through congressional hearings is that a hearing indicates that Congress is considering the issue, but not necessarily that it has worked out differences of opinion about how (or whether) to proceed with the legislation. Additionally, Congress can hold hearings on existing poverty-related programs in order to assess whether they are responding to increased need. As a result, hearings are a sign of congressional attention to the problem of poverty, not necessarily congressional agreement on how to address it.

However, there is no evidence that Congress is responsive to the poor through hearings. Figure 4.3 shows that the percentage of congressional hearings on poverty-related issues does not rise and fall in a pattern similar to the increases and decreases in poverty. In fact, the lagged national poverty rate and the percentage of poverty-related hearings are correlated at –0.49, which is robust if examined contemporaneously or with a longer lag to allow Congress more time to respond.[8] Indeed, the

---

[8] The correlation between congressional action and contemporaneous poverty is –0.45, and the correlation is –0.54 and –0.57 if one allows a two year lag or three year lag for Congress to act, respectively. As an additional check on the robustness of the relationship,

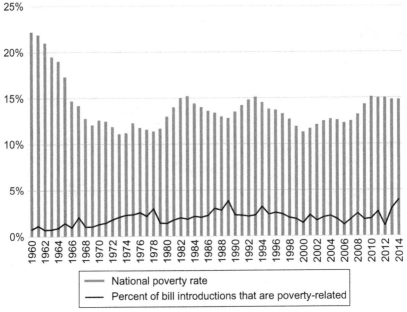

FIGURE 4.4 Congressional responsiveness to the poor: bills introduced, 1960–2014

highest portion of congressional hearings on poverty-related issues were held in the mid–late 1970s, a period during which the fewest people were living in poverty. In contrast, Congress was particularly inactive from 2011 to 2013, when the number of poor was at its highest levels (see Figure 4.3).

Lastly, I examine the composition of the congressional agenda for signs of responsiveness to poverty (see Figure 4.4). Specifically, I ask whether Congress responds to higher national poverty rates by introducing more bills related to poverty as a percentage of all bills introduced. Expectations of responsiveness are heightened because bill introductions are the least costly of congressional activity, requiring no coordination or agreement within Congress. Individual members of Congress independently decide what type of legislation they want to introduce, and they are free to introduce as many (or as few) bills on whatever policy topics as they wish.

the correlation between the lagged (one year) number of poor people (as compared to the national poverty rate) and the number of congressional, poverty-related hearings (as compared to the percentage of hearings dedicated to poverty issues) is –0.43.

TABLE 4.1 *Average annual congressional activity on poverty-related issues by party control of Congress, 1960–2014*

	Percentage of bills introduced	Percentage of hearings held	Percentage of laws passed
Unified Democratic Congress ($n = 33$)	2.70	2.63	1.86
Unified Republican Congress ($n = 12$)	2.72	2.10	0.85
Divided Congress ($n = 10$)	2.94	2.86	1.18
Comparison of Means Tests			
Dem vs. Rep control	$t = 0.064$	$t = -0.054$	$t = -01.86$
Dem vs. Divided	$t = -0.739$	$t = -0.883$	$t = 0.488$
Rep vs. Divided	$t = -0.917$	$t = -2.930^*$	$t = -1.130$

* Denotes significance at $p < 0.05$ level.

Despite this different measure of congressional action, the same pattern emerges. Figure 4.4 provides no evidence that Congress responds to a higher national poverty rate by devoting more agenda space to poverty-related issues. Specifically, when poverty levels rise, there is no parallel increase in the proportion of bills introduced to address poverty. Rather, the data suggest that, to the extent that there is any relationship between national poverty rates and congressional activity, it continues to be a negative relationship. In the case of bill introductions, the percentages of the agenda dedicated to poverty and the national poverty rate are correlated at –0.54, which is again robust to alternate lagged timing.[9]

The lack of systematic evidence of congressional responsiveness to the poor across all three types of congressional activity runs against expectations that Congress will exhibit some degree of macro-responsiveness to poor Americans. One possible explanation is that party polarization and political gridlock make it hard for Congress to accomplish much on poverty-related issues. As a first look at this possibility, in Table 4.1, I compare summaries of congressional activity levels under unified Democratic, unified Republican, and divided control of Congress.

[9] The correlation is –0.51 when using a contemporaneous poverty rate, –0.55 when using poverty rates lagged by two years, and –0.57 when using poverty rates lagged by three years. In addition, the correlation between the number of poor and the number of poverty-related bills introduced (as compared to percentage measures) is –0.51 for both contemporaneous and one year lagged data.

The data presented in Table 4.1, however, indicate that congressional activity is remarkably similar, regardless of whether Congress is controlled by Democrats, Republicans, or is divided between the parties. Examples exist of minimal levels of representation of the poor under divided government (e.g., the 97th Congress, 1981–1982, and the 112th Congress, 2011–2012) as well as under unified Democratic control (e.g., 91st Congress, 1969–1970, and 96th Congress 1979–1980), and unified Republican control (e.g., 106th Congress, 1999–2000, and 108th Congress, 2003–2004). Additionally, these similar summary statistics of congressional activity are based on percentages, which account for differences in the overall number of bills passed, and so the differences are not an artifact of differences in overall congressional production.

A Model of Congressional Responsiveness to the Poor

Next, I account for the potential impact of the political environment and national economic conditions in order to more completely assess whether Congress is unresponsive to the poor. The dependent variables are the same three indicators of congressional activity used previously (laws, hearings, and bills introduced), but now it is possible to consider alternate explanations in a manner that a bivariate approach does not allow. A potentially relevant feature of the broader environment is whether the United States is engaged in a war. During times of war I expect to find less congressional action on poverty-related issues, all else equal, because Congress is forced to devote greater legislative energy to issues related to the war, which may crowd out attention to domestic issues like poverty. Indeed, this notion of trade-offs is reflected in the classic macroeconomic model of a production-possibility frontier where a nation must choose between devoting resources to "guns vs. butter." Therefore, I include a dichotomous variable that indicates whether the United States was in a federally designated "period of war" in a given year, which is taken from the Congressional Research Service (CRS) report on dates of war and military conflicts.

The political and partisan context in which Congress exists also has potential implications for the amount of congressional activity for the poor. Notwithstanding the earlier bivariate tests, I consider whether unified or divided party control of government shapes what Congress, as a whole, does on issues related to poverty. In general, unified control of Congress and the White House is expected to increase passage of legislation, because agreement across the two branches of government is facilitated by shared party control (e.g., Binder 1999; Mayhew 1991). However, since congressional activity on poverty issues is measured as a percentage of all laws passed, I expect that any improved productivity under unified government may increase both the number of poverty-focused bills passed as well as the total number of bills passed, resulting in little change in the percentage of laws passed that address poverty-relevant issues. Additionally, congressional activities that occur earlier in the lawmaking process (e.g., the composition of the legislative agenda and congressional hearings) are even less likely to be affected by unified (or divided) government, because they do not require the involvement of the president. Nevertheless, I include in the model a dummy variable for unified Democratic party control of both the legislative and executive branches, and another dummy variable for unified Republican party control of the two branches (with divided government as the referent).

Although the earlier bivariate examination suggests that party control does not affect congressional activity on poverty-related issues (see Table 4.1), I explore party control of Congress (i.e., the House and the Senate) in a multivariate context. I expect that the potential for poverty-related congressional activity is greater during a unified Congress than a divided Congress. The advantages associated with unified partisan control of Congress are rooted in the greater ease with which the House and Senate can coordinate on legislative priorities and preferences, thereby making it easier to pass legislation. However, it is not exclusively an institutional argument, as I expect that unified Democratic control of Congress is distinctly more favorable for congressional activity on poverty-related issues than unified Republican control of Congress. Issues related to poverty are more closely identified with Democrats, and this issue ownership provides incentives for the party to be active on that issue (Bawn et al. 2012; Petrocik 1996). As a result, I argue that the effect of unified government is conditional on the party in control, and include two dummy variables for unified Democratic control of Congress and unified Republican control of Congress (where the referent group is divided control of Congress).

Lastly, another factor that may shape congressional activity on poverty-related issues is the general condition of the national economy (separate of national poverty rates). If the overall economy is doing well, then Congress may be less likely to focus on issues affecting the poor, because public and media attention is focused on the positive economic news. In contrast, when the economy is slowing down, I anticipate that Congress will focus more on poverty-relevant issues, because there is likely to be greater public attention to these issues as more people feel economically vulnerable. I employ the percentage change in GDP as the primary measure of changing national economic conditions.[10]

I estimate a series of three regression models where the dependent variables are: (1) the percentage of bills introduced in Congress on poverty-related issues, (2) the percentage of congressional hearings held on poverty issues, and (3) the percentage of laws passed that are poverty-related. Each dependent variable is measured as a percentage of all bills introduced (or hearings held, or laws passed) in a given year in order to control for variation in the overall activity levels of Congress during the period from 1960 to 2014. I estimate an ordinary least squares (OLS) regression model with robust standard errors. Since Congress may be delayed in its response to changes in poverty, I employ a one year lag on the measure of national poverty rate. This allows for a more realistic notion of congressional responsiveness, as compared to assuming that Congress has a simultaneous response. Similarly I lag the GDP growth rate variable by one year to allow for economic conditions to take effect before expecting them to shape congressional activity.[11] Finally, since the data are annual, but the legislative cycle is two years, I include an indicator for the second year in a congressional session when members of Congress spend more time in their districts campaigning.[12] The results of these models are presented in Table 4.2.

The clear conclusion to be drawn from Table 4.2 is that Congress does not respond to increased poverty with more action on issues relevant to the poor even when controlling for the overall economic and political environment. The estimated findings in Table 4.2 provide no evidence that Congress is responsive to the number of poor Americans when it comes to poverty-related issues on the legislative agenda, or the percentage of poverty-focused laws that pass (see column 3). Moreover, there is evidence that Congress actually introduces fewer bills and holds fewer hearings on issues that affect the poor (as a percentage of all congressional

---

[10] Specifically, I use the US Bureau of Economic Analysis (www.bea.gov/national/xls/gdpchg.xls) figures for the annual percentage change in GDP based on chained 2009 dollars and lagged by one year. This measure is not strongly correlated with the poverty rate, and has a correlation coefficient of 0.11.

[11] The findings for poverty and economic growth presented below are substantively and statistically unchanged if contemporaneous data is used rather than lagged data, or if a longer lag of two years is employed.

[12] Alternately, one might combine the annual data into congresses, but this would result in half the number of observations.

TABLE 4.2 *Congressional responsiveness to poverty*

	Bills introductions	Hearings	Laws
National poverty rate (lagged)	−0.123* (0.033)	−0.136* (0.044)	−0.068 (0.036)
GDP growth rate (lagged)	−0.0002 (0.003)	−0.001 (0.0004)	−0.0001 (0.0004)
Country at war	−0.007* (0.003)	−0.008* (0.002)	−0.004* (0.002)
Unified Congress – Democrat	0.001 (0.004)	0.002 (0.002)	0.005 (0.003)
Unified Cong – Republican	−0.006 (0.003)	−0.01* (0.003)	−0.004 (0.004)
Unified Govt – Democrat	−0.004 (0.003)	−0.003 (0.003)	−0.005* (0.003)
Unified Govt – Republican	0.005 (0.004)	0.003 (0.003)	−0.0004 (0.004)
Second year of session	−0.001 (0.002)	−0.002 (0.002)	−0.004* (0.002)
Constant	0.051* (0.005)	0.051* (0.006)	0.26* (0.006)
Number of observations	55	55	55
F-statistic (8, 46)	8.62	14.11	4.28

Models are estimated using OLS estimation. The dependent variable is poverty-related activity as a percentage of total congressional activity.
* Denotes significance at $p < 0.05$ level.

hearings held) in response to higher levels of poverty in the preceding year (columns 1 and 2).[13] Put differently, when more people live in poverty, Congress does not respond by devoting more of its agenda to relevant issues, nor does it hold more hearings on issues like affordable housing, unemployment, or food assistance – or pass more legislation to address poverty.

These results are based on a relatively small number of observations, but contribute a new perspective to our understanding of macro-responsiveness and economic inequality. The evidence that multiple types of congressional activity are not responsive to the poor is compatible with

[13] When estimating these models with a count version of the dependent variable (i.e., the number of poverty-related bills introduced, hearings held, and laws passed), the coefficient estimates on poverty rates again either fail to achieve conventional standards of significance or are negatively signed.

previous conclusions that policy outcomes are more responsive to the preferences of the rich. However, the findings here are distinctive both in their emphasis on the poor and the actions examined. Two of the three dependent variables emphasize the legislative process over outcomes (i.e., congressional hearings and bill introductions) and do not require Congress to choose the poor over the wealthy in order to register activity on poverty-related issues. For instance, there is nothing to prevent Congress from offering legislation to address poverty-relevant issues and to address the interests of the wealthy. On these measures of lawmaking activity, then, Congress can call attention to issues related to poverty, and also be active on issues of importance to the wealthy. Yet, Congress still does very little on behalf of the poor.

Among the other findings in Table 4.2, perhaps the strongest one is that Congress does less on issues related to poverty in years when the country is engaged in war. For example, when the United States is not in a period of war, Congress devotes an average of 3 percent of hearings to topics related to poverty, but this falls to 2.3 percent during periods of war, which is a statistically meaningful decline.[14] This is to be expected, because congressional time and resources are constrained, but that does not diminish the potentially harmful impact on the poor, especially given the duration of the United States involvement in prolonged conflicts like Vietnam and Afghanistan. Another notable finding presented in Table 4.2 is that there is no evidence that Congress responds to broader economic growth or decline. The estimated coefficient on lagged GDP growth is negative, but does not achieve conventional levels of statistical significance in any model. This is noteworthy, because the lack of responsiveness to the poor might have been mitigated if Congress was instead responsive to the broader economic climate. Finally, the data in Table 4.2 also indicate that unified partisan control of Congress – and of government – matters very little for congressional activity on poverty issues. There is no evidence of a significant difference in what Congress does on issues related to the poor under unified Democratic control, unified Republican control, and divided party control of Congress.[15] Also as expected, there is no evidence that whether one party controls the

---

[14] A difference of means test concludes that this difference in proportion of hearings is significant at conventional standards (t-statistic = 3.12, $p < 0.01$).

[15] The only exception is that when Republicans have a majority of seats in both the House and the Senate, Congress holds slightly more hearings on poverty than under divided party control.

legislative and executive branches affects congressional activity early in the lawmaking process (bills introduced or hearings held).

Taken together, these analyses provide further evidence that Congress as a whole is not responsive to fluctuations in the number of people living in poverty over time. When the national poverty rate increases, Congress does not respond with increased legislative activity. In fact, in some cases, Congress responds to increasing levels of poverty by actually doing less to address related policies. The reason behind this negative relationship is unclear, although it may reflect the fact that during these times Congress is particularly active on certain other issues, which has the effect of reducing the percentage of bills or hearings devoted to poverty-relevant issues. Regardless, for an elected representative body this is disheartening news that undermines previous conclusions that Congress is generally responsive to the public. Before concluding that Congress as a whole is unresponsive to levels of national poverty, I next consider the possibility of responsiveness to the geographic dispersion of poverty.

CONGRESSIONAL UNRESPONSIVENESS TO THE DISTRIBUTION OF THE POOR

Here I recast the question as whether Congress is responsive to the *distribution* of the poor. I argue that the national poverty rate is not the only way to think about the representation of the poor, because it may mask significant variation in the amount of poverty experienced in places around the country, including in congressional districts. For instance, a national poverty rate of 15 percent could be distributed evenly, with 15 percent poverty in all congressional districts, or it could be that some districts have 25 percent poverty, while other districts have only 5 percent poverty. These two scenarios have different implications for representation in a majoritarian institution like the US Congress, where a key to legislative success is building sufficient support for one's proposal so that it can gain majority approval. For purposes of representation, then, it is important to think about how the poor map onto congressional districts, and how these districts aggregate to build the type of political coalition that political economists argue is critical to producing congressional action.

Although the term "distribution" is not always used, scholars often think about how interests are distributed across congressional districts and the implications of this for political representation (e.g., Bailey 2001; Clemens et al. 2015; Lee 1998, 2003, 2004; Schiller 1999). Examples of constituency interests that can be characterized as geographically distributed in ways that shape their political representation include racial minorities, economic interests (e.g., military bases, firms) and even partisan voters (most notably in the context of evaluating redistricting plans). Indeed, the Congressional District Dataset (Adler 2002) and the Congressional District Demographic and Political Data (Lublin 1997b) are prime examples of attention to the distribution of various constituencies by congressional district. However, there has been little attention to how the tens of millions of poor in American are spread across congressional districts.

A classic illustration of the importance of geography in the US Congress is the differential influence of agricultural interests in the House, where they are concentrated in a relatively small percentage of House districts, as compared to the Senate, where they are dispersed across a greater number of states. As a result of this different political geography, legislation that emerges from the Senate is often more representative of rural and agricultural interests, as illustrated by the Senate's greater support for ethanol in energy legislation and larger farm subsidies for crops like corn and soybeans (Rogers 2012). Schiller's (1999) work on US trade policy reveals similar differences in the way that the distribution of trade-sensitive industries combines with the different geographic structure of the two chambers to the benefit of different industries.

The focus here is on the House, which is based on geographic representation, and so the focus is on the distribution of the poor across congressional districts. In the parlance of political economy scholars, this would be called the political dispersion (or political concentration) of the poor (see Busch and Reinhardt 1999; Caves 1976; Pincus 1975; Trefler 1993). When an industry is politically dispersed, it has a presence across more House districts, which means that more legislators have a direct, constituency-based interest in advocating for their interests. Optimal interest dispersion requires that the industry is sufficiently large in each district to be noticed by the legislator, and to compel them to act on their behalf (Rogowski 2002). The greater base of support increases the likelihood of successfully building a majority coalition to advance industry interests in Congress (Chase 2015).[16]

---

[16] Another perspective in the political economy literature emphasizes geographic concentration of interests, arguing that, when industries are in close proximity to one another, trade policy outcomes are more likely to reflect their interests (e.g., Busch and

At the heart of thinking about the representation of the poor from a political economy perspective is the central tension between the risk of too much concentration, which can result in too few supportive legislators to achieve policy goals, and the risk of too much dispersion, which can result in the dilution of an interest's political power. As Rogowski (2002) argues, there is a representation "sweet spot" where an interest is sufficiently dispersed to matter to a significant number of legislators, but is not spread so thin that it is only a small presence in those districts. The question is whether the distribution of the poor meets this description.

In order to evaluate the extent to which the distribution of poverty affects overall congressional activity on poverty-related issues, I first determine how poverty maps onto congressional districts. Are the poor concentrated in a few extremely high poverty districts, or are they spread out across many districts? These two different distributions have political consequences for how much Congress as a whole does, as well as for which legislators act for the poor, which is the focus of Chapters 5 and 6. Here I consider how the distribution of the poor affects the size of the group of legislators seeking to represent the interests of the poor in the House. Passing legislation in the House requires at least 218 votes so if the poor are distributed across a larger number of congressional districts, it should be easier to build a coalition in support of poverty-related legislation. However, if many legislators represent only a modest number of poor people, then that may not be enough to bring together sufficient support to move legislation forward in the House. Recognizing this balance of distribution and intensity, we might expect that, as the number of districts with levels of poverty above the national average increases, Congress should also be more likely to act on poverty-related legislation.

Data on poverty by congressional district is not as prevalent as one might expect. The US Census is the source for data on the number of people living in poverty, but the comprehensive decennial data is more readily available at the national, state, and even county levels than congressional district level. A subset of Census data, however, is aggregated

Reinhardt 1999; McGillivray 2004; Pincus 1975; Ray 1981; Trefler 1993). In a comparative context, there is evidence that the effects of geographic concentration of industries depends on institutional features like party systems (McGillivray 1997) and electoral systems (Rickard 2012). However, this perspective says little about how the distribution of an industry maps onto the congressional political geography that determines representation. Additionally, some of the evidence that geographically concentrated industries are more successful (e.g., Busch and Reinhardt 1999) is based on studies of firms receiving non-tariff barriers, which are not typically legislated by Congress.

at the congressional district level, and is available either in hard copy volumes published by the Census Bureau or published online in more recent years. It is from these Census reports that I built the data on the distribution of the poor by congressional district that is used here and in subsequent chapters. Here I focus on four points in time – the first congressional election after the new Census measures are taken (e.g., 1983–1984, 1993–1994, 2003–2004, and 2013–2014). Although this provides just four observations, it nevertheless provides a sense of the changes in the distribution of poverty over the decades.

Once poverty is measured at the district level, it quickly becomes apparent that there is considerable variation in the number of poor constituents across the 435 House districts since 1980. Concerns that the national poverty figures may mask variation across the country are supported by the data. Looking at snapshots of the four congresses immediately after each decennial Census was completed, Figure 4.5 presents maps of congressional districts shaded to reflect the level of poverty in the district. These maps are based on Census data and GIS software to create visual depictions of the distribution of the poor across districts and over time. It is clear that, at any point in time, some congressional districts experience very low levels of poverty (less than 5 percent), while other districts in the country have one-quarter or more of their population living in poverty.

Figure 4.5 also reveals that there is a significant subset of districts characterized by moderate-to-high levels of poverty, from where we would expect the collective demand for action on issues relevant to poor constituents to come. In terms of the political economy literature, the poor seem to be a constituency that lies in the middle ground described by Rogowski (2002) as well-suited for representation: they are widely dispersed enough to build support, and they are also a sizeable presence in numerous districts, such that they should not be overlooked by legislators. Given the distribution of the poor, then, we should expect at least some congressional action on their behalf.

A political economy approach to the case of the poor raises the question of how much poverty in a district is sufficient to spur legislative activity and political representation. To investigate this, I employ two thresholds to evaluate how the distribution of the poor affects congressional responsiveness. First, I look at the number of districts (or House seats) with high levels of poverty, which I define here as when 20 percent or more of the district population lives in poverty. This threshold means that members of Congress from districts where one out of every five

(a) Poverty Levels by Congressional Districts, 1980s

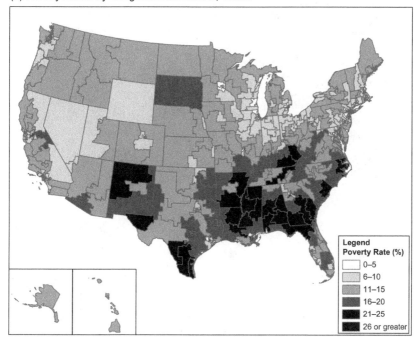

(b) Poverty Levels by Congressional Districts, 1990s

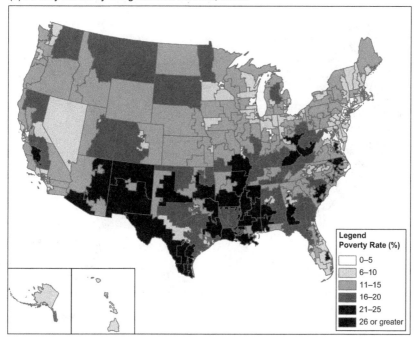

FIGURE 4.5 Distribution of poverty across congressional districts, 1983–2014

(c) Poverty Levels by Congressional Districts, 2000s

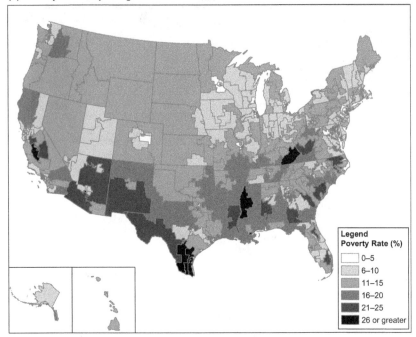

(d) Poverty Levels by Congressional Districts, 2010s

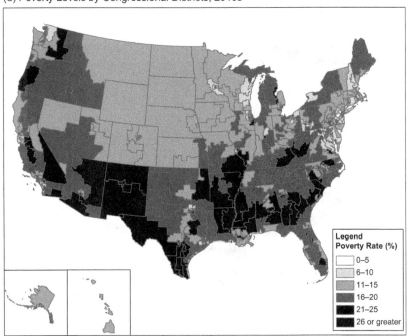

FIGURE 4.5 *(cont.)*

TABLE 4.3 *Responsiveness to the distribution of high poverty districts*

Congress	High poverty districts	Poverty-related laws	Poverty-related hearings	Poverty-related bills
98th (1983–1984)	48	11 (1.8% of all laws)	113 (3.2% of all hearings)	279 (3.0% of all bills introduced)
103rd (1993–1994)	63	5 (1.1%)	100 (2.7%)	267 (3.7%)
108th (2003–2004)	46	5 (1.0%)	54 (2.0%)	260 (3.0%)
113th (2013–2014)	89	2 (1.1%)	34 (1.9%)	296 (3.5%)

constituents is poor are expected to work together to address issues of poverty. As Table 4.3 shows, the number of high poverty districts ranges from forty-six districts after the 1980 Census (or 11 percent of House seats) to eighty-nine districts (or 20 percent of seats) in the 2010 Census.

The rightmost three columns in Table 4.3 once again show that Congress does very little to address poverty in each of the selected congresses. Most importantly, this is true regardless of the number of legislators representing high poverty districts (first column). Across these limited cases, the number of high poverty districts is negatively associated with the number of laws passed or hearings held.[17] However, when there are more districts with high levels of poverty, more legislators propose poverty-relevant legislation. The key distinction is that hearings and laws both require institutional action and cooperation among legislators, whereas introducing bills to Congress can be done by legislators acting alone, a distinction that I will return to in Chapter 7. As a result, an increase in the number of legislators representing high-poverty districts can perhaps impact the number of bills introduced, even if there is not enough support to form a majority coalition to advance legislation further.

I next assume that a lower threshold of poverty might be sufficient to compel legislators to action. In other words, a successful coalition may be built among legislators who represent districts with significant poverty, but not necessarily high poverty, as defined previously. Table 4.4, therefore,

---

[17] The number of high poverty districts is negative correlated with the number of poverty-related laws and hearings, at more than −0.55, but this is based on only four observations and, thus, should be interpreted with some caution.

TABLE 4.4 *Responsiveness to the distribution of significant poverty districts*

Congress	Significant poverty districts	Poverty-related laws	Poverty-related hearings	Poverty-related bills
98th (1983–1984)	110	11 (1.8% of all laws)	113 (3.2% of all hearings)	279 (3.0% of all bills introduced)
103rd (1993–1994)	137	5 (1.1%)	100 (2.7%)	267 (3.7%)
108th (2003–2004)	168	5 (1.0%)	54 (2.0%)	260 (3.0%)
113th (2013–2014)	234	2 (1.1%)	34 (1.9%)	296 (3.5%)

reports the number of districts with poverty rates above the national poverty rate at that time. For instance, during the 98th Congress (1983–1984), the national poverty rate was 14.8 percent, and there were 110 districts with district-level poverty rates of 14.8 percent or more.[18] These "significant poverty" districts make up a much larger portion of the House than the "high poverty" districts. In fact, the number of districts in which poverty is concentrated at or above the national average in the 113th Congress (2013–2014) increases to 234 districts (or 54 percent of House seats). This indicates that, at least in recent years, there are enough legislators with a stake in poverty-related legislation that Congress should be able to take action.

Despite this lower threshold, the patterns are remarkably similar. There is no evidence that Congress passes more laws or holds more hearings when more districts have significant numbers of poor constituents. In fact, there is a negative association, which indicates that, as the number of districts with significant poverty increases, the number of laws and hearings on poverty issues decline. However, as the number of districts with above average poverty rates increases, so does the percentage of the congressional agenda dedicated to poverty-related issues. The positive correlation between the number of districts with higher poverty rates and the number of poverty-focused bills introduced again

---

[18] The national population is not evenly divided into the 435 House districts, and there is significant variation in the population of congressional districts, which means that there are not necessarily 217 districts with above average levels of poverty. For instance, the 2010 Census reports that the total population for districts in the 113th Congress (2013–2014) vary in size from 526,283 (Rhode Island's first district) to 989,415 (Montana's at-large district).

suggests that individual legislators may respond to higher rates of poverty by increasing their individual activity on poverty-related issues, which is the subject to which I turn in Chapter 5.

A closer look begins to offer some preliminary insights into why the distribution of the poor across congressional districts may not translate into laws and hearings in the way that political economy theories would predict. Implicit in political economy theories of how the distribution of constituents translates into policy outcomes is the assumption that legislators from both parties will work together to advance the interests of the constituent group. However, this expectation neglects the fierce partisanship in Congress that can preclude legislators from working together. As Republicans are increasingly likely to be elected from districts with significant poor populations, it is possible that the split between Democrats and Republicans may hamper Congress' ability to work together on poverty-related issues, despite the fact that more legislators come from districts with significant poverty.[19]

The power of partisanship to thwart legislative activity on poverty issues is exemplified in the 113th Congress (2013–2014), which occurred in the aftermath of the Great Recession, when many Americans were still struggling to recover from the economic downturn. These conditions gave rise to a majority of House members (234) representing constituencies with poverty rates at or above the national average, including 104 Democrats and 120 Republicans. However, despite this potentially large coalition, only two poverty-related laws passed: PL 113–128, which amended the Workforce Investment Act of 1998, and PL 113–186, which reauthorized the Child Care and Development Block Grant of 1990. During this same congress, only thirty-four congressional hearings were held on poverty-relevant issues, and important policy areas like education for underprivileged children received no congressional attention. Given the highly partisan and polarized political climate, it is perhaps unrealistic to expect that Republicans and Democrats would come together to represent the poor. If legislators work only with their copartisan colleagues, then the majority described above quickly disappears. The suggestive evidence that partisan politics shape how Congress responds to the poor foreshadows a partisan dynamic of the representation of the poor by members of Congress, which will be examined in greater detail in Chapters 5–7.

---

[19] In the 108th Congress (2003–2004), Republicans represented nearly one quarter (23 percent) of districts with poverty rates greater than 15 percent. In the 113th Congress (2013–2014), Republicans represented half of all districts with 15 percent poverty or more.

CONCLUSION

Overall, the fact that Congress as a whole does so little on poverty-related issues, even when poverty is increasing over time or across districts, demonstrates a surprising lack of responsiveness. When the national poverty rate increases, there is not a similar increase in the number of bills introduced, hearings held, or laws passed that address poverty-related issues, despite the fact that Congress has generally been found to be responsive to shifts in the public mood (e.g., Stimson 1999). When poverty spreads such that more House members come from districts with high levels of poverty, there appears to be some increase in the number of poverty-relevant bills introduced, but no comparable increase in congressional hearings or laws passed. I argue that partisanship undermines the political economy expectation of coalition-building by legislators who share the distinction of coming from poorer districts. Indeed, the aggregate patterns hint at the differences between Democratic and Republican legislators that I examine in greater detail in upcoming chapters.

Rather than conclude that the poor are not represented in Congress, based on the macro-level patterns, I argue that it is necessary to shift perspectives from the collective representation provided by Congress as a whole to the dyadic representation between individual legislators and poor constituents in their districts. From the dyadic perspective, congressional representation is made up of hundreds of representative relationships between members of Congress and their constituents. These relationships are at the heart of normative theories about the obligations and expectations in a representative democracy (e.g., Burke 1790; Mill 1861; Pitkin 1967). Shifting the focus in this way moves the study of poverty from macro-responsiveness to the classic framework for studying congressional representation as between individual legislators and their constituents. Thus, in Chapter 5, I examine whether the considerable variation in the distribution of district-level poverty produces variation in individual legislators' behavior. Namely, do House members who represent districts with more poor constituents do more on their behalf than their colleagues who represent fewer poor constituents? Given the evidence that Congress as a whole is not responsive to the poor, turning to the individual members of Congress opens up the possibility of uncovering some degree of representation between elected representatives and their poor constituents.

5

Legislators' Unresponsiveness to the Poor

The scarce evidence of collective representation of the poor is cause for concern. However, how to interpret this overall inactivity depends on the process that leads to these outcomes. One possibility is that collective representation of the poor falls short because no individual legislators take up or advance these policies, but that is not the only explanation. Perhaps individual legislators are acting in ways that represent the interests of the poor, even if their efforts do not produce successful legislation. Therefore, the lack of collective representation evident in the preceding chapter needs to be re-examined at the level of its component parts – the individual legislators. The way to more comprehensively assess congressional responsiveness to the poor is to break apart the black box of the institution, and to examine the decisions and behaviors within.

Central to congressional representation is the relationship between an elected legislator and the people in his district. This type of "dyadic" representation is rooted in the electoral structure of Congress that ties legislators' fortunes to the votes of those individuals who live in their geographic district. Everyone has "their" member of Congress, and every Member has "their" constituents to whom they are accountable. This dyadic link means that constituents expect their member to make their interests heard in Washington, and legislators know that failing to meet those expectations has potential consequences.

As a result, the members who do most of the work of representing the poor in Congress should be those whose districts include more constituents living in poverty. Legislators from districts with more poor constituents have rational incentives, as well as a normative obligation, to act on their behalf. As a result, it is possible for dyadic representation of the poor to exist despite the low levels of collective representation. That is, individual legislators from high poverty districts may introduce legislation and cast votes on poverty-related issues, even if their actions do not sway the outcomes of Congress as a whole. If this is the case, then the poor are being represented in Congress in a manner consistent with the notion of political representation as having one's interests made present in government (Pitkin 1967).

Despite this potential, the analyses in this chapter uncover no consistent evidence of dyadic representation of the poor. That is, legislators who come from districts with more poor constituents do not pursue more poverty-related legislative actions. Only if a legislator represents one of the very poorest districts in the country is such activity at all more likely, and, even then, taking legislative action on poverty issues remains unlikely. Instead, there emerge a few legislators who do the work of representing the poor, despite not having a district connection, notably Democrats, women, and minorities. These findings bode poorly for dyadic representation, but motivate the surrogate theory of representation advanced in Chapter 6.

DYADIC REPRESENTATION IN CONGRESS

There is a long history of thinking about constituency representation as the specific relationship between an individual Member of Congress and the people in the district that he or she represents.[1] In their classic research on congressional representation, Miller and Stokes (1963) refer to this as "dyadic" representation (see also Weissberg 1978). As Ansolabehere and Jones write, "this is what is most often meant by representation in the United States. The often personal relationship between the individual representative and his or her constituency is perhaps the most distinctive aspect of the U.S. Congress" (2011, 293).

The dyadic model of representation is critical to understanding how well the poor are represented in Congress because it focuses on who is acting for the poor. Moreover, it allows one to examine whether those who represent more poor constituents are more active on poverty-relevant issues. Although this type of responsiveness is well-established for nearly all other constituencies, its applicability to the poor remains

---

[1] See also Hill, Jordan, and Hurley 2015 for a review of the literature.

unknown, and this is a critical gap in our understanding of the representation of an important, understudied constituency.

Dyadic Representation of Constituent Groups

Scholars have produced an extensive literature on dyadic representation in Congress, wherein the district is treated as a collection of subconstituencies rather than a single median (e.g., Fenno 1978; Fiorina 1974; Hall 1996; Kingdon 1989; Miler 2010). However, although many subconstituencies are examined, including some politically underrepresented groups, the poor is not one of them. Instead, scholars frequently focus on constituencies based on party affiliation or identity. For instance, studies conclude that legislators are more likely to represent the preferences of co-partisans in the district (e.g., Ansolabehere, Snyder, and Stewart 2001; Bishin 2000; Clinton 2006; Hill and Hurley 2003; Kastellac, Lax, and Phillips 2010). In a similar vein, female legislators are more likely to represent female constituents, especially on issues relevant to women (e.g., Griffin and Newman 2013; Griffin, Newman, and Wolbrecht 2012; Swers 2002a, 2002b). Likewise, African American legislators are more active on issues of concern to racial minorities, particularly when they represent more black constituents (e.g., Canon 1999; Cobb and Jenkins 2001; Griffin and Newman 2008, 2013; Hutchings 1998; Hutchings, McClerking, and Charles 2004; Tate 2003; Whitby 1997). There is additional evidence that legislators are responsive to policy-specific constituencies too (e.g., Adler 2002; Adler and Lapinski 1997; Hall 1996; Hansen and Truel 2015; Miler 2007, 2010; Schiller 1995). Across all of these different constituency groups, the conclusion is the same: members of Congress represent the constituents they have in the district. We do not know if the same can be said for the poor.

As suggested earlier, legislators from districts with more poor constituents should be more likely to act on behalf of the poor. Not only are the poor a salient constituency, but legislators also face strong electoral incentives to act on their behalf. The more poor constituents in a district, the more voters that are at stake for the legislator to win – or to leave on the table for a potential challenger (e.g., Arnold 1990; Fiorina 1974; Mayhew 1974; Sulkin 2005). Furthermore, this type of rational calculation is reinforced by the normative expectation that a member of the House is responsible for giving voice to the people he represents. Many, if not most, legislators believe that part of their role as an elected representative is to respond to their constituents (Fenno 1978, 1996, 2003,

2006; Miler 2010; Miller and Stokes 1963). Therefore, the electoral incentives and normative considerations that promote dyadic representation in general also should apply to the poor.

Dyadic Representation and Class

Although the poor are generally overlooked as a constituency group in congressional research, a few scholars have begun to examine the positional congruence between individual legislators' voting behavior and the preferences (derived from public opinion data) of three economic subconstituencies: the upper class, middle class, and lower class (e.g., Bartels 2008; Ellis 2013). These studies are an important departure from the macro-level studies of inequality in Congress discussed in Chapter 4, because the attention is on individual members of Congress, rather than Congress as a whole. However, they come to somewhat mixed conclusions.

The most frequent finding is that legislators are most responsive to the wealthy in their district. In his influential book on inequality in American politics, Bartels (2008) shows that economic forces and the parties' policy decisions have increased the income gap between the upper class and the lower class. As part of his broader argument, Bartels examines class-based policy congruence in the US Senate by comparing individual senators' general vote patterns (NOMINATE scores) and specific roll-call votes with constituents' self-reported ideology from survey data.[2] Bartels finds evidence of unequal responsiveness, as senators from both parties are responsive to the ideological preferences of the upper class, while neither party is responsive to the preferences of low-income constituents.[3]

Others echo the finding that Members of Congress are most responsive to the wealthy.[4] Of particular note, Griffin and Newman (2013) examine a series of nine key votes during the 109th Congress (2005–2006), and conclude that legislators vote more often in the way high-income constituents prefer as compared to low-income constituents. Similarly, Ellis (2013) finds that, during the 110th Congress (2007–2008), legislators

---

[2] Measures of constituency ideology are taken from the NES Senate Election Study conducted from 1988 to 1992.

[3] Bartels divides the public into thirds, based on income. Bhatti and Erikson 2011 reexamine Bartels findings and conclude that the general relationship holds, although they caution that there is greater nuance than conveyed in the original study.

[4] See Carnes 2012, 2013, Ellis 2012, 2013, Griffin and Newman 2005, 2008, 2013, and Hayes 2012.

were typically in greater agreement with their wealthier constituents, based on legislators' votes and the preferences of their upper-income, middle-income, and low-income constituents. Hayes (2012) also examines congruence between public opinion and roll call votes in the Senate, and finds that senators are more responsive to the preferences of high income constituents. In addition, several case studies find that legislators' votes are consistent with the preferences of their wealthier constituents on issues such as the Bush tax cuts, repeal of the estate tax, marriage penalty tax, and minimum wage (Bartels 2008; Gilens 2005; Hussey and Zaller 2011; Jacobs and Page 2005; Kelly 2009).

On the other hand, a few studies find legislators to be at least somewhat responsive to the preferences of lower-income citizens. Barrett and Lomax-Cook (1991) examine whether legislators' support for social welfare programs reflects the degree of economic hardship in their districts, and find a modest relationship between the two. In other work, they find a positive relationship between district poverty and legislators' anti-poverty votes, although their conclusions are somewhat tempered by the limited scope of the data (Lomax-Cook and Barrett 1992). This more optimistic conclusion that legislators reflect class constituents is in keeping with the aggregate-level studies that find policy outputs to be responsive to the preferences of lower-income individuals, along with other individuals (e.g., Ura and Ellis 2009; Wlezien and Soroka 2011). Together these studies represent important steps towards bridging the gap between studies of inequality and studies of congressional representation. However, more work remains to be done. Specifically, we need to build upon the existing focus on the political advantages of the wealthy, and instead examine the ways in which those at the bottom are – or are not – represented.

CONGRESSIONAL REPRESENTATION OF THE POOR

In this and the next two chapters, I take up the task of examining the dyadic representation of the poor, and offer an approach that breaks from existing research in three important ways. First, I shine the spotlight directly on the poor, rather than focusing on the advantages of the wealthy few. Second, the interests of the poor, rather than their opinions or their ideological predisposition, serve as the basis for evaluating dyadic representation. Third, I examine legislators' behavior on behalf of their poor constituents in terms of the bills they sponsor, as well as the votes they cast. This systematic shift in focus requires a different empirical approach than previous studies, and raises distinct normative questions about congressional representation.

Focusing on the Poor

As discussed in Chapter 1, scholarly research and the popular press tend to emphasize the wealthy and the extent to which they are advantaged at the expense of (1) the 99 percent or (2) the middle class, as the stand-in for the average American. The concentration of wealth is undoubtedly an important part of understanding how economic inequality is manifested in politics. However, dyadic representation of the poor is not the inverse of representing the wealthy. For example, a legislator may not be particularly responsive to wealthy constituents, but this does not automatically mean that he will be active on behalf of the poor in his district. In turn, a legislator may advocate for the interests of the wealthy, as well as for policies that help the poor. Similarly, attention to the needs of the middle class does not reveal much about a legislator's attentiveness to the unique interests of the poor. Therefore, examining which legislators act on behalf of the poor offers a much needed, complementary perspective to the existing focus on the wealthy.

Representing Constituency Interests

The expectation of dyadic representation of the poor is rooted in the notion that a legislator should take actions that reflect the interests of his constituents back in the district. The focus on interests rather than preferences is an important distinction, both theoretically and empirically. As Bentham argues, "the representative's duty toward his constituents is 'a devotion to their interests *rather than* to their opinions'."[5] Legislators are not expected to react to the changing wishes of their constituents, but rather to deliberate and debate political solutions to address the interests of their constituents (see Pitkin 1967). In this way, interests are more akin to the needs, or the objective conditions experienced by constituents, as opposed to their opinions, which can be fickle, subjective, and even erroneous.[6]

Dyadic representation based on interests has implications for the role of elections and the subsequent impact on reelection-minded legislators'

---

[5] Italics in the original. Pitkin 1967, 176, quoting Bentham.
[6] On this point, see especially Pitkin's 1967 discussion of Burke in chapter 9.

behavior. As Mansbridge (2003) discusses, focusing on interests posits a model of representation wherein citizens evaluate their legislators retrospectively and legislators work to anticipate their constituents' needs (see also Arnold 1990; Page 1978). Put differently, a legislator takes action on issues that are consistent with the interests of his constituents, in anticipation that these efforts will be rewarded in the next election. This contrasts with a preference-based model of dyadic representation in which constituents' preferences lead the legislator's subsequent actions in office.

The difference between representation based on interests versus preferences also has implications for how dyadic representation is conceptualized and measured. The most common approach to representation is what Baumgartner and Jones (2004) refer to as "positional policy congruence," or whether members of Congress vote consistently with the majority district opinion on a given policy (e.g., Baumgartner, DeBoeuf, and Boydstun 2008; Brady and Schwartz 1995; Gilens 2012; Holian, Krebs, and Walsh 1997; Theriault 2005; Woon 2009). Similarly, legislators' voting records have been found to reflect the ideological preferences of their constituents (e.g., Bafumi and Herron 2010; Caughey and Warshaw 2016; Clinton 2006; Ellis and Stimson 2012; Hayes 2012).

However, others argue that citizens' political knowledge is insufficient to make public opinion measures meaningful indicators of constituency preferences, and, hence, of representation. The shortcomings of individuals' political knowledge are well-documented and affect both measures of ideology and specific policy preferences (e.g., Converse 1964; Delli Carpini and Keeter 1997; Jacobs and Shapiro 2005). In more recent work, Broockman (2016) argues that aggregated measures of ideology as a measure of congruence are flawed and can be misleading, which makes them a poor choice for evaluating representation. Furthermore, these concerns are amplified when looking at the poor, who generally are less informed about politics than other Americans.[7]

---

[7] In addition, Berinsky 2004 finds that higher non-response rates among the poor may underrepresent their preferences in public opinion. Furthermore, the limited availability of survey data by congressional district means that survey-based measures may depend on a small number of observations per district or combining multiple surveys, both of which reduce confidence in the subsequent findings. In response to these problems, there is a small but growing literature that uses various statistical techniques, including multilevel regression and poststratification, data imputation, and simulations, to arrive at constituency preferences (e.g., Ardoin and Garand 2003; Lax and Phillips 2009; Park, Gelman, and Bafumi 2004; Tausanovitch and Warshaw 2013; Warshaw and Rodden 2012).

Scholars who argue for an interest-based approach to representation instead use demographics to capture constituency interests, such as the percentage of the district that is rural, or the number of constituents employed in a given industry (see especially Adler's Congressional District Data). These measures can be compared to legislators' behavior, in order to evaluate dyadic representation in both the US Congress (e.g., Adler 2000; Barrett and Lomax-Cook 1991; Hall 1996; Lazarus 2013; Lublin 1997a; Miler 2010, 2011) and in cross-national settings as well (e.g., Blidook and Kerby 2011; Hibbing and Marsh 1987; Soroka, Penner, and Blidook 2009).[8] Additionally, an interest-based approach to examining the representation of the poor has the advantage of bypassing worries about constituents' information levels inherent to survey-based preference measures.

Beyond Voting

Lastly, I argue that representation of the poor is not only about voting outcomes. As discussed in Chapter 3, the congressional representation literature has expanded, beyond the long-standing focus on voting behavior to include other ways in which a member of Congress can represent his constituents, such as bill introductions, cosponsored legislation, participation in congressional committees, and participation in the floor debate (e.g., Hall 1996; Miler 2010; Minta 2009, 2011). These various forms of "non-roll call position taking behavior" (Highton and Rocca 2005) reflect the many discretionary choices legislators make about when and how to represent their constituents. Since dyadic representation calls attention to who does the actual work of representing the poor, I focus on which legislators make the effort to introduce poverty-focused legislation, as well as on their voting behavior. These complementary behaviors probe two rather different activities that occur at different moments in the legislative process.

There are many reasons that a legislator might sponsor a bill on behalf of his constituents. Introducing a bill allows a legislator to place an issue on the legislative agenda, which calls attention to that issue both within

---

[8] A similar approach leads scholars to evaluate constituency representation using observed political leanings of the district. Electoral returns – most commonly partisan vote in presidential elections – are used to measure constituents' general political choices instead of public opinion (e.g., Ansolabehere et al. 2001; Canes-Wrone, Brady, and Cogan 2002; Erikson and Wright 1980; Miler 2016).

Congress and beyond.[9] When a legislator authors a piece of legislation, he has tangible evidence of his attention to his constituents. Indeed, there is strong evidence that members of Congress sponsor legislation that reflects their constituents' interests, especially larger constituency groups (e.g., Barnello and Bratton 2007; Hall 1996; Highton and Rocca 2005; Lazarus 2013; Miler 2011; Sulkin 2005; Wawro 2000). The poor are such a constituency for some members. Additionally, the introduction of a bill can legitimize the issue in a way that few other behaviors can. This role of bill introductions may be less critical when issues are already prominent on the congressional agenda. However, for constituents who are under-represented in the political system, such as the poor, bill introductions are particularly valuable, because they acknowledge that one's interests deserve space on the congressional agenda. In short, when a legislator authors a bill, it gives poor constituents a seat at the legislative table.

The value of expanding how we study constituency representation to include non-voting behaviors is clear, yet legislators' votes on poverty-relevant issues also remain an important measure of the representation of the poor. Early studies of dyadic representation tended to focus on legislators' voting records, not only because the data were available, but also because votes on the final passage of a bill are meaningful. When a legislator casts his vote, it is a clear statement of his position, and helps to determine whether that bill becomes law. Like bill introductions, roll call votes are documented actions to which a legislator can point to show his constituents that he is working on their behalf, which make votes an important behavior for dyadic representation. This chapter, then, first examines the bills that each legislator introduces, and then turns to the votes each legislator casts on poverty-focused legislation.

WHO SPONSORS POVERTY-RELEVANT LEGISLATION?

Given the myriad demands on their time, legislators cannot write legislation on all policy areas. Instead, legislators prioritize and actively partici-pate in the legislative process in some areas more than others. If classic

---

[9] All House members, regardless of committee membership, seniority, or party, can intro-duce a bill, and party leaders do not play a gatekeeping role when it comes to sponsoring legislation. Additionally, a legislator's decision to offer poverty-focused legislation does not preclude him from introducing legislation in other policy areas. Authoring a bill requires some commitment, since it is a moderately costly activity, but legislators do not have to provide extensive policy details, which makes it possible to avoid controversial details (such as costs or funding sources) when introducing legislation.

notions of dyadic representation are at work, then members who have more poor constituents in their district should sponsor more poverty-focused legislation. As a result, the primary hypothesis is that as the number of poor in a congressional district increases that legislator will be more likely to introduce legislation relevant to the interests of the poor. The main explanatory variable in the upcoming regression estimates, as well as subsequent estimates of voting, is the poverty rate in a legislator's district.[10]

In order to determine who puts poverty-focused issues on the House agenda, I analyze the sponsorship activity of all members of the US House of Representatives over a thirty-two year period from the 98th Congress (1983–1984) through the 113th Congress (2013–2014). As described in Chapter 3, poverty-relevant legislation includes a range of economic, housing, education, and social service issues that affect those living in poverty.[11] As a result, bills are categorized in a party-neutral manner, and are based on the content, not the valence, of the legislative proposal. A bill proposing that a social program be converted to a block grant would be coded as poverty-relevant legislation, just the same as a bill calling for increased funding for Head Start.

I use three bill introduction variables in the analyses of dyadic representation. I first assess whether a given legislator offers any poverty-relevant legislation in a given congress. This is followed by a second measure, which is a count of how many poverty-related bills the member sponsors in a given congress. Third, I create a count of the number of "serious" poverty-related bills a legislator sponsors in each congress, where "serious" is defined as a bill referred to a committee on which the sponsor serves. This measure reflects the fact that few bills offered by non-committee members are taken up by the committee in the modern House (e.g., Adler and Wilkerson 2012; Volden and Wiseman 2014). As a result, serious sponsorship addresses the possibility that some legislators may sponsor legislation that they know has no chance of going anywhere, and distinguishes such proposals from those where the legislator is a committee member and expects their proposal to be advanced to committee.

---

[10] As was discussed in greater detail in Chapter 3, these data come from the US Census Bureau.

[11] Table 3.1 provides a more detailed list of these categories, which are based on the substantive coding scheme employed by the Policy Agendas Project.

Initial Patterns

An initial survey of the empirical patterns of legislators' activity shows that the overwhelming majority of House members do not sponsor any legislation related to poverty (see Figure 5.1). On average, 77 percent of House members (or 335 of 435 legislators) are completely inactive, and do not sponsor a single poverty-relevant bill in a given congress. Another 16 percent of legislators (which equates to seventy legislators) sponsors just one poverty-focused bill, and only 7 percent (or thirty legislators) sponsor two or more relevant bills. If one uses the more restrictive measure of "serious" bills sponsored by committee members, the proportion of active legislators drops to just 7 percent (one poverty-focused bill) and 3 percent (two or more bills). The fact that so few legislators are active participants in this policy area is consistent with the aggregate-level findings in Chapters 3 and 4, as well as Hall's (1996) conclusion that few House members avail themselves of the opportunities to participate.

Yet perhaps these low activity rates are neither surprising nor alarming if the inactive legislators have few poor constituents, and, therefore, have fewer incentives and less normative responsibility to offer poverty-related

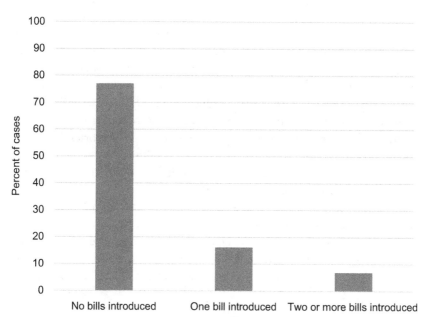

FIGURE 5.1 Distribution of poverty-related bills introduced to the House of Representatives, 1983–2014

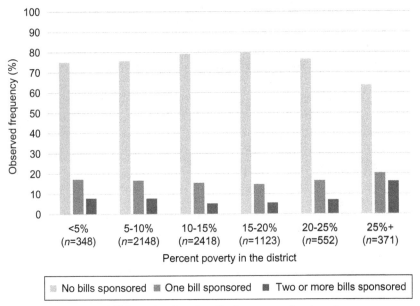

FIGURE 5.2 Bill introductions by district poverty level, 1983–2014

legislation. As a preliminary probe of this relationship, Figure 5.2 illustrates the observed likelihood that a legislator sponsors a poverty-related bill based on the level of poverty in the district.[12] This depiction reveals only very slight differences in the activity levels of legislators from districts with poverty levels ranging from 0 to 25 percent, which encompasses 95 percent of all House members. Indeed, the observed probability that a legislator from these types of districts fails to introduce a bill is consistently between 75 and 80 percent across the first five categories. Similarly, these legislators appear to be quite similar when they do sponsor poverty-related legislation: 15–17 percent sponsor just one bill, and 5–8 percent sponsor two or more bills.

The patterns begin to diverge somewhat when looking at members from those few districts with very high poverty levels (25 percent poverty or greater). Legislators in this relatively small group are slightly more likely to sponsor one poverty-related bill, with one-fifth of legislators from very poor districts offering at a single poverty-related bill. However,

---

[12] The categories of district poverty level are the same as used in the maps of district-level poverty over time presented in Chapter 4.

there is a notable increase in the probability of offering multiple bills: 16 percent of legislators from districts with the highest poverty rates sponsor two or more poverty bills.[13] Therefore, without taking into account any other factors, it appears as though at least a few legislators from the very poorest districts introduce more pieces of poverty-related legislation to the congressional agenda. The next logical question is whether this particular positive relationship remains once other factors that affect legislative behavior are taken into account.

Additional Expectations

Members differ in the attributes they bring to the table, as well as the types of districts they represent. Legislators' sponsorship of poverty-related legislation, therefore, is expected to be shaped by a number of personal and political characteristics, including their background,[14] legislative experience, and party affiliation. First, a legislator's racial and ethnic identity is expected to shape his behavior on poverty relevant issues. African Americans and Latinos experience higher rates of poverty than white Americans, and today the poverty rate among blacks (26%) and Latinos (23%) is more than double that of whites (12%).[15] As a result, minority members of Congress likely bring to office a greater awareness and understanding of issues related to poverty, which may compel them to address these issues in office. Additionally, there is

---

[13] The likelihood of a legislator from a district with less than 25 percent poverty sponsoring two or more poverty-focused bills is 6.3 percent, as compared to 16.2 percent for a legislator from a district with greater than 25 percent poverty. A difference of means test shows this difference is statistically significant at conventional levels ($t = -7.33, p < 0.01$)

[14] Legislators' personal economic experiences are an important influence on their behavior in office (e.g., Burden 2007; Butler 2014; Carnes 2012, 2013), but the empirical reality is that there are very few legislators with personal experience to bring to bear on issues related to poverty. Important recent work by Carnes (2013) finds that fewer than 2 percent of members of Congress come from a working class background (based on data from 1998 to 2008), and consequently a working class perspective is missing in Congress. Given the extremely laborious task of coding the class backgrounds of all House members over more than three decades and the expectation that such efforts would result in the identification of only a few legislators with personal experience with poverty, I do not include a measure of legislator's own class background in these models. In addition, members of the US House of Representatives receive a salary that puts them well-above the poverty line. In 1984, a House member's salary was $72,600 (or $166,846 in 2016 dollars), and they are paid $174,000 (in 2016 dollars) today.

[15] For instance, the US Census Bureau reports that, for the period from 2007 to 2011, the national poverty rate was 11.7 percent for whites, 23.2 percent for Hispanics, and 25.8 percent for African Americans (Macartney et al. 2013).

evidence that poverty-related issues, including unemployment, are particularly important to African Americans, which should further increase the likelihood that African American legislators will sponsor poverty-related legislation (e.g., Haynie 2001; Kinder and Winter 2001; Minta 2009; Tate 2003; Whitby 1989, 1997). It is less clear that poverty-related issues are a similar focal point for Latinos, as Swers and Rouse note that "there is no consensus on which issues reflect Latino interest" (2011, 247). There is, however, some evidence that Latinos are more supportive of larger government, and see education and economic security as particularly pressing issues (Casellas 2011; Griffin and Newman 2008). Thus, African American and Latino legislators are expected to be more active on poverty issues, independent of the poverty rate in their districts. Based on the official biographies maintained by the Office of the Historian for the US House of Representatives, I include two separate indicator variables for African American and Latino legislators.[16]

Female legislators should also be more likely to sponsor poverty-focused legislation. There is considerable overlap between issues that are relevant to the poor, such as education and family assistance, and those issues traditionally considered to be "women's issues" (e.g., Dodson 2006; Hawkesworth 2003; Swers 1998, 2002a). Therefore, since female legislators are more likely to be active on "women's issues" (e.g., Dodson 1991; Gerrity, Osborn, and Mendez 2007; Reingold 2000, 2008; Thomas 1994), they should also be particularly active on poverty-related issues. In addition, women typically are more supportive of social spending, and a government-provided social net, due to the traditional gender role of women as caregivers (e.g., Norton 2002; Shogan 2001; Walsh 2002).

Whether legislators come from urban districts, which traditionally have higher rates of concentrated poverty (Kneebone 2014), is another factor expected to increase the likelihood that a legislator sponsors poverty-related legislation. Following from the discussion in Chapter 1, I argue that constituents in more urban districts are likely to have greater awareness and familiarity with poverty, independent of the poverty rate in the district, and, thus, will expect their legislator to do more to address poverty-related issues. For instance, a legislator from an urban district that includes wealthier neighborhoods within the city will still be more likely to introduce poverty-related legislation because issues of poverty are salient to the legislator and his constituents. In order to assess whether

---

[16] Note that the percentage of the district that is black or non-white is not included in the model, because of the high correlation with legislators' own race and ethnicity.

the urban versus rural nature of a legislator's district affects his behavior, I include a measure of the percentage of the district that is urban, as determined by the US Census Bureau.

A legislator's experience, as well as his electoral security, are also expected to shape his likelihood of offering poverty-focused legislation. First, more senior legislators are expected to be more active in the legislative process (e.g., Hall 1996; Volden and Wiseman 2014). As legislators gain experience in the institution, the costs associated with introducing a bill are lower. Thus, more senior legislators are more likely to sponsor legislation, including poverty-related legislation, than junior colleagues. A measure of the number of years served prior to the congress in question is included in the model. Additionally, although all legislators are interested in reelection, those who were elected with a lower percentage of the vote should be especially concerned with growing their support to ensure reelection. On the one hand, they may sponsor more legislation as tangible evidence that they are working hard on their district's behalf. On the other hand, they instead may spend more time campaigning in the district rather than legislating on Capitol Hill. To account for these conflicting expectations, I include a variable for electoral security, which is measured as the percentage of the vote with which legislators were most recently elected to the House. Data on electoral security comes from the CQ Voting and Elections Archive.[17]

The most obvious political characteristic of each legislator is his party affiliation. Even though the dependent variable is designed to accommodate different approaches to poverty, I nevertheless expect that Democrats should be more likely to sponsor poverty-focused legislation than their Republican colleagues. This is because Democrats are seen as better able to handle the issue of social welfare and poverty-related policies as compared to Republicans (Petrocik 1996; Stonecash 2000) and have a history of attention to the issue. As a result, individual Democratic legislators are expected to act consistently with their party, both because they are likely to share the party's position and because their electoral

---

[17] Committee membership may also affect legislators' propensity to sponsor legislation. I address this possibility by using the "serious" bill sponsorship dependent variable, which counts only bills introduced by members of the committee to which it is referred. I argue that such an approach is theoretically preferable to the inclusion of a committee dummy variable in the model, especially given the wide-ranging definition of poverty-relevant issues and subsequently complicated decision of designating a relevant committee to include in the model.

fortunes are tied to the success of the party brand (e.g., Cox and McCubbins 1993; Jacobson 2004).[18]

Although I expect legislators of both parties to be responsive to greater numbers of poor constituents, one might also wonder if Democrats and Republicans react differently to large numbers of poor in the district. In particular, Democrats might be more responsive to higher levels of district poverty because they "own" the issue, which provides greater incentives to take action in response to more poor constituents (see Petrocik 1996). On the other hand, Republicans might not react to higher poverty rates in the district in the same way as Democrats, because poverty-focused issues do not play to Republican legislators' political advantage. In order to explore this possible differential responsiveness, I also estimate the primary model for Democrats and Republicans separately, to see whether responsiveness might indeed vary by party.

A legislator's party also matters in another way – as a determinant of majority or minority party status in the House. Members of the majority party enjoy procedural benefits in the House (e.g., more seats on congressional committees) and majority party leaders have many procedural powers that allow them to control the legislative agenda (e.g., Aldrich and Rohde 1998; Cox and McCubbins 1993, 2005; Krehbiel 1991; Pearson and Schickler 2009; Rohde 1991; Sinclair 1983). Consequently, legislators who are in the majority party will be more likely to offer legislation in general, including poverty-related legislation, than minority party members. During the period examined (1983–2014), Democrats and Republicans were each in the majority in the House for eight congresses, and this is denoted with an indicator variable.

In addition to a legislator's own attributes and partisanship, the decision to introduce poverty-focused bills may also be affected by the economic environment in the district, specifically the distribution of income among residents. The median household income in each district provides insight into this economic distribution, and helps to put the number of poor constituents in a broader context (see Ellis 2013; Gelman et al. 2007, 2008).[19] Legislators who represent districts with lower median incomes

---

[18] In the rare cases where a Member is neither a Democrat nor a Republican, I code the legislator according to the party with which they caucus.

[19] District median income is, in part, affected by the level of poverty in the district, but it provides unique information about the overall distribution of income. For instance, a district with 15 percent poverty could have a median income of $40,000, which indicates that many of the non-poor in the district have moderate incomes, whereas another district with 15 percent poverty could have a median income of $60,000, which indicates that in

should be more active on poverty-related issues, because more of their constituents are economically vulnerable, *ceteris paribus*. When more constituents have lower incomes, even if they are not poor, they are more likely to either have personal experience with poverty, be exposed to poverty in their daily lives, or worry about being a few strokes of misfortune away from poverty themselves.[20]

National economic conditions may also affect a member's decision to take legislative action on poverty-related issues. When the national economy is struggling, all legislators should be more likely to offer legislation addressing issues related to poverty, *ceteris paribus*. This is because tougher economic times increase demands for Congress to help unemployed Americans, as well as to avoid more people losing their jobs and possibly falling into poverty. The annual national unemployment rate, which is taken from the Bureau of Labor Statistics, is included as an indicator of the economic conditions in the country.

Empirical Tests and Findings

To predict dyadic representation of the poor in the form of bill introductions, I employ a multi-level mixed effects model. My data include 435 House members for each of sixteen congresses, which means that standard assumptions about the independence of observations do not hold in two notable ways. First, some legislators serve several terms in the House, and, thus, the multiple observations for those individuals share certain information and are non-independent. Second, there is likely some dependence among the 435 observations in a given Congress, which reflects the common features of the political environment that jointly affect all House members during that congress. Accordingly, I use the multi-level mixed effects model, which is a type of hierarchical model that incorporates both fixed effects – which are similar to the effects in standard regression models – and random effects. This specification employs a random intercept for each legislator, which accounts for the personal differences that exist across House members, including any idiosyncratic

---

addition to the poor in the district there are also many upper-income residents. If only poverty rate is examined, these two districts would seem the same, but the addition of median income means that we can distinguish between a district with overall modest incomes and one with incomes at the high and low extremes.

[20] Data on household median income by congressional district is taken from the US Census Bureau.

features of a legislator, and dummy variables for each congress, except one, to address congress-specific variation.[21]

Table 5.1 presents the estimated results for three separate models – one for each dependent-variable measure. Because the first model predicts whether a legislator sponsored any poverty-related legislation at all during a given two-year congress, I employ a logit estimator. The other two measures of legislative activity are counts of the number of poverty-related bills sponsored (second model) and the number of "serious" poverty bills introduced (third model), and are estimated using a Poisson estimator.

The first and most important finding in the first column of Table 5.1 is the lack of evidence that legislators who represent districts with more poor constituents are more likely to introduce poverty-related legislation. Similarly, there is no evidence that legislators with more poor constituents introduce more bills, or more serious bills, addressing issues related to poverty (columns 2 and 3). The absence of any relationship between the policies a legislator proposes and the poor he represents is remarkable. It means that, when it comes to sponsoring poverty-relevant bills, a legislator who represents a district with 22 percent poverty does not act differently than a legislator who represents a district with 12 percent poverty, or even 2 percent poverty. Furthermore, the overall lack of responsiveness to the poor in the district is robust across three decades.[22] This finding was foreshadowed by the simple patterns in the data (see Figures 5.1 and 5.2), but that does not diminish the striking disconnect between the lack of evidence of dyadic responsiveness uncovered here and the large body of research that establishes the representational link between constituents and their legislators' behavior.

When looking in detail at legislators across districts with moderate-to-high levels of poverty, for instance, it becomes clear that most of them do not sponsor poverty-focused legislation. On average, only about 21 percent of legislators from districts with 15–25 percent poverty decide to offer legislation addressing the interests of the poor, and, when they do, they generally

---

[21] Because the data are not nested in the standard sense of hierarchical models, it is not appropriate to estimate a model with random effects by legislator nested within random effects by congress. Instead, a series of dummy variables are included to take into account any congress-specific effects on the likelihood of sponsoring poverty-relevant legislation (or the number of poverty-relevant bills sponsored).

[22] The null finding is robust when the model is estimated only for each decade, which offers further evidence for the lack of responsiveness to the poor throughout the period.

TABLE 5.1 *Poverty-related bill introductions, 1983–2014*

	Sponsored any bills	Number of bills sponsored	Number of "serious" bills sponsored
District poverty rate	−0.018 (0.014)	−0.004 (0.004)	0.0002 (0.002)
District median income ($1,000s)	0.002 (0.008)	−0.0001 (0.002)	0.002 (0.001)
District percentage urban	0.005* (0.042)	0.001 (0.001)	0.00003 (0.0004)
National unemployment rate	−0.243* (0.112)	−0.059* (0.028)	0.023 (0.019)
Democratic legislator	0.269* (0.126)	0.065* (0.093)	0.010 (0.021)
Majority party legislator	0.199* (0.078)	0.078* (0.018)	0.095* (0.013)
Seniority	0.014* (0.006)	0.005* (0.002)	0.005* (0.001)
Electoral safety	0.006* (0.003)	0.001 (0.001)	0.0001 (0.001)
African American legislator	0.752* (0.262)	0.303* (0.071)	0.114* (0.046)
Latino legislator	0.494 (0.315)	0.145 (0.085)	0.106 (0.056)
Female legislator	0.335* (0.172)	0.107* (0.048)	0.034 (0.031)
Constant	−0.610 (1.16)	0.586* (0.297)	−0.272 (0.199)
Random effects (legislator)	01.49* (0.073)	0.446* (0.014)	0.285* (0.008)
N	6,960	6,960	6,960
Wald Chi^2 (25)	134.47	157.17	129.35

Column 1: Multilevel logit model with random-effects estimated for legislators and fixed congress effects.
Columns 2–3: Multilevel Poisson model with random-effects estimated for legislators and fixed congress effects.
* Denotes significance at $p < 0.05$ level.

offer just one bill.[23] For the most part, knowing the degree of poverty in a congressional district does not reliably predict which legislators take steps to represent the interests of the poor and which do not.

[23] Among House members from districts with 15–25 percent poverty rates who sponsor poverty-related legislation, the median number of bills offered is one, and the mean number of proposals is 1.5.

Examples abound of legislators whose behavior is at odds with
what one would expect based on the extent of poverty in their districts.
One such case is Republican Hal Rogers from the 5th District of
Kentucky, which is a rural, white district with a consistently high rate
of poverty of nearly one-quarter of the constituency. Despite representing the 5th District during all sixteen terms examined, Representative
Rogers never offered a single bill on any poverty-related issues, such
as food assistance, work and training programs for welfare recipients,
or low-income housing.[24] Similarly, Democrat Ed Pastor, who for
twenty-four years represented the 4th District of Arizona,[25] a largely
urban, majority Latino district around Phoenix with similarly high
poverty levels, likewise failed to introduce any poverty-related legislation. The decisions made by them, and many others like them, runs
counter to the expectation that House members are responsive to their
constituents.

However, at the very highest levels of poverty there appears to be a
unique constituency impact on some legislators. The empirical patterns
presented earlier (see Figure 5.2) suggested that the small group of
legislators from districts with poverty rates exceeding 25 percent might
sponsor more poverty-relevant legislation. To further examine this
possibility of dyadic representation of the poor at the extreme levels
of district poverty, I re-estimate the models of bill sponsorship with
two changes. First, I add a quadratic term that allows for district-level
poverty rates to have a non-linear effect on legislative behavior. These
results are presented in the first three columns of Table 5.2. They show
that at increasingly high levels of poverty, legislators are in fact somewhat more responsive to large numbers of poor constituents, and this is
true across all three measures of bill introductions. Second, to probe
further the level at which greater responsiveness might begin, a dummy
variable is included that indicates whether the district has a very high
level of poverty (25 percent or more). The final three columns of
Table 5.2 reveal that legislators from extremely poor districts do
tend to offer more bills, and more serious bills, related to poverty than

[24] One exception is during the government shutdown in October 2013, Congressman
Rogers, in his role as the chairman of the House Appropriations committee, authored a
joint resolution (H.J. Res. 84) for "making continuing appropriations for Head Start for
fiscal year 2014, and for other purposes."
[25] Prior to representing the 4th district of Arizona, Rep. Pastor represented the 2nd district
of Arizona from 1991 to 2002.

TABLE 5.2 *Poverty-related bill introductions and high poverty districts, 1983–2014*

	Any bills	Number of bills	Number of "serious" bills	Any bills	Number of bills	Number of "serious" bills
District poverty rate	-0.080* (0.035)	-0.022* (0.009)	-0.013* (0.006)	—	—	—
District poverty rate squared	0.002* (0.001)	0.001* (0.0002)	0.0004* (0.0002)	—	—	—
Very high poverty district	—	—	—	0.393 (0.231)	0.186* (0.062)	0.146* (0.041)
District median income ($1,000s)	-0.002 (0.009)	-0.001 (0.002)	0.001 (0.001)	0.010 (0.007)	0.002 (0.002)	0.003* (0.001)
District percentage urban	0.005 (0.003)	0.001 (0.001)	-0.0001 (0.0004)	0.005* (0.003)	0.001 (0.001)	-0.00004 (0.0004)
National unemployment rate	-0.269* (0.113)	-0.067* (0.029)	0.018 (0.019)	-0.206 (0.110)	-0.049 (0.028)	0.026 (0.019)
Democratic legislator	0.293* (0.126)	0.071* (0.033)	0.014 (0.021)	0.238* (0.120)	0.057 (0.032)	0.063 (0.160)
Majority party legislator	0.203* (0.078)	0.079* (0.019)	0.096* (0.013)	0.201* (0.078)	0.080* (0.019)	0.096* (0.013)
Seniority	0.014 (0.006)	0.005* (0.002)	0.005* (0.001)	0.013* (0.006)	0.004* (0.002)	0.005* (0.001)
Electoral safety	0.006 (0.003)	0.001 (0.001)	0.0001 (0.001)	0.006 (0.003)	0.001 (0.001)	0.0001 (0.001)
African American legislator	0.705* (0.262)	0.286* (0.071)	0.102* (0.047)	0.513* (0.252)	0.225* (0.069)	0.073 (0.045)

(continued)

TABLE 5.2 (continued)

	Any bills	Number of bills	Number of "serious" bills	Any bills	Number of bills	Number of "serious" bills
Latino legislator	0.417 (0.317)	0.120 (0.086)	0.089 (0.056)	0.260 (0.301)	0.072 (0.082)	0.071 (0.053)
Female legislator	0.340* (0.172)	0.108* (0.045)	0.035 (0.031)	0.329 (0.177)	0.105* (0.048)	0.033 (0.031)
Constant	−0.361 (1.26)	0.865* (0.321)	−0.079 (0.215)	−01.51 (1.00)	0.357 (0.256)	−0.322* (0.171)
Random effects (legislator)	01.48* (0.073)	0.445* (0.014)	0.286* (0.008)	01.48* (0.073)	0.445* (0.014)	0.285* (0.008)
N	6,960	6,960	6,960	6,960	6,960	6,960
Wald Chi² (26)	138.10	162.67	135.04	136.04	165.48	142.16

Multilevel logit models (columns 1 & 4) and multilevel Poisson models (all other columns) with random-effects estimated for legislators and fixed congress effects.

* Denotes significance at $p < 0.05$ level.

their colleagues.[26] The evidence of responsiveness, however, is sensitive to the definition of high poverty used. If the threshold for defining "high poverty" districts is instead lowered to 20 percent poverty, or even 22.5 percent poverty, then the relationship no longer achieves significance at the 95 percent level of confidence. Moreover, these findings are tempered by the reality that only about 5 percent of districts fall into this highest poverty category, and only one-third of even these members sponsor any poverty-focused legislation.[27]

In fact, the relative few who do introduce poverty-relevant legislation represent districts with vastly different numbers of poor people. During the 102nd Congress (1991–1992), for instance, Democrats Barney Frank (MA), John (Pat) Williams (MT), and Charles Rangel (NY) each sponsored four poverty-related bills, despite the fact that Rep. Frank represented a district with 7.2 percent poverty, Rep. Williams represented a district where 12.1 percent of residents lived in poverty, and Rep. Rangel's district had 33.4 percent poverty. Similarly, among Republican House members during the 109th Congress (2005–2006), Representatives Melissa Hart (R-PA) and Wally Herger (R-CA) each proposed two poverty-related bills, despite the fact that they represented districts with poverty rates of 7.5 percent and 17 percent, respectively. If legislators were responsive to the poor in their district, we should see legislators like Rep. Williams, Rep. Rangel, and Rep. Herger systematically introducing more bills to address poverty than members like Rep. Frank and Rep. Hart.

Another way to think about the findings is to understand that there are some legislators who have little constituent-based reason to offer poverty-relevant legislation, but sometimes do just that. These legislators also behave in ways that do not reflect the constituents in their district, although in a way that is perhaps normatively more palatable. As an illustrative example, for more than a decade Republican Representative Marge Roukema represented the 5th District of New Jersey, a mixed rural–suburban district with a largely white constituency and less than 4 percent poverty rate. However, across six congresses, Rep. Roukema

---

[26] Note that the likelihood that a legislator sponsors at least one poverty bill is not affected by extreme levels of poverty in the district (Table 5.2, column 4), even though there is evidence that extreme district poverty increases the number of bills offered (Table 5.2, columns 5 and 6).

[27] However, the fact that 35 percent of legislators who represent districts with the very highest poverty rates sponsor at least one poverty-focused bill is a noticeable improvement over the average rate of 23 percent.

chose to introduce several pieces of poverty-relevant legislation addressing issues like affordable housing, childhood immunizations, and
reauthorizing welfare grants to states. In a district with very low poverty
rates, it is difficult to attribute Rep. Roukema's actions as responding to
the needs of her constituency or providing classic dyadic representation.
Instances of legislators like Representative Roukema, who take action
despite the lack of a district connection, are the focus of Chapter 6, which
examines the role of surrogate representation of the poor.

The findings presented in the primary model in Table 5.1 also reveal
several other patterns about which legislators introduce poverty-relevant
legislation. In particular, a legislator's personal identity affects their decision to address poverty issues separately of district-level poverty. As
expected, African American and female legislators contribute more
poverty-related proposals to the congressional agenda, regardless of the
amount of poverty in their own districts. Indeed, race accounts for
the largest difference in the predicted probability that a legislator will
introduce poverty-relevant legislation (see Figure 5.3). African American
members are 11.5 percentage points more likely to sponsor at least one

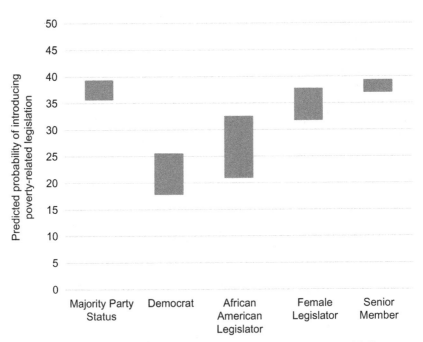

FIGURE 5.3 Predicted effects of selected variables on poverty-related bill
introductions

bill as compared to their colleagues. Female legislators are six percentage points more likely to introduce poverty legislation than male legislators, all else equal. The results in Table 5.1 also indicate that Latino legislators may be more inclined to sponsor poverty-related bills, but the coefficient estimates fall short of conventional standards for statistical significance.

As anticipated, Democratic legislators also are more likely to sponsor legislation related to poverty than their Republican colleagues, regardless of the degree of poverty in their districts (Table 5.1, column 1). In fact, the predicted probability that a Democratic legislator sponsors poverty legislation is one in four, or 25 percent (see Figure 5.3), whereas for Republicans it is 17 percent. The second column of Table 5.1 shows that Democratic legislators also sponsor a greater number of poverty-relevant bills than Republicans, although this relationship does not extend to the introduction of "serious bills" (see column 3).

In light of Democratic legislators' greater propensity to sponsor poverty-relevant legislation in general, might Democrats also respond differently than Republicans to a large number of poor constituents in the district? If this is the case, the null finding for legislators' responsiveness to the poor in their districts may be masking interesting partisan differences. Therefore, in Table 5.3 (columns 1 and 2), I re-estimate the model separately for Democratic and Republican legislators, and the results are noteworthy in two ways.

First, there is no evidence that Democrats are responsive to the number of poor in their district. This is somewhat surprising, and suggests that, even if Democrats are associated with poverty-related issues, this does not compel Democratic legislators from high-poverty districts to offer more legislation than Democrats from districts with lower poverty rates. Therefore, even though Democratic House members are more likely to introduce poverty-relevant legislation than Republicans, *ceteris paribus*, among Democrats there is no evidence that these legislators are responsive to a greater number of poor in their districts.

Second, Republicans' behavior is inversely related to district-level poverty. That is, not only are all Republicans less likely to offer poverty-focused bills than Democrats, but Republicans from districts with a large number of poor constituents are even less likely to introduce legislation than their co-partisans from districts with lower levels of poverty. The curious relationship between Republicans and their poor constituents affords the unusual situation of legislators actively not representing those in their district. This behavior, I argue, reflects the polarization of the parties, as well as the dominance of the Republican Party in the South and

TABLE 5.3 *Poverty-related bill introductions by legislator subgroups, 1983–2014*

	Democratic legislators	Republican legislators	Women legislators	African American legislators	Latino legislators
District poverty rate	0.005 (0.017)	-0.075* (0.027)	-0.043 (0.044)	0.107* (0.043)	-0.031 (0.066)
District median income ($1,000s)	0.005 (0.011)	-0.013 (0.013)	0.005 (0.023)	0.061 (0.044)	-0.052 (0.084)
District percentage urban	0.007* (0.003)	0.002 (0.004)	-0.002 (0.008)	0.014 (0.012)	0.010 (0.019)
National unemployment rate	-0.143 (0.158)	-0.393* (0.167)	-0.041 (0.276)	0.014 (0.331)	-0.515 (0.577)
Democratic legislator	—	—	0.253 (0.389)	-11.20 (305.3)	2.48* (0.990)
Majority party legislator	0.173 (0.346)	-0.270 (0.398)	0.130 (0.238)	-10.06 (305.3)	-0.877 (0.791)
Seniority	-0.002 (0.008)	0.032* (0.009)	0.056* (0.022)	0.032 (0.020)	0.029 (0.030)
Electoral safety	0.007 (0.004)	0.002 (0.004)	0.017 (0.011)	0.028* (0.013)	-0.007 (0.016)
African American legislator	0.493 (0.289)	1.00 (1.24)	1.12 (0.603)	—	—
Latino legislator	0.511 (0.366)	-1.09 (0.846)	0.689 (0.730)	—	—
Female legislator	0.173 (0.225)	0.461 (0.289)	—	0.619 (0.454)	0.265 (0.814)
Constant	-1.22 (1.63)	2.55 (2.01)	-2.30 (3.05)	1.72 (305.3)	3.16 (8.08)
Random effects (legislator)	1.52* (0.100)	1.41* (0.109)	1.48* (0.193)	1.25* (0.251)	1.53* (0.394)
N	3,688	3,272	805	533	303
Wald Chi² (23)	108.48	55.56	34.38	47.24	23.80

Multilevel logit model with random-effects estimated for legislators and fixed congress effects (not shown).
* Denotes significance at $p < 0.05$ level.

in rural areas. In the next chapter, I take up these party dynamics in greater detail, and discuss why partisans differ in their responsiveness to the poor.

I also examine whether female legislators, African American legislators, and Latino legislators respond differently to district poverty than their white or male colleagues. Again, the logic is that these legislators' predisposition toward poverty-related issues might make them uniquely responsive to large numbers of poor people in their districts. Therefore, I replicate the primary analyses by estimating the model separately for only female legislators, African American legislators, and Latino legislators. The results are presented in the final three columns of Table 5.3.

Across these estimations, I find no evidence that Latino legislators or female legislators are responsive to the level of poverty in their district. When looking only at Latino House members, for instance, those who come from districts with more poor constituents are not distinguishable from Latino legislators who represent fewer poor constituents (see Table 5.3, column 5). This holds true when looking only at female House members as well (column 3). The one exception is that African American legislators who come from districts with high levels of poverty tend to be more likely to sponsor poverty-relevant legislation than other African American legislators. This finding in part reflects the fact that African American legislators represent a considerable number of those few districts with the very highest poverty rates.[28] As noted in Chapter 1, there is also a unique relationship between race and poverty in America that affects these dynamics, and which is examined in greater detail in Chapter 6.

Finally, the main results presented in Table 5.1 also reveal that House members who have served in the chamber for longer are more likely to offer poverty-related legislation. The fact that more senior legislators introduce more poverty-related legislation is consistent with the expectation that their familiarity with the lawmaking process makes participation less costly for them as compared to a junior colleague. This is especially true for "serious" bills, since legislators who have a longer career in the House may be better able to anticipate the committees to which a bill will be referred, and to understand the benefits of being on the committee that takes up the proposed legislation. Another significant determinant of bill introductions, including serious bills, is party status,

---

[28] African American legislators represent approximately half of congressional districts with poverty levels of more than 25 percent.

which reflects the procedural power of the majority party in the House in advancing legislation through the House (Volden and Wiseman 2014). I also find that legislators from urban districts are generally not more active in sponsoring poverty-related legislation, once controlling for other factors, nor is there evidence that the broader economic environment affects legislators' decisions about introducing poverty-focused legislation.

Overall, there is very little evidence that legislators are more likely to offer poverty-focused legislation as the number of poor constituents in their district increases. The only evidence of this type of responsiveness to the poor occurs among the fairly small subset of legislators from the very poorest districts, and among African American legislators, who are also more likely to represent these districts. To find such limited evidence of dyadic representation of the poor is at odds with the conventional wisdom that legislators are responsive to their constituents.

WHO VOTES FOR POVERTY-RELEVANT LEGISLATION?

The lack of dyadic representation evident in bill introductions raises the question of whether this failure is specific to bill sponsorship, or whether it also holds across other forms of legislative activity, namely voting behavior. One can imagine that a legislator might not take the initiative to sponsor poverty-relevant bills on behalf of his poor constituents, but, nevertheless, will vote to support policies to reduce poverty if faced with a vote.

Legislators' voting records provide an interesting second opportunity for legislators to take actions to represent their districts, precisely because they are different in many ways from bill sponsorship. Notably, casting a vote requires little effort by a legislator, and does not require much investment of time or resources. Additionally, voting "matters" because it explicitly determines the fate of legislation. Whereas other forms of legislative behavior are sometimes dismissed as not having direct policy effects (e.g., cosponsorship, floor statements, etc.), the impact of votes is clear.

Legislators have considerable discretion in how they cast their vote, even if they do not control which bills come to a floor vote.[29] How a legislator votes on poverty-focused legislation is expected to be influenced

---

[29] Which bills come to a floor vote is managed by the Speaker of the House and majority party leaders. Technically, legislators can choose to abstain from a vote, but this is

by the number of poor constituents in his district, attributes of the legislator himself, and broader economic conditions. These are the same explanations used to predict which legislators sponsor poverty-relevant legislation, and I anticipate they will have similar effects on legislators' votes. Two factors in particular, constituency and party, are expected to heavily shape legislators' vote choice, because of the strong electoral incentive to please their constituents and advance their party (e.g., Cox and McCubbins 1993, 2005; Kingdon 1989).

In order to determine whether House members vote in support of the interests of their poor constituents, I examine legislators' "poverty score," as developed by the the Sargent Shriver National Center on Poverty Law. The Shriver Center is a charitable organization focused on policy and legal solutions to "increase justice and opportunity for low-income people and to ensure that their voices are heard in the making of public decisions that affect them."[30] This makes their evaluations particularly well-suited for the task of assessing congressional representation of the poor. Each year they identify key poverty-related legislation considered by Congress, and rate all House members based on whether they voted with the Center's position or not. As noted in Chapter 3, the Shriver Center defines poverty-relevant issues as "multi-faceted and complex," and includes education, housing, employment, health, and traditional social welfare issues. A legislator's poverty score then reflects the percentage of the time that they voted in agreement with the position of the Shriver Center that year. These scores are made publicly available on their website for use by other organizations, media outlets, and the public.

I compile legislators' poverty scores for all available congresses, which includes 2007–2014 (the 110th–113th congresses).[31] Legislators' scores range from 9 to 100 percent agreement, and the average score during this period is a 60 percent agreement with the Shriver Center's positions. The overall distribution of poverty scores (see Figure 5.4) reveals a bimodal

---

uncommon, as excessive absenteeism can be presented to constituents as a failure to do one's job.

[30] www.povertylaw.org/media

[31] As is convention, annual vote scores are averaged to create a score for each congress. For example, a legislator's score in the 110th Congress is the average of his score in 2007 and his score in 2008. Note the total number of cases does not equal 435 in each congress. A total of sixty-nine cases are missing across the four congresses, which includes thirty-six Republican House members and thirty-three Democratic House members. The reasons for the missing poverty scores include party leaders who generally do not cast roll call votes (i.e., Speaker of the House) or legislators who departed or joined the House mid-session and did not make enough votes to be scored.

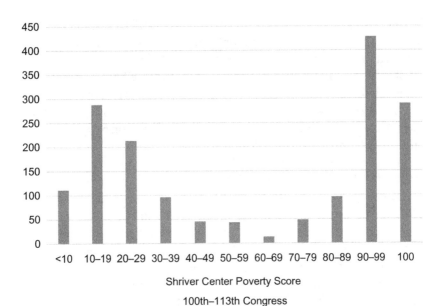

FIGURE 5.4 Distribution of poverty scores in the House of Representatives, 2007–2014

distribution, with a notable number of legislators scoring highly. This itself is interesting, because it suggests that the Shriver Center's poverty score is capturing support among some House members for policies that help the poor to an extent not seen when looking at bill introductions. The bimodal distribution of legislators' voting behavior is also quite different from that for legislators' bill sponsorship activity, and hints at the role of party in determining legislators' votes, a relationship explored in the multivariate model.

Of primary interest is the extent to which higher voting scores are more likely among legislators who come from districts with higher levels of poverty. Figure 5.5 presents an initial, bivariate relationship between district-level poverty and the votes cast by House members. These initial data suggest that there may be a positive relationship between the voting support for poverty legislation and the degree of poverty in the district. Legislators from districts with higher levels of poverty, on average, have higher scores. There is not a clear pattern across districts with 0–20 percent poverty, but there is a noticeable increase when looking at legislators from districts with 20–25 percent poverty, and then another increase when looking at the districts with the very highest levels of poverty (greater than 25 percent). As noted earlier, however, there are a

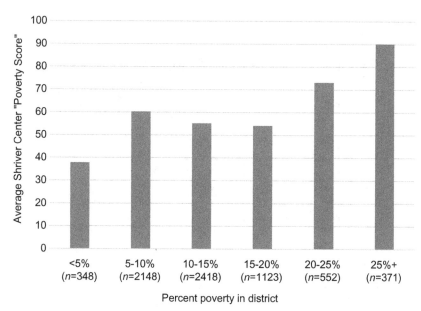

FIGURE 5.5 Relationship between district poverty level and vote score, 2007–2014

number of other factors that may affect voting behavior, especially party, that need to be examined along with district poverty before concluding that the poor benefit from dyadic representation when it comes to voting behavior.

The multivariate analyses in this section parallel those from earlier in the chapter, with the question this time being whether legislators who represent more poor constituents have a stronger voting record in support of the poor. Based on the suggestive data (see Figure 5.5), I expect that, as the poverty rate in a district increases, a legislator's "poverty score" is likely to rise. Again, this expectation is rooted in the long literature on the importance of the "electoral connection" (Mayhew 1974), and the vast evidence that legislators are more likely to act on behalf of their constituents when there are a greater number of affected constituents in the district.

The model specification presented in Table 5.4 is identical to the one for bill sponsorship, except that the singular dependent variable here is the Shriver Center poverty score for each legislator in each congress. The first column analyzes legislators' voting behavior over multiple congresses; thus, individual legislators can be in the data more than once, and there may be congress-specific effects, both of which make the mixed

TABLE 5.4 *Voting support for poverty legislation, 2007–2014*

	All terms (2007–2014)	110th Congress (2007–2008)	111th Congress (2009–2010)	112th Congress (2011–2012)	113th Congress (2013–2014)
District poverty rate	-0.043 (0.095)	-0.222 (0.194)	-0.164 (0.200)	-0.348* (0.154)	-0.128 (0.135)
District median income ($1,000s)	0.032 (0.046)	-0.058 (0.119)	-0.074 (0.079)	-0.071 (0.069)	0.036 (0.053)
District percentage urban	0.079* (0.022)	0.037 (0.042)	0.135* (0.035)	0.085* (0.036)	0.060* (0.031)
National unemployment rate	0.628 (0.344)	—	—	—	—
Democratic legislator	66.34* (0.864)	58.89* (1.49)	69.49* (1.26)	72.53* (1.34)	71.36* (1.13)
Majority party legislator	-3.09* (0.374)	—	—	—	—
Seniority	0.139* (0.040)	0.270* (0.072)	0.137* (0.051)	0.071 (0.048)	0.055 (0.046)
Electoral safety	-0.006 (0.021)	-0.074 (0.047)	-0.053 (0.046)	0.013 (0.039)	0.017 (0.036)
African American legislator	3.36* (1.68)	5.50* (1.39)	1.84 (1.43)	5.52* (1.51)	3.95* (0.965)
Latino legislator	4.86* (1.78)	9.54* (3.39)	5.34* (2.52)	5.60* (2.25)	3.73* (1.57)
Female legislator	1.59 (1.08)	2.23 (1.62)	0.576 (1.13)	2.29* (1.08)	1.12 (0.676)
Constant	10.40* (5.21)	41.02* (6.09)	20.18* (4.50)	19.06* (5.33)	12.43* (5.27)
Random effects (legislator)	8.86* (0.324)	—	—	—	—
N	1,671	409	414	415	433
Wald Chi² (13)	8,832.99	225.51	505.65	1,136.16	1,808.63

Column 1: Multilevel OLS model with random-effects estimated for legislators and fixed congress effects. Columns 2–5: OLS model with robust standard errors.
* Denotes significance at $p < 0.05$ level.

effects, multi-level model used previously appropriate here as well. However, the model is also estimated for each single congress in which data is available (columns 2–5), which conveys the consistency of the findings across Democratic and Republican majorities in the House. For these models, I use an OLS regression with robust standard errors, which is more appropriate for the cross-sectional data. Additionally, in these single-congress models, independent variables that do not vary within a single congress (such as the national unemployment rate) are omitted.

Despite the promise suggested by the collection of high vote scores in the raw data, there is no evidence in Table 5.4 that legislators who represent large numbers of poor constituents are more supportive of anti-poverty policies in their voting. The percentage of the constituency living in poverty is not systematically related to a legislator's vote score, with coefficient estimates signed in both directions and never approaching conventional levels of statistical significance. Holding other factors constant, a legislator who represents a district with low poverty and a legislator who represents a district with high levels of poverty are statistically indistinguishable when it comes to their voting record in favor of policies designed to help the poor.

Furthermore, the absence of a relationship between poor constituents and a legislator's voting record is evident in every single congress (see columns 2–5 in Table 5.4). The robustness of the null finding is especially notable considering that the House was controlled by the Democrats for two congresses (110th and 111th) and by the Republicans for two congresses (112th and 113th). Additionally, these congresses capture the period of the Great Recession and subsequent slow recovery, which is exactly the period in which one might expect elected members of Congress to be especially responsive to issues related to poverty.[32] However, even with high poverty rates nationally and spikes in many congressional districts, there is no evidence that legislators responded by voting in favor of more poverty-focused legislation.

An illustrative case again sheds light on the real world workings of this absence of dyadic representation. For six terms, Representative Rodney Alexander was a Republican House member from the 5th District of Louisiana, which encompasses the northeast portion of the state, and combines rural areas with the small cities of Monroe and Alexandria. Approximately one-quarter of Rep. Alexander's constituents live in

---

[32] The National Bureau of Economic Research defines the Great Recession as occurring from December 2007 to June 2009.

TABLE 5.5 *High poverty districts and voting support for poverty legislation, 2007–2014*

	Shriver Center poverty score	
District poverty rate	−0.231 (0.230)	—
District poverty rate squared	0.005 (0.006)	—
Very high poverty district (25% or greater)	—	0.181 (1.18)
District median income ($1,000s)	0.024 (0.047)	0.047 (0.035)
District percentage urban	0.078* (0.022)	0.078* (0.022)
National unemployment rate	0.581 (0.348)	0.670* (0.316)
Democratic legislator	66.36* (0.863)	66.29* (0.861)
Majority party legislator	−3.01* (0.384)	−3.07* (0.379)
Seniority	0.139* (0.040)	0.138* (0.040)
Electoral safety	−0.007 (0.021)	−0.007 (0.021)
African American legislator	3.20 (1.65)	3.11 (1.64)
Latino legislator	4.66* (1.80)	4.58* (1.72)
Female legislator	1.64 (1.08)	1.59 (1.08)
Constant	12.67* (5.78)	8.68* (3.79)
Random effects (legislator)	8.85* (0.324)	8.86* (0.324)
N	1,671	1,671
Wald Chi^2 (14)	8,847.75	8,822.23

Multilevel OLS model with random-effects estimated for legislators and fixed congress effects (not shown).
* Denotes significance at $p < 0.05$ level.
Dependent variable is Shriver Center Poverty Score, which goes from 0 to 100.

poverty, which puts his district above the 90th percentile of poverty in congressional districts. Despite very high levels of poverty among his constituents, he voted "to fight poverty" only 30 percent of the time, on average, and his Shriver Center score never eclipsed thirty-six.[33] It is hard to see how Rep. Alexander was representing the interests of his more than 180,000 poor constituents with this low level of support.

In light of the earlier finding that legislators from the very poorest districts were somewhat more likely to introduce legislation, I next examine whether vote-based representation might function similarly among legislators from districts with high poverty. I first estimate the core voting model with both the district poverty rate and the poverty rate squared included. In this instance, both terms fail to achieve conventional levels of statistical significance (see Table 5.5, column 1). Based on Figure 5.5, which hints at the relationship between legislators' votes and the highest levels of district

[33] From 2007 to 2013 (110th–112th Congresses), Representative Alexander's scores from the Shriver Center were: 23.5, 33, and 35.5.

poverty, I then estimate legislators' poverty scores with the inclusion of a dummy variable to indicate that a district has a poverty rate of 25 percent or greater. Once again, there is no evidence of vote-based responsiveness at this highest level of district poverty (column 2), nor is there if the threshold is relaxed to 20 percent poverty (not shown). In other words, even specifying the model to allow for the very poorest districts to have a unique impact fails to reveal evidence of a relationship between how a legislator votes on poverty issues, and who lives in his district.

As was the case when examining bill introductions, the results displayed in Table 5.4 reveal that some types of legislators do vote in support of anti-poverty legislation. By far the most influential factor is the party of the legislator. Democratic House members score much higher on the poverty scorecard than their Republican colleagues, even controlling for other factors. It is worth noting that the Shriver poverty scores are based on recent congresses when the House is highly polarized. In this climate where even issues previously thought of as non-ideological are being made partisan (see Lee 2009), it is not surprising to see a strong partisan component to poverty and social welfare voting. In fact, the marginal effect of party on legislators' vote scores is much larger than any other factor (see Figure 5.6).

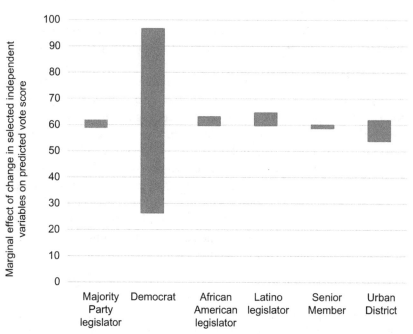

FIGURE 5.6 Predicted effects of selected variables on Shriver poverty vote score

This estimated effect holds district poverty levels (and all other variables) constant, which means that a Republican and a Democrat who come from equally poor districts are expected to have vastly different voting patterns on poverty legislation. In the next chapter, I examine more fully the relationship between party and who represents the interests of the poor.

There is also strong evidence that a legislator's own racial identity is important. Both African American and Latino legislators are consistently more likely to have a record of supporting the Shriver Center's positions on fighting poverty (see Table 5.4). Moreover, the significant impact of race and ethnicity exists, even after controlling for the legislator's party, and, therefore, cannot be attributed to the greater likelihood that minority legislators are Democrats. Figure 5.6 illustrates the marginal effects of legislator's identity, with African American and Latino legislators scoring approximately 3.5 percentage points and 5 percentage points higher, respectively, than their colleagues. This higher level of support for anti-poverty policies among African American and Latino legislators is consistent with the findings earlier in this chapter that minority legislators, particularly African Americans, sponsor more poverty-focused bills than other legislators. The emerging unique relationship between a legislator's race and their actions on poverty-focused issues is the subject of further examination in the next chapter.

The data in Tables 5.4 and 5.5 also illustrate that more senior legislators tend to be more supportive of the anti-poverty policies promoted by the Shriver Center. The magnitude of this relationship, however, is modest, and the marginal impact of serving ten terms in the House (as compared to a freshman legislator) amounts to only a 1.4 percentage point increase on a legislator's poverty score. Legislators who come from more urban districts are also more likely to vote in favor of anti-poverty legislation, and this is true holding party, race, and ethnicity constant. Here, the marginal effect of a legislator who comes from an overwhelmingly urban district as compared to a rural district is approximately 6 percentage points (see Figure 5.6).[34] In Chapter 6, I take up the question of whether legislators from urban and rural districts differ in their response to poverty-related issues, including potential differences between Republican and Democratic legislators.

---

[34] The predicted Shriver poverty vote score for a legislator from a district that is 90 percent urban is 61.0, as compared to a predicted vote score of 54.7 for a legislator from a district that is only 10 percent urban, *ceteris paribus*.

Since legislators from five subgroups – Democrats, Republicans, African Americans, Latinos, and women – have demonstrated a tendency to be more active on issues relevant to the poor, I once again analyze whether these groups of legislators might respond differently, in terms of their voting behavior, to large numbers of poor constituents in their districts. It is possible that grouping all legislators together, which results in the null relationship between district-level poverty and voting presented in Table 5.4, may be masking responsiveness among one or more of these subgroups of legislators. In order to get a clearer picture, I replicate the model for each subset of legislators separately, and present the results in Table 5.6.

First, when looking only among Democrats (column 1), those legislators whose districts contain a greater number of poor constituents do not have more supportive voting records than their Democratic colleagues from less poor districts. The same is true when looking only at Republican legislators (column 2). In short, once again, there is no evidence that legislators of either party are responsive to higher poverty rates in their districts. These same-party estimations (columns 1 and 2) also confirm the importance of legislators' own racial and ethnic backgrounds. Among Democrats, for instance, African American and Latino legislators are more supportive of legislation to end poverty by more than 2 percentage points as compared to their white Democratic colleagues (column 1). Likewise, among Republicans, Latino Republicans score 11 percentage points higher on the poverty scorecard than white Republicans (column 2), which is consistent with the conventional image of Latino Republicans as more moderate than their copartisans.[35]

Second, Table 5.6 also examines the voting reactions of African American legislators, Latino legislators, and female legislators to district-level poverty. There is no evidence that the number of poor constituents shapes the votes of any of these subsets of legislators. Among African American legislators, the voting patterns of those who represent more poor constituents are not discernibly different from the voting patterns of members from less poor districts (column 4). The same is true when looking only at Latino legislators (column 5), as well as only among female legislators (column 3). Table 5.6 also reveals that party remains a strikingly strong predictor of voting behavior for all three subsets of legislators.

---

[35] Note that there were only four African American Republican members during this period, Representatives Gary Franks (CT), Tim Scott (SC), J.C. Watts (OK), and Allen West (FL).

TABLE 5.6 *Voting support for poverty legislation by legislator subgroups, 2007–2014*

	Democratic legislators	Republican legislators	Women legislators	African American legislators	Latino legislators
District poverty rate	-0.109 (0.080)	0.059 (0.182)	-0.039 (0.197)	-0.034 (0.059)	-0.484 (0.3104)
District median income ($1,000s)	0.040 (0.038)	0.841 (0.079)	-0.049 (0.093)	0.003 (0.045)	-0.308 (0.302)
District percentage urban	0.109* (0.019)	0.035 (0.038)	0.135* (0.048)	0.012 (0.014)	0.284* (0.102)
National unemployment rate	1.58* (0.349)	0.071 (0.551)	1.22 (0.693)	1.39* (0.307)	0.047 (1.67)
Democratic legislator	—	—	66.09* (1.73)	72.25* (2.33)	54.46* (2.68)
Majority party legislator	-0.801 (0.738)	-4.48* (1.14)	-5.41* (0.862)	-2.50* (0.741)	-7.59* (1.84)
Seniority	0.074* (0.032)	0.222* (0.076)	0.144 (0.089)	0.003 (0.020)	0.124 (0.159)
Electoral safety	0.066* (0.020)	-0.063 (0.037)	0.031 (0.050)	-0.007 (0.016)	0.054 (0.069)
African American legislator	2.42* (1.07)	4.26 (13.44)	-1.03 (2.37)	—	—
Latino legislator	2.89* (0.780)	11.36* (4.13)	4.13* (2.49)	—	—
Female legislator	1.09 (0.780)	1.03 (2.33)	—	-1.27* (0.415)	1.81 (2.62)
Constant	64.49* (4.84)	19.73* (9.10)	6.13 (10.67)	13.0* (4.73)	29.41 (28.16)
Random effects (legislator)	4.85* (0.290)	11.27* (0.557)	5.48* (0.567)	< 0.0001 (0.001)	4.79* (1.02)
N	852	819	275	159	109
Wald Chi² (10)	298.83	603.27	2,685.38	1,270.63	784.28

Multilevel OLS model with random-effects estimated for legislators and fixed congress effects (not shown).
Dependent variable is Shriver Center Poverty Score, which goes from 0 to 100.
* Denotes significance at $p < 0.05$ level.

The overall picture conveyed by the vote-based data, then, is of no dyadic representation when it comes to a legislator responding to his own poor constituents. This means that legislators with many poor constituents in their district are not more likely to vote to pass legislation aimed at helping the poor than legislators with few poor constituents. This is normatively troubling, because it suggests that members of the House are not acting in the interest of their poor constituents. However, the absence of a clear relationship between legislators and the number of poor in the district also means that some legislators from districts with low-to-moderate poverty are casting votes in favor of proposals intended to help the poor, regardless of whether their districts include many poor constituents. These legislators are behaving in ways that do not conform to a dyadic approach to constituency representation, but instead to a surrogate model where the legislators addressing poverty do not have an electoral connection to the poor. In the next chapter, then, I discuss surrogate representation and the implications of this type of representative relationship.

CONCLUSION

Legislators are not responsive to the number of poor constituents in their districts, and this is true when looking at legislators' choices about what types of bills to propose, as well as how to cast their votes. More than three-quarters of the members of the House are entirely inactive on poverty-focused issues in any given Congress, including many members who represent districts with high levels of poverty. Moreover, the actions legislators do take on poverty-relevant issues are largely unrelated to the number of poor constituents in their district. In the case of legislators sponsoring poverty-focused legislation, only those legislators from the very poorest district are responsive at all to the interests of their constituents who live in poverty, but these cases make up a small fraction of congressional districts. One implication of these findings is that there are many districts with tens, if not hundreds, of thousands of poor Americans whose interests are not being represented by their elected House member, whether in terms of the congressional agenda or votes cast. Furthermore, the underrepresentation of the poor is particularly prevalent among Republican legislators. A second implication, however, is that some legislators from districts with low poverty are active and supportive of issues such as job training programs, investment in schools in low-income communities, efforts to meet the basic needs of the homeless, and the development of new approaches to ending childhood hunger.

There is some promise, then, in the fact that at least a few legislators introduce bills and cast votes in the interest of the poor, even if these legislators are not electorally connected to the poor themselves. This type of surrogate representation is not the way congressional scholars, or the American public, usually think about constituency representation in Congress. However, in light of the overwhelming absence of district-based, electorally-motivated dyadic representation, it may be the only way in which the interests of the poor are represented in Congress. The next chapter, then, continues to ask who in Congress does the actual work of representing the poor, but it concentrates on those mostly surrogate legislators who champion the poor, without the district connection that is at the heart of dyadic representation.

6

Surrogate Champions for the Poor

The poor, like all constituent groups, need strong advocates in Congress. They need legislators who will devote their time to issues related to poverty, and who will advance legislation to address poverty-relevant issues. Without these legislative champions, it is unlikely that the interests of the poor will be raised on Capitol Hill. Without this initial recognition, it is unlikely that the House will pursue policies intended to help the poor. As Williams writes, "before government can act in a manner that is responsive to the interest of individual citizens, those interest must be articulated by a representative in a decision-making body such as a legislature" (1998, 24). Therefore, this chapter identifies and discusses these "champions for the poor."

The previous three chapters reveal that some poverty-related legislation is introduced in the House, and that certain legislators are more likely to offer such legislation. However, these chapters also make clear that the representation of the poor in Congress is not straightforward. To the extent that it occurs, it does not follow the classical paths of collective or dyadic representation. Put differently, the champions of the poor are not the usual suspects. In this chapter, I examine an alternate pathway of representation – surrogate representation – wherein a legislator represents constituents beyond his own district. I establish the role surrogate representatives play in giving the poor a political voice, and show that surrogate representation is central to how the poor are represented in Congress.

This focus on surrogate champions shifts attention to the activity of legislators throughout their careers in the House, rather than at one moment in time. My examination of nearly 1,400 House members uncovers a group of thirty-five consistent champions of the poor, nearly all of whom serve as surrogate representatives, and many of whom are women and African Americans. These "consistent champions" of the poor are the strongest advocates for the poor, and can be counted on to introduce multiple bills related to poverty on a regular basis. This reliability distinguishes them from legislators who never or only periodically offer poverty legislation, and makes them essential to the representation of the poor. A closer analysis of these legislators reveals four types of consistent champions: Old-School Democrats, Democratic Women, Indigo Republicans, and Urban Black Democrats. Later in the chapter, I identify the champions in each group and detail the types of poverty-related legislation they offer.

I then consider another type of advocate on poverty issues, the "occasional champions." These legislators exhibit significant activity on such issues, but are not as reliably active as the consistent champions. Expanding the definition of champions uncovers many similarities between the two groups, and suggests that some of the occasional champions could become an even stronger voice for the poor. It also reveals that many Latino legislators are part-time advocates on poverty issues, which is noteworthy given their shortage among consistent champions and the high rates of poverty within the Latino population. Lastly, I consider the "missing champions," those legislators who have much in common with the champions, but have chosen not to be active on poverty-related issues. Their prevalence tempers the findings about how well the poor are being represented, and highlights both the importance of surrogate champions and how much more could be done on behalf of the poor.

SURROGATE REPRESENTATION OF THE POOR

The sparse evidence of dyadic representation does not necessarily mean that the poor go unrepresented, but simply that they do not receive the type of representation normally afforded constituents. Instead, they receive what Mansbridge (1999, 2003) has called "surrogate representation." This type of representation occurs when a legislator represents constituents who reside outside his own district. Mansbridge argues that surrogate representation is common in the US Congress because of the use of single-member plurality districts, which leave constituents with minority interests looking for representation from legislators beyond their district. An inherent feature of surrogate representation is that there is no electoral connection between the representative and the represented. Put differently, surrogate representation is an informal, or "noninstitutional arrangement," in which the represented cannot hold the legislator accountable via elections (Mansbridge 2003, 523).

The idea that a legislator may act on behalf of constituents beyond his geographic district is rooted in Burke's notion of virtual representation. He describes this as occurring when "there is a communion of interest and sympathy in feelings and desires between those who act in the name of any description of people and the people in whose name they act, although the trustees are not actually chosen by them."[1] For Burke, virtual representation is an important complement to direct representation because it allows the substantive representation of constituencies whose grievances are not reflected in legislative deliberations.[2] Saward similarly claims that the primary benefit of surrogate representation is the ability to "bring into the legislative arena interests and perspectives that are widely held, but, due to formal territorial representation, do not have the political voice that their numbers or significance merit" (2010, 22). Thus, surrogate representation can enhance a legislature's ability to provide deliberative representation to all constituents. This normative standard of deliberation does not rely on the representativeness of outcomes, but instead requires that "the perspectives most relevant to a decision [to be] represented in key decisions" (Mansbridge 2003, 524). Thus, deliberative representation for the poor would mean that their interests are represented by surrogate legislators, and are part of the dialog when Congress considers legislation that directly affects them.[3]

Particularly relevant for the poor is Mansbridge's discussion of "descriptive surrogate representation" (1999, 651). Here she argues that legislators who are descriptive representatives on account of shared identity (e.g., race, ethnicity, gender) with constituents in their district, are also likely to serve as surrogate representatives for members of that identity group beyond the district. For instance, African American members of Congress are descriptive representatives for their own black constituents, but also serve as descriptive surrogate representatives for African Americans across the country (Mansbridge 1999, 2003). She similarly

---

[1] Burke, as quoted in Pitkin 1967, 173.
[2] See also Williams 1998.
[3] Mansbridge also establishes "an aggregative criterion" for surrogate representation, which is that it promotes proportional representation of interests in the chamber as a whole (see Mansbridge 2003, 524, as well as the discussion in Mansbridge 2011).

notes that female and LGBT members of Congress serve a dual role as descriptive and surrogate representatives for women and members of the LGBT community, respectively. These legislators' sense of responsibility as a surrogate representative is enhanced further by group consciousness or linked fate, which has been identified as a critical element of the representation of underrepresented groups such as African Americans (e.g., Dawson 1995; Fenno 2003; Gamble 2007; Hall 1996; Hall and Heflin 1994; Minta 2011; Swain 1993; Tate 2003; Whitby 1997), Latinos (e.g., Bratton 2006; Minta 2011; Rouse 2013; Sanchez 2006; Welch and Hibbing 1984), and women (e.g., Bratton and Haynie 1999; Carroll 2002; Hall 1996; Hawkesworth 2003; Reingold 1992; Swers 2002a; Thomas 1994).

The absence of working class and poor members of Congress (e.g., Carnes 2012, 2013; Grumbach 2015) means that the poor are exceedingly unlikely to have such descriptive representatives in Congress. Therefore, legislators who act on behalf of the poor beyond their districts will not be *descriptive* surrogate representatives, because they do not share the experiences of poverty. According to Mansbridge, this means that these surrogate representatives will not have that strong sense of responsibility to the poor that comes with shared identity or group consciousness. In the absence of descriptive surrogate representatives for the poor, anyone can be a surrogate for the poor, since it is based on what legislators do on poverty-relevant issues, not who they are.

I argue that descriptive representatives of other underrepresented groups are particularly likely to be surrogates for the poor because their issues overlap. When the poor have shared policy interests with other types of constituents, there can be positive spillover that produces strong surrogate representation for the poor as well. Additionally, legislators who are already descriptive representatives for another underrepresented group are familiar with the idea of representing constituents beyond their own district, and being a surrogate for poor individuals across the country may easily be incorporated into how they see their role as a representative.

For instance, African American legislators' beliefs about linked fate produces a strong sense of responsibility to represent black constituents, especially on issues of concern to the black community. Many of these "black issues" overlap with poverty issues, such as welfare, education, housing, social services, and job training (e.g., Gamble 2007; Haynie 2005; Minta 2011). As a result, I argue that African American legislators are more likely to be active on poverty-relevant issues as well, which results in black legislators functioning as surrogate representatives of the poor. Similarly, female legislators are descriptive surrogate representatives for women, and there is important overlap between so-called "women's issues" and the interests of the poor, including on issues related to education, families, and hunger (e.g., Carroll 2002; Norton 2002; Swers 1998, 2002a, 2002b; Thomas 1994). As a result, I also expect that female legislators are more likely to be surrogate representatives for the poor, because their representative relationship to the poor is strengthened by their role as descriptive surrogates for women.

DEFINING CONSISTENT CHAMPIONS OF THE POOR

How do we identify the champions of the poor? Legislative champions are those who do much of the work necessary to advance policy proposals, beginning with introducing the legislation (e.g., Hall 1996; Kingdon 1984; Krutz 2005; Volden and Wiseman 2014; Wawro 2000; see also Schiller 1995). Introducing legislation is an important step, both because it brings the issue to the attention of Congress and it is the official beginning of the legislative process. If no member takes the initiative to offer legislation on a given issue, Congress will not consider it. Legislative champions also bring a commitment to the issue that ensures that it will not fade from congressional view. They reliably introduce poverty-related legislation from one term to the next. Thus, I argue that we need to consider the entirety of a legislator's career, not just occasional moments of action. Moreover, because the poor cannot apply electoral pressure on their surrogates (since they do not come from the district), dependable champions are an especially valuable ally.

To identify the consistent champions of the poor, I examine the career of every legislator who served in the House of Representatives during the period from 1983 to 2014 (98th–113th Congress). There were 1,399 House members during this time, with a near equal number of Democrats (708) and Republicans (691). I examine each legislator's history of sponsoring poverty-relevant bills during their tenure in the House. As detailed in Chapter 3, there are many types of legislation that are considered poverty-related, including bills addressing unemployment, the Earned Income Tax Credit (EITC) or other tax-based programs, food assistance, education for low-income children, social welfare programs, and housing assistance, among others. Additionally, the bills sponsored could advance pilot programs, suggest revisions to existing programs, or propose new policies. Thus, the determination of champions is made using a wide-ranging measure of what it means to advocate for the poor.

TABLE 6.1 *List of consistent champions of the poor*

Rep. Mario Biaggi (D-NY)	Rep. Richard Ottinger (D-NY)
Rep. Matthew Cartwright (D-PA)	Rep. Leon Panetta (D-CA)
Rep. Rodney Davis (R-IL)	Rep. Erik Paulsen (R-MN)
Rep. Joseph DioGuardi (D-NY)	Rep. Donald Payne, Jr. (D-NJ)
Rep. Robert Dold (R-IL)	Rep. Jared Polis (D-CO)
Rep. Gary Franks (R-CT)	Rep. Charles Rangel (D-NY)
Rep. William Goodling (R-PA)	Rep. Tom Reed (R-NY)
Rep. Melissa Hart (R-PA)	Rep. Charles Schumer (D-NY)
Rep. Augustus Hawkins (D-CA)	Rep. Joe Sestak (D-PA)
Rep. Barbara Kennelly (D-CT)	Rep. Ronnie Shows (D-MS)
Rep. Rick Lazio (R-NY)	Rep. Marlin Stutzman (R-IN)
Rep. Barbara Lee (D-CA)	Rep. Dina Titus (D-NV)
Rep. George Leland (D-TX)	Rep. Bruce Vento (D-MN)
Rep. Matthew Martinez (D-CA)	Rep. Theodore Weiss (D-NY)
Rep. David McKinley (R-WV)	Rep. John Williams (D-MT)
Rep. Patsy Mink (D-HI)	Rep. Frederica Wilson (D-FL)
Rep. Gwen Moore (D-WI)	Rep. Lynn Woolsey (D-CA)
Rep. William Orton (D-UT)	

I identify consistent champions based on whether a legislator sponsors an average of two or more poverty-related bills per term over their career in the House. This measure sets a relatively high threshold, and creates a definition that is strict enough to make the notion of "champions" meaningful. Yet, it is also flexible enough to include legislators with long careers who may have had a term or two in which they were less active than the rest of their career. Based on this definition, thirty-five legislators are identified as consistent champions for the poor (see Table 6.1).[4]

Figure 6.1 shows the distribution of all legislators on this average-sponsorship measure, and illustrates the distinctiveness of this group of consistent champions. The group of legislators who are reliably active on poverty-related issues (i.e., average two or more bill introductions) is set off at the far right of the figure from the hundreds of other legislators. Moreover, among those who do sponsor at least some poverty-related legislation, most legislators average less than half a bill each two-year term in Congress. Also notable is the fact that 698 House members, or nearly half of those who serve during this period, never sponsor a single poverty-related bill.

---

[4] Legislators who serve only one term in the House are excluded from the definition of consistent champions.

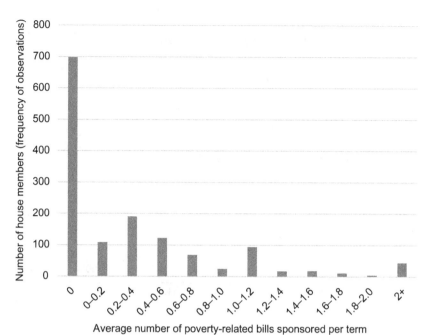

FIGURE 6.1 Distribution of poverty-related bill introductions

I first identify the basic characteristics of all of these champions before discussing the four types of consistent champions in detail. The previous chapter provides a valuable starting point, since it revealed that, in any given congress, Democrats, African Americans, and women were more likely to sponsor a bill. The question here is whether these features also explain sustained activity on poverty-related issues. Figure 6.2 illustrates how the consistent champions as a group compare on these and other variables to all House members. It shows that they are far from a representative cross-section of the full chamber.

As expected, Democrats, African Americans, and women are disproportionately represented among the consistent champions. The first comparison presented in Figure 6.2 reveals that 71 percent of the consistent champions for the poor are Democrats, despite making up only about half of all House members. Indeed, party remains an important factor when discussing the four types of consistent champions, all of which are defined, in part, by party identification. African American legislators also make up a much larger portion of the consistent champions (20%), as compared to their presence in the overall House membership (7%).

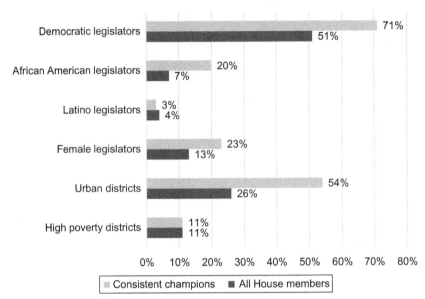

FIGURE 6.2 Average characteristics of consistent champions

Similarly, female legislators are almost twice as prominent among consistent champions of the poor as they are in the House as a whole, accounting for 23 percent of the champions, but only 13 percent of House members. In contrast, only one Latino legislator is identified as a consistent champion for the poor, a point to which I later return.

I also explore the nature of the district each legislator represents, considering first the urban (or rural) composition of each legislator's district. I take the average value of the variable over each legislator's career.[5] Figure 6.2 reveals that consistent champions are more than twice as likely to come from urban districts as House members in general (54% vs 26%).[6] The most notable pattern among the thirty-five

---

[5] The variable measures the percentage of the district that is classified as urban. Since 1950, the US Census Bureau has defined urban areas as including large metro areas, cities, suburban areas, and also clusters of predominantly large towns. Based on this definition, the Census reports that the national population has been more than two-thirds urban since 1960.

[6] Consistent with the US Census Bureau, "rural" and "mostly rural" populations are defined here as districts where less than 50 percent of residents live in urban or urbanized areas, "mostly urban" districts are defined as having 50–95 percent of the population residing in urban areas or urbanized clusters, and "urban" districts are defined by 95 percent or more of the residents living in urban or urbanized areas. Using this definition, approximately one quarter of House members come from districts that are

consistent champions is that they are overwhelmingly surrogate representatives, or legislators who do not come from high poverty districts. Figure 6.2 shows that consistent champions are no more likely to come from high poverty districts than the average House member. Only four (of thirty-five) consistent champions come from districts with very high poverty rates of 25 percent or more, which is the same proportion as found among all House members. In contrast, twenty-two consistent champions come from districts with less than 15 percent district poverty, including thirteen champions from districts with single-digit poverty rates. Thus, while a few consistent champions come from poor districts, there are many more champions from low and moderate poverty districts.

TYPOLOGIES OF CONSISTENT CHAMPIONS

Although the consistent champions can be described in terms of particular characteristics, when one steps back to look at the collection of thirty-five individuals, four types of champions for the poor emerge. These typologies reflect more than a single variable, and highlight the way that certain characteristics come together to provide a more complete picture of who are the champions for the poor. These groups of champions are the "Old-School Democrats," "Democratic Women," "Indigo Republicans," and "Urban Black Democrats." The types of poverty-related legislation offered by each of these archetypes varies, but all four groups of consistent champions illustrate the importance of surrogate representation for the representation of the poor.[7]

Old-School Democrats

The first type of consistent champion is the group of legislators I refer to as the "Old-School Democrats" (see Table 6.2). These eleven legislators are white, male Democrats who nearly all come from urban districts (ten of eleven). The majority of these champions come from northeastern states like New York, New Jersey, and Pennsylvania. Most importantly,

---

rural or mostly rural, one half of members come from districts that are mostly urban, and one quarter come from districts that are fully urban.

[7] Nearly all thirty-five consistent champions fit well into these groups. Only two members, Rep. Ronnie Shows (D-MS) and Rep. Matthew Martinez (D-CA), do not fit into the typologies and, thus, are not listed in Tables 6.2–6.5.

TABLE 6.2 *List of Old-School Democrat champions*

Rep. Mario Biaggi	Rep. Charles (Chuck) Schumer
Rep. Matthew Cartwright	Rep. Joe Sestak
Rep. William Orton	Rep. Bruce Vento
Rep. Richard Ottinger	Rep. Theodore (Ted) Weiss
Rep. Leon Panetta	Rep. John (Pat) Williams
Rep. Jared Polis	

all represent districts with poverty rates of 15 percent or below, which means they are surrogate representatives.

Notably, the Old-School Democrats are primarily of an earlier generation of House members. Nearly three-quarters of these champions (eight of eleven) were first elected to the House in, or prior to, 1990.[8] Thus, the Old-School Democrats began their careers during the long period of Democratic control of the House, and before the extreme partisan polarization and electoral competition of today (e.g., Lee 2016; Sinclair 2014). These legislators reflect an earlier era of Democratic politics, and their activity on behalf of the poor is shaped by that earlier period. Of particular relevance is that many Old-School Democrats predate the rise of the centrist New Democrats. This has implications for their behavior on poverty-relevant policy. The proposals offered by Old-School Democrats reflect the more traditional Democratic priorities of the New Deal and Great Society, rather than the Clinton-era "triangulation" approach to welfare and social policy, which positioned itself as a hybrid of Democratic and Republican approaches.[9]

Collectively, the Old-School Democrats introduce legislation focused primarily on issues such as housing policy and food assistance. These two topics, in fact, make up two-thirds of the bills introduced by these consistent champions. Many of the bills offered by Old-School Democrats focus on preserving and expanding housing assistance for poor citizens, including Rep. Bruce Vento's (D-MN) proposal authorizing the Department of Housing and Urban Development to make grants to states to

---

[8] In comparison, only half of the 707 Democrats who served in the House during this period were elected in, or prior to, 1990.

[9] The "triangulation" approach to welfare pursued by President Bill Clinton is attributed to his advisor, Dick Morris, and entailed combining elements of Democratic proposals (e.g., provisions for food assistance and child care) with elements of Republican proposals (e.g., work requirements, time limits on benefits) to create a winning outcome. See Berman 2011.

preserve existing low-income housing (HR 4838, 105th Congress). Likewise, legislation from Rep. Richard Ottinger (D-NY) requests increased funding for the Low Income Home Energy Assistance Program (LIHEAP), which helps the poor maintain basic heating and cooling (HR 2439, 98th Congress).

The Old-School Democrats are also particularly active on another core anti-poverty issue, hunger. This is best illustrated by the legislation introduced by Rep. Leon Panetta (D-CA) over his career in the House. Of the fourteen poverty-relevant bills he introduced, eleven of them addressed food assistance by calling for the expansion or increased funding of programs for low-income people and the unemployed. Another example of Old-School Democrats' attention to expanding food assistance programs is Rep. Mario Biaggi's (D-NY) proposal to facilitate the distribution of excess agricultural commodities through the school lunch and other food assistance programs (HR 1513, 98th Congress).

Representative Theodore (Ted) Weiss (D-NY) is an exemplary illustration of an Old-School Democrat, and the types of issues to which these consistent champions devote their efforts. Rep. Weiss was first elected to the US House of Representatives in 1976, to represent the west side of Manhattan. Rep. Weiss' own story provides context for his political beliefs about the role of government in helping the poor. As a child, Weiss had fled the Nazi invasion of Hungary and immigrated to the United States in 1938. After serving in the Army, he attended Syracuse University on the GI Bill and earned his bachelor's degree and a law degree. Weiss's political career began on the New York City Council (1962–1976) before replacing Bella S. Abzug in the House, where he served until his death in 1992.

Weiss was a liberal Democrat who saw the merits of an active government that was willing and able to help its citizens in need. As such, he believed in an active, socially conscious government that took its cue from the New Deal and Great Society programs. Indeed, Weiss greatly admired Eleanor Roosevelt, whose photograph he hung in his congressional office (Dao 1992). During his career in Congress, Weiss was known as a "liberal stalwart in the House," "the conscience of the House," and "a congressional crusader for social programs and human rights" (Dao 1992; "U.S. Rep. Ted Weiss, 64, Dies" 1992).

As a champion of liberal causes, Weiss focused much of his legislative energy on various programs fighting poverty and homelessness. He proposed and defended federal funding of poverty-related programs, even in the face of increasing budget and political pressures to reduce spending on social services. Contrary to the political winds of the 1980s and 1990s that called for tighter restrictions on social welfare programs, Weiss worked to make federal poverty programs more accessible. He focused on practical ways to promote participation in existing programs, such as allowing children to receive food assistance without requiring all adults in a household to provide Social Security numbers, or allowing for child care costs to be deducted before determining food stamp eligibility. In addition to proposing such legislation, Weiss also used his committee position as "a forum for hearings that often called in government bureaucrats to account for inattentiveness to the victims of poverty, drugs, and other social conditions" ("U.S. Rep. Ted Weiss, 64, Dies" 1992). For instance, from his position on the Government Operations' Subcommittee on Human Resources and Intergovernmental Relations, Weiss commissioned a study and report on homelessness in 1985 (Fogel 1985).

Rep. Weiss also illustrates the surrogate nature of Old-School Democrats' actions for the poor. Weiss came from a district that was not particularly poor, but it was liberal, and many of his constituents shared Weiss' beliefs in the role of government in reducing poverty and homelessness. Indeed, his district was described as being made up of "New Yorkers of many races and ethnicities who still believe that government can – and should – work to promote social and economic equality" (Frazer 1992). Additionally, as an urban district in New York City, Rep. Weiss and his constituents likely were aware of the deeper poverty elsewhere in the city, which may have reinforced his commitment to poverty-relevant issues. As a surrogate champion and an Old-School Democrat, Rep. Weiss called attention to core issues related to poverty, and championed the poor outside his district.

Democratic Women

The second type of consistent champion that emerges is the "Democratic Women" (see Table 6.3). These female legislators make up 20 percent of the consistent champions for the poor, despite constituting only 9 percent of the overall House membership. The Democratic Women come from urban and mostly urban districts (six of seven legislators) and from a range of states outside the South. As discussed earlier, there is considerable overlap in the substance of women's issues and poverty-relevant issues, which creates a subset of gendered poverty issues focused primarily around the traditional role of women as mothers and caregivers (e.g., Carroll 2002; Hawkesworth 2003; Kathlene 1994; Norton 2002;

TABLE 6.3 *List of Democratic Women champions*

Rep. Barbara Kennelly
Rep. Barbara Lee
Rep. Patsy Mink
Rep. Gwen Moore
Rep. Dina Titus
Rep. Frederica Wilson
Rep. Lynn Woolsey

Pearson and Dancey 2011; Shogan 2001; Swers 1998, 2002a, 2002b; Walsh 2002).[10] The result of this intersection between gender and poverty is that the Democratic Women are particularly active on poverty issues related to child care and education and play a dual role as surrogates for both women and the poor.[11]

Many of the poverty-related bills introduced by the Democratic Women highlight gendered issues relevant to poverty, including those affecting families. For example, Representative Lynn Woolsey (D-CA) introduced legislation to allow the loss of childcare to be included as a legitimate cause for a single parent quitting a job without losing assistance under welfare work requirements (HR 1615, 105th Congress). Given that children in single-parent households are nearly six times more likely to live only with their mother than their father (US Census Bureau 2016), this legislation addressed a problem faced primarily by poor women.[12] The role of women as caregivers is also reflected in legislation focused on children. For instance, Rep. Dina Titus (D-NV) proposed legislation to expand the school lunch program to provide food to at-risk children on holidays and weekends (HR 4249, 113th Congress).

Some of the proposals offered by Democratic women focus on poor women, but from a less family-oriented perspective. For instance,

---

[10] Previous scholarship also shows that Democratic women are especially active on women's issues, and this partisan difference is also reflected in female legislators' activity on poverty-related issues. Only one female Republican legislator is identified as a consistent champion.

[11] On issues of intersectionality and the unique challenges of representation for groups who are underrepresented on multiple dimensions of identity, see Hawkesworth 2003 and Strolovitch 2006, 2007.

[12] "The Majority of Children Live with Two Parents, Census Bureau Reports." Press Release from the U.S. Census Bureau, CB16–192. November 17, 2016.

Rep. Gwen Moore (D-WI) proposed legislation to require states to address domestic and sexual violence among individuals receiving support through the Temporary Assistance for Needy Families (TANF) program (HR 4978, 111th Congress). Addressing the challenges that women face in (re)entering the work force, Rep. Barbara Kennelly (D-CT) proposed legislation that would give employers a tax credit for hiring displaced homemakers, who are disproportionately women (HR 2127, 98th Congress). These female champions not only add more voices calling attention to poverty-relevant issues in Congress, but they also emphasize different aspects of poverty. In this way, female champions contribute to a more multi-dimensional poverty focused agenda, and help to give voice to the perspective of poor women.

It is important to note that the nature of such representation by Democratic Women differs by race. The non-black women in this group of champions come from districts with an average poverty rate of 10 percent, and so their role is primarily as a surrogate representative for the poor.[13] In comparison, the three African American female champions here, Representatives Barbara Lee (D-CA), Gwen Moore (D-WI) and Frederica Wilson (D-FL), come from districts with an average of 22 percent poverty.[14] For these legislators, their activity on poverty-related issues reflects their dual roles as both dyadic and surrogate representatives of the poor.

To further illuminate the role of Democratic Women champions, particularly the ways in which their multiple representative roles come together on poverty-relevant issues, I turn to the career of Representative Patsy Mink of Hawaii. Like other minority members of Congress, she is at once a district representative, descriptive representative, and surrogate representative. In Rep. Mink's case, she was also the first Asian American woman to serve in Congress. Her advocacy on behalf of the poor reflects her commitment to poverty-related issues, as well as the overlap between her role as a surrogate for the poor and a descriptive surrogate for women.

Patsy Mink's elected political career began in state politics, and she served in the territorial government of Hawaii from 1956 to 1964. After a failed bid for the US House in 1959, Mink was elected to Congress in

---

[13] Consistent champions who are white women come from districts with poverty rates ranging from 7.6 to 14.8 percent.

[14] Consistent champions who are African American women come from districts with poverty rates ranging from 17.1 to 26.3 percent.

1964 when Hawaii gained a second congressional seat. She chose to retire in 1976 to pursue an unsuccessful bid for the US Senate. However, she then returned to the US House in 1990 by winning a special election, and served in the House until her death in September 2002. Upon her death, Mink was celebrated for her work on behalf of "the people of her state, and for the forgotten, the disenfranchised, the poor."[15]

Throughout her career in the US Congress, Mink was a strong voice for women and for the poor. Although she served in the House during two very different periods, 1965–1976 and 1990–2002, her legislative priorities and how she approached her responsibilities as a representative remained constant. For Mink, issues related to poverty were largely national in scope, since her own district experienced relatively low poverty of approximately 10 percent. Indeed, Mink believed that members of Congress had a responsibility to be a voice for constituents nationwide: "You were not elected to Congress, in my interpretation of things, to represent your district, period. You are national legislators."[16] This conviction that a representative should speak both for her district and for broader constituencies guided Rep. Mink's career.

Mink came to Washington as a strong supporter of President Johnson's Great Society programs, and she continued to promote liberal causes and a role for government in addressing the country's social problems. During her second turn in Congress, Rep. Mink remained a liberal activist, despite other Democrats' quiet shift toward the political middle on social programs.[17] Described as having an "unwavering commitment to social causes,"[18] she fought against the welfare reform deal brokered by House Speaker Newt Gingrich (R-GA) and President Bill Clinton. She proposed substitute legislation that would have replaced the Republican proposal, and her legislation (H.Amdt. 328 to HR 4) was one of only two Democratic alternatives that received a vote on the House floor. When that failed, she became a leading voice urging President Clinton to veto the welfare reform legislation.[19] In the aftermath of the welfare overhaul, Mink continued as a surrogate representative to help poor Americans within the structure of the new welfare system. For instance, she proposed legislation to increase job opportunities and training programs (HR 1250,

---

[15] Norman Mineta, as quoted in "Hawai'i, nation lose 'a powerful voice'," 2002.
[16] Mink, as quoted in Davidson 1994.
[17] Ibid.
[18] "Hawai'i, nation lose a 'powerful voice'," 2002.
[19] Library of Congress, Manuscript Reading Room, "Patsy T. Mink Papers."

104th Congress), to allow welfare benefits earned based on employment to be treated as income for purposes of the EITC (HR 1045, 105th Congress), and to make changes to the requirements and penalties under TANF during its reauthorization (HR 3113, 107th Congress).

In addition to her support for social programs in general, Mink believed that many issues related to poverty were also women's issues. She provided a voice for poor women saying, "Women are the ones that are the most severely damaged by poverty, whether it's as single heads of households or mothers of dependent children, or as working women who belong to the very bottom of the wage scale. So women had a great stake in the success of the program."[20] During her later terms in the House, Mink proposed twenty-one poverty-relevant bills, the majority of which (eleven) addressed issues that affect poor women and children. For instance, during the 103rd Congress (1993–1994), Rep. Mink introduced legislation to greatly expand early childhood education programs, including through establishing model federal programs and providing staff development programs (HR 3201). Mink also authored multiple bills to increase federal support for childcare, increase benefits for poor children through Supplemental Security Income (SSI), and expand the school breakfast program. Mink also proposed legislation to protect individuals who leave a job due to sexual harassment from losing Food Stamps under the work requirements of TANF (HR 4487, 105th Congress).

As Rep. Mink's career illustrates, the Democratic Women champions bring together their roles as descriptive surrogate representatives for women, as well as surrogate representatives for the poor. They provide a unique perspective on certain aspects of poverty that affect women and families. The overlap between women's issues and poverty issues facilitates acting in this dual role. Rep. Mink's career also reveals an awareness of her role as a national, surrogate representative that is typical of many consistent champions.

Indigo Republicans

The third group of consistent champions are those I call the "Indigo Republicans." These are Republican House members from largely blue (Democratic) and occasionally purple (mixed party) states, who demonstrate a commitment to poverty-relevant issues through their regular

---

[20] Mink, as quoted in Davidson 1994, 145–6.

TABLE 6.4 *List of Indigo Republican champions*

Rep. Rodney Davis	Rep. Rick Lazio
Rep. Joseph DioGuardi	Rep. David McKinley
Rep. Robert Dold	Rep. Erik Paulsen
Rep. Gary Franks	Rep. Tom Reed
Rep. William Goodling	Rep. Marlin Stutzman
Rep. Melissa Hart	

introduction of related legislation. There are eleven Indigo Republicans, who together constitute just over 30 percent of all consistent champions (see Table 6.4). This is a smaller percentage than the general Republican composition of the House (49 percent), but, nevertheless, is larger than some might expect, based on perceptions of the two parties and the findings in Chapter 5.

Geographically, the Indigo Republicans largely hail from states such as New York, Pennsylvania, and Illinois. The member who comes from the furthest south is Rep. David McKinley, who represents the First District of West Virginia, which runs along the Pennsylvania border. In addition, Indigo Republicans are more likely than other Republicans to come from metropolitan areas, with all but one representing an urban or mostly urban district, including those around New York, Chicago, and Minneapolis.[21]

Notably, like the other types of champions discussed previously, Indigo Republicans function as surrogate representatives for the poor. These legislators do not come from districts with many poor residents – the average district poverty rate among them is 10.5 percent. Only three Republican champions come from districts where the poverty rate is greater than 15 percent, with none greater than 20 percent. Thus, the picture of the Indigo Republican champions is reminiscent of an earlier generation of Rockefeller Republicans, who were largely Northern moderates with fiscally conservative and socially progressive positions.

As compared to other types of constituent champions for the poor, Indigo Republicans have a distinctive approach to poverty-related issues. This reflects the underlying differences in the way that the two parties view the role of government, and the best policy tools for reducing

---

[21] The 691 Republicans who served from 1983 to 2014 come from districts that are, on average, 67 percent urban, according to the US Census Bureau. In comparison, the eleven Republican consistent champions come from districts that average 76 percent urban.

poverty in the United States. These Republican surrogates tend to propose legislation that uses devices like the tax code to address issues related to poverty. For instance, Rep. Bill Goodling (R-PA) introduced legislation to increase the Earned Income Tax Credit (EITC), which helps low-income workers (HR 2637, 101st Congress). Rep. Bob Dold (R-IL), likewise, offered legislation to change the tax code to encourage employers to hire unemployed individuals (HR 2868, 112th Congress.).

Indigo Republicans also favor policies that reduce the role of the federal government, in favor of either giving more power to states or to the private and nonprofit sectors to address poverty. For instance, legislation offered by Rep. Melissa Hart (R-PA) would have allowed states to extend the use of welfare block grants to support infant safe haven programs (HR 2018, 107th Congress). Another example is Rep. Tom Reed (R-IN)'s request for a revised formula to allocate Low Income Home Energy Assistance (LIHEAP) funds to the states (HR 3860, 113th Congress). Illustrating Republicans' preference for a larger non-government role, Rep. Erik Paulsen (R-MN) proposed allowing food stamps to be redeemed through nonprofit food purchasing and delivery services, as compared to traditional, welfare-approved retail stores (HR 3860, 111th Congress).

Indigo Republicans are also more likely than other consistent champions to take a more business-oriented approach, which is to be expected for Republican legislators. For instance, Rep. Joseph DioGuardi (R-NY) sponsored numerous bills addressing affordable housing, including bills addressing the calculation of fair market rates (HR 1499, 100th Congress) and providing for rent adjustments in low-income housing to reflect capital investments (HR 1501, 100th Congress). Other proposals focus on job training and the role of businesses and employers in helping low-income individuals. One example of this approach is Rep. Bill Goodling's (R-PA) proposal to develop a vocational training system and local skill centers (HR 5288, 102nd Congress).

In addition to these more distinctively Republican proposals, Indigo Republicans sometimes offer more general legislation bolstering and expanding poverty-relevant programs. Examples include Rep. DioGuardi's call for increased housing assistance and services for the homeless (HR 1502, 100th Congress) and Rep. Goodling's appeal for improvements to Head Start (HR 1528, 103rd Congress). While these types of proposals may be less distinctive as compared to proposals by other consistent champions, they set these Indigo Republicans apart from their party more generally.

TABLE 6.5 *List of Urban Black Democrat champions*

Rep. Augustus (Gus) Hawkins
Rep. Barbara Lee
Rep. George (Mickey) Leland
Rep. Gwen Moore
Rep. Donald Payne, Jr.
Rep. Charles Rangel
Rep. Frederica Wilson

As a whole, Indigo Republicans' unique contribution to the consistent champions is that they combine traditionally Republican policy approaches with a commitment to addressing issues related to poverty. These legislators' proposals complement those by the mostly Democratic consistent champions, and provide important diversity in the perspectives brought to policy conversations.

Urban Black Democrats

A smaller group, that I refer to as the "Urban Black Democrats," are the final subset of legislators that act as a consistent champion for the poor (see Table 6.5). Although African American legislators, in general, are more likely than other Democrats to represent urban districts (77 percent compared to 38 percent), every one of these seven consistent champions is from a heavily urban district, including ones in New York, Los Angeles, Chicago, Miami, Houston, and Milwaukee.[22] Most notably, Urban Black Democrats come from districts with high levels of poverty, which means that, in addition to a surrogate role, they also engage in dyadic representation when they act on behalf of the poor. Thus, Urban Black Democrats reflect the ways in which race, poverty, and place are inter-twined in the United States.

The surrogate role of Urban Black Democrats is complex, because they serve as representatives of two under-represented populations: African Americans and the poor. Their responsibilities to these two constituencies are facilitated by the overlap between "black issues" and issues relevant to the poor, such as welfare, education, housing, social services, and job

[22] I consider heavily urban districts as those in which 95 percent of the residents live in urban areas.

training (e.g., Gamble 2007; Haynie 2005; Minta 2011). When Urban Black Democrats are active on these issues, they are able to act on behalf of both constituencies. However, unlike Democratic Women, whose legislative activity highlights a subset of gendered poverty issues, Urban Black Democrats sponsor a significant amount of general anti-poverty legislation. To the extent that general programs like the Job Training Partnership Act (JTPA) or tax incentives to promote employment also benefit poor minority constituents, these legislators are acting both as champions of the poor and also as "race representatives" (Haynie 2005).

Additionally, unlike the other consistent champions, Urban Black Democrats come from districts with substantial poverty; the average district poverty rate among Urban Black Democrats is 23 percent.[23] Thus, Urban Black Democrats are both district representatives for the poor in addition to being surrogates. One implication is that these legislators are electorally accountable to their poor constituents in a way that many other champions are not. The fact that poor constituents have the power to affect Urban Black Democrats' electoral fortunes should make these legislators particularly attentive to the interests of the poor.

The bills they sponsor reflect this responsibility to represent a combination of their own constituents in the district, African Americans nationwide, and the poor nationwide. For instance, Rep. Frederica Wilson (D-FL) proposed legislation to address unemployment both locally in her Miami district and nationwide, including calling for a pilot program to give grants to local governments and community-based organizations to help create jobs (HR 2574, 112th Congress). Similarly, Rep. Gwen Moore (D-WI) sponsored legislation to make grants to help low-income families gain access to affordable automobiles, which would not only help her Milwaukee-based district, but the many poor nationwide who live in areas with limited public transit (HR 3599, 110th Congress).

This overlap between their district and surrogate roles is also reflected in the bills Urban Black Democrats sponsor to address low-income housing. For instance, Representative Charlie Rangel (D-NY) represents part of New York City, and has sponsored multiple bills addressing affordable and public housing. This is an issue relevant to his own poor constituents, as well as to Americans living in poverty nationwide. Another illustration is Rep. Mickey Leland's (D-TX) commitment to issues related to homelessness, which affected his Houston-area district,

---

[23] The lowest district poverty rate among Urban Black Democratic champions is 17.7 percent.

as well as districts across the country.[24] Throughout this period, Leland sponsored eighteen bills that proposed extending a variety of social services to the homeless, such as education, food assistance, and housing assistance.

A closer look at the career of Representative Augustus "Gus" Hawkins of California provides further insight into the unique role that Urban Black Democrats play in representing the poor in Congress. Hawkins was born in Louisiana in 1907, endured the Great Depression, and supported President Franklin D. Roosevelt and his New Deal programs. Indeed, decades later, Hawkins would still be described as "an old-fashioned New Deal liberal" (Eaton 1990). After nearly thirty years in the California Assembly, he was elected to represent a new majority black district in Los Angeles in 1962. Rep. Hawkins served in the US House representing Los Angeles from 1963 until his retirement in January 1991.

Rep. Hawkins was widely regarded as a committed advocate for the poor and disadvantaged, but also a pragmatic legislator (Trescott 1990). Hawkins preferred the behind-the-scenes work of legislating to the media limelight, and was willing to work with a range of colleagues, including Republicans, to accomplish policy goals. Although he helped to found the Congressional Black Caucus (CBC), he often broke with its members over its more combative style (*Black Americans in Congress* 2008; Herszenhorn 2007). Indeed, colleagues called Hawkins the "Silent Warrior" (*Black Americans in Congress* 2008), which reflects his beliefs about effective representation: "the leadership belongs not to the loudest, not to those who beat the drum or blow the trumpets, but to those who day in and day out, in all seasons, work for the practical realization of a better world – those who have the stamina to persist and remain dedicated."[25]

A distinguishing feature of Rep. Hawkins' long career – and of all Urban Black Democrats – is that they serve multiple representative roles when it comes to poverty issues. Rep. Hawkins is a district representative for the many poor, minority constituents in his central Los Angeles district, and also a surrogate representative for the poor (and African Americans) across the country. As a result, Rep. Hawkins addressed the needs of both his district and his national constituency through his actions

---

[24] Reports in the mid-1980s estimated that between 250,000 and 2 million Americans were homeless (Alter 1984).

[25] Rep. Gus Hawkins, *Congressional Record*, US House of Representatives, 101st Congress, 2nd session. October 27, 1990. As quoted in *Black Americans in Congress, 1870–2007*, 2008.

on poverty-related issues. Similarly, his activity in Congress reflected his commitment to represent both African Americans and the poor. In playing these multiple roles, Rep. Hawkins' efforts on behalf of the poor often did not have an explicit racial focus, but their effect was also to help poor minorities.

Two substantive areas – education and employment – are central to Rep. Hawkins' legislative career, including his position on the House Committee on Education and Labor, which he eventually chaired. In the area of education, Rep. Hawkins championed educational opportunities for disadvantaged children, which would help children both in his district and across the country. He was a noted proponent of the Head Start early education program from its inception as part of President Lyndon Johnson's Great Society programs (Eaton 1990). Later in his career, he authored the Hawkins-Stafford Act of 1988, which provided funding to close the achievement gap between children from low-income families and children from middle- and upper-class households nationwide. President Ronald Reagan lauded the legislation at the White House signing ceremony, saying "It will extend programs for the disadvantaged and other students with special needs ... and focus program benefits on those with the greatest need."[26] Rep. Hawkins also sponsored numerous bills calling for greater federal funding for education for disadvantaged children over his career, which again would benefit the children in his Los Angeles district as well as around the country. For instance, he proposed legislation to improve the educational opportunities of "educationally deprived children" that tied federal funding to localities based on the number of children living in poverty (HR 950, 100th Congress). Indeed, when Rep. Hawkins retired from Congress, he was praised by David Leiderman, the former executive director of the Child Welfare League of America: "When I think of Gus Hawkins, I think of the congressman who is the real champion of poor kids in this country" (Trescott 1990).

Rep. Hawkins' advocacy for the poor also extended to his work on issues of job training, employment, and discrimination. Early in his career, he helped to write the law barring discrimination in hiring and creating the Equal Employment Opportunity Commission (EEOC) as part of the Civil Rights Act of 1964. Once again, this national legislation

---

[26] President Ronald Reagan. "Remarks on Signing the Augustus F. Hawkins – Robert T. Stafford Elementary and Secondary School Improvement Amendments of 1988." April 28, 1988. Accessed via The American Presidency Project, University of California-Santa Barbara. www.presidency.ucsb.edu/ws/?pid=35745

also benefited those in his district, notably his many African American constituents who were likely to face discrimination in the workplace. Another major legislative success was the passage of the Humphrey-Hawkins Act in 1978 (also known as the Full Employment and Balanced Growth Act of 1978), which proposed comprehensive efforts to reduce unemployment, including federal jobs programs. More generally, he offered many pieces of legislation over his career to provide job-training and employment opportunities, especially for families receiving public-assistance, which included many of his district constituents. For instance, Rep. Hawkins sponsored legislation focused on providing employment opportunities to long-term unemployed in high-unemployment areas, such as his own district, and called for these projects to involve renovating and repairing community facilities (HR 1036, 98th Congress). The local focus of this proposal – both in targeting high-unemployment communities and pinpointing projects that improve neighborhoods – captures the way in which Rep. Hawkins advocated for the poor in his own district, as well as his work as a surrogate representative for the poor nationwide.

THE OCCASIONAL CHAMPIONS

I now consider a different type of champion, one who has demonstrated a willingness to call attention to poverty issues, but who has not done so consistently over his career. I call these legislators "occasional champions," which captures both their inclination to sponsor poverty-relevant bills, as well as the irregularity of their activity. This broader definition recognizes that there is more than one way to identify legislative champions, and the primary measure of consistent champions is somewhat restrictive. There is also value in knowing how similar the consistent champions and occasional champions are to one another. If both types of champions have many shared traits, then the occasional champions at some point may become more consistent champions. Finally, of particular interest is whether an expanded definition reveals heightened activity among Latino House members, since they were notably absent from the ranks of consistent champions.

Occasional champions include two types of legislators that are excluded from the list of consistent champions because their activity is either irregular or infrequent. First are legislators who have a burst of activity on poverty issues, but do not sustain this level of activity. In order to capture these legislators, I determine the maximum number of poverty-related bills each legislator sponsored in a single congress, and identify all legislators who ever sponsored four or more bills in a single session.[27] Their inclusion recognizes the potential impact that legislators can have based on a flurry of activity.

Second are legislators who have introduced numerous but sporadic poverty-related bills over their careers. To identify these legislators, I look at the total number of poverty-relevant bills sponsored by each House member, and then select all legislators who sponsored a total of ten or more bills, regardless of how these proposals are distributed over their careers. This approach captures legislators who develop a portfolio of poverty-relevant legislation over time, even if they do not average two bills per congress or never have the type of burst captured by the previous measurement approach.[28] Combining these two new measures (and omitting any legislators who have already been identified as consistent champions) produces a list of forty-five "occasional champions" (see Table 6.6).

Figure 6.3 illustrates that, for the most part, these occasional champions have characteristics that are both very similar to the consistent champions, as well as quite distinct from the membership of the House as whole. For instance, both the occasional and consistent champions are overwhelmingly Democrats (73 percent and 71 percent, respectively), which contrasts with the near equal partisan split among all House members (see Figure 6.3). Female and African American legislators also comprise similarly-elevated proportions of the occasional and consistent champions as compared to the total House membership. Figure 6.3 also reveals that a large majority of occasional champions likewise come from urban districts (62 percent), which contrasts sharply with the mere 26 percent of House members who come from similarly urban districts. Lastly, occasional champions are not more likely to come from districts with very high poverty rates as compared to the House overall. Only five (of forty-five) occasional champions represent districts with poverty rates of 25 percent or more, while sixteen occasional champions come from districts where the poverty rate is in the single digits. Thus, the occasional champions for the poor are overwhelmingly surrogate representatives, with most coming from districts with low to moderate poverty.

---

[27] This produces a list of twenty-three new legislative champions, as well as twenty-seven legislators who are already identified as consistent champions.

[28] This measure identifies thirty-six new occasional champions, including sixteen House members that were previously identified as consistent champions.

TABLE 6.6 *List of occasional champions of the poor*

Rep. Robert Andrews (D-NJ)	Rep. James McDermott (D-WA)
Rep. Michael Bilirakis (R-FL)	Rep. Howard McKeon (R-CA)
Rep. Michael Castle (R-DE)	Rep. Bob Michel (R-IL)
Rep. Cardiss Collins (D-IL)	Rep. George Miller (D-CA)
Rep. John Conyers (D-MI)	Rep. James Moran (D-VA)
Rep. Rosa DeLauro (D-CT)	Rep. Major Owens (D-NY)
Rep. Keith Ellison (D-MN)	Rep. Carl Perkins (D-KY)
Rep. John Erlenborn (R-IL)	Rep. Thomas Petri (R-WI)
Rep. Bob Filner (D-CA)	Rep. Marge Roukema (R-NJ)
Rep. Barney Frank (D-MA)	Rep. Edward Roybal (D-CA)
Rep. Raul Grijalva (D-AZ)	Rep. Jose Serrano (D-NY)
Rep. Tony Hall (D-OH)	Rep. Christopher Shays (R-CT)
Rep. Alcee Hastings (D-FL)	Rep. Albio Sires (D-NJ)
Rep. Wally Herger (R-CA)	Rep. Hilda Solis (D-CA)
Rep. Andrew Jacobs Jr. (D-IN)	Rep. Pete Stark (D-CA)
Rep. Nancy Johnson (R-CT)	Rep. Robert Torricelli (D-NJ)
Rep. Marcy Kaptur (D-OH)	Rep. Edolphus Towns (D-NY)
Rep. Dale Kildee (D-MI)	Rep. Nydia Velazquez (D-NY)
Rep. Joseph Knollenberg (R-MI)	Rep. Maxine Waters (D-CA)
Rep. John Lewis (D-GA)	Rep. Anthony Weiner (D-NY)
Rep. Nita Lowey (D-NY)	Rep. Jerry Weller (R-IL)
Rep. Carolyn Maloney (D-NY)	Rep. Ron Wyden (D-OR)
Rep. Carolyn McCarthy (D-NY)	

It is on the dimension of ethnicity, however, where an important substantive difference exists between the consistent and occasional champions. Although there was only one Latino member of Congress identified as a consistent champion, Representative Matthew Martinez (D-CA), six Latino legislators are found among the occasional champions: Representatives Raul Grijalva (D-AZ), Edward Roybal (D-CA), Jose Serrano (D-NY), Albio Sires (D-NJ), Hilda Solis (D-CA), and Nydia Velazquez (D-NY). The addition of Latino occasional champions is important in part because Latino members of Congress have the potential to serve as both district representatives and surrogate representatives for the poor.

The fact that Latino legislators make up a greater proportion of the occasional champions than the consistent champions is in keeping with the more varied nature of "Latino issues" (see Swers and Rouse 2011). Whereas black issues and women's issues are more clearly defined and exhibit considerable overlap with poverty-relevant issues, there is far less consensus as to what constitutes Latino issues. Moreover, the diversity of the Latino population further complicates the development of a clear

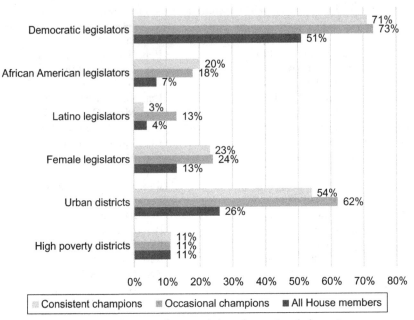

FIGURE 6.3 Average characteristics of occasional champions

Latino agenda (e.g., Rocca et al. 2008; Sanchez 2006). As a result, there is less synergy between Latino legislators' roles as district representatives, descriptive representatives for Latino constituents, and surrogate representatives for the poor. This, in turn, divides their legislative attention and makes them more likely to be occasional, rather than consistent, champions on poverty issues.

When they do offer poverty-relevant legislation, Latino occasional champions divide their efforts between issues that reflect certain interests of poor Latino constituents and more general poverty-related issues. First, like female legislative champions who focus on gendered poverty issues, Latino occasional champions tend to focus on issues that exist at the intersection of Latino issues and poverty-related issues. For instance, Rep. Grijalva (D-AZ), Rep. Martinez (D-CA), and Rep. Solis (D-CA) all sponsored legislation addressing issues of dual language education in low-income communities, which is an issue of particular relevance to poor Latino constituents. Additionally, Rep. Velazquez (D-NY) sponsored legislation to encourage teachers of limited English speaking students by reducing their loan repayments (HR 2861, 110th Congress).

Moving from education to employment, Latino occasional champions again focus on policies that have a unique impact on Latinos living in poverty, as well as affecting the poor more generally. One such example is legislation authored by Rep. Grijalva (D-AZ) to foster job creation that explicitly targets border communities (HR 3049, 112th Congress). Rep. Grijalva is advocating on behalf of constituents in his own district, AZ-03, which includes 300 miles of the US–Mexico border, as well as the many unemployed Latinos who live in districts along the southern border.

However, Latino champions also sponsor general poverty-relevant legislation. For instance, Rep. Sires (D-NJ) sponsored legislation to increase funding for public housing, which is an issue that affects the poor across districts, and across race and ethnicity (HR 3521, 110th Congress). Similarly, Rep. Velazquez sponsored legislation to increase affordable housing for low-income families (HR 4218, 112th Congress) and provide financial counseling to families facing foreclosure (HR 5855, 110th Congress). Both of these proposals would benefit many poor constituents, not only Latino ones.

Overall, Latino occasional champions behave quite similarly to both African American champions and female champions. All of these groups must balance their roles as dyadic representatives, descriptive representatives, as well as surrogate representatives for the poor. However, the more fractured Latino political agenda means that there is less consistent overlap with poverty-related issues, which, in turn, requires that Latino House members divide their legislative activity between more issues.

THE MISSING CHAMPIONS

A final group that I investigate are the "missing champions" for the poor. These are the legislators who have much in common with the consistent and occasional champions, but who are not active on poverty-related issues. Their inaction is an essential part of understanding how Congress does, and does not, represent the poor. Recall that the champions of the poor, of either type, constitute just 6 percent of House members, and most of them are surrogates whose districts do not have high poverty. Thus, there are many legislators from districts with high poverty rates who are neither consistent nor occasional champions. Closer inspection reveals that 165 of the 183 House members (90 percent) who come from districts where at least 20 percent of residents live in poverty are neither consistent nor occasional champions.

Similar dynamics characterize findings about specific groups of champions. For instance, Urban Black Democrats comprise a significant number of consistent champions (six of thirty-five), but a more complete picture should also include the twenty-three African American House members from districts with very high poverty rates who are not champions of any type. Likewise, Latino House members make up 13 percent of the occasional champions (as compared to 4 percent of all House members), but these occasional champions are only a fraction of all Latinos in the House during this period. Indeed, forty-eight of fifty-five Latino House members are neither consistent champions nor occasional champions for poverty-relevant issues, including twenty-three Latino legislators who never offer any poverty focused legislation. Thus, some of the initial optimism about the role of legislative champions for the poor, including African American consistent champions and Latino occasional champions, is tempered by the reality that there are many more missing champions among each of these groups.

Perhaps the most important case of missing champions are Republican legislators who represent low-income areas. Most notably, none of the forty-four Republican House members who come from districts with poverty rates of 20 percent or more emerge as consistent or occasional champions of the poor. This is nothing short of astounding. These Republican legislators come from districts where at least one out of five of their constituents is living in poverty, but not a single one of them is sufficiently active on poverty-related issues to be identified by even the more relaxed criteria that defines occasional champions. Not only are these legislators neglecting their responsibility to represent their district constituents, but this also means that the burden for giving voice to the millions of poor who live in their districts is being passed on to surrogate representatives.

Digging deeper, there is a striking absence of activity by Republican legislators from rural districts. If one focuses on rural districts with high poverty rates in particular, none of the eighteen Republicans from these districts are legislative champions on poverty-related issues. In fact, thirteen of them did not sponsor a single poverty-relevant bill during their careers in the House, despite coming from districts with high poverty rates of 20 percent or more. More generally, there is a lack of action by nearly all rural Republican legislators. Of the 168 Republican House members from mostly or entirely rural districts, only two legislators are consistent or occasional champions: Representatives Bill Goodling (R-PA) and Thomas Petri (R-WI).

The silence of rural Republican legislators on issues relevant to poverty is significant because the rate of poverty in rural America consistently exceeds the poverty rate in urban areas.[29] Furthermore, Republicans are more likely to represent rural districts.[30] As a result, many rural poor constituents are left without a political voice.[31] This is especially critical when it comes to poverty-related issues where the problems or policy solutions differ between rural and urban settings. For instance, the interests of the rural poor on housing assistance policy are quite different from those of the urban poor. Policies intended to address weaknesses in the provision of affordable housing, such as rent support or tax incentives for construction, have different real-world application in rural and urban settings where population density, land availability, and real estate investment differ starkly. Even programs with wide benefit to families living in poverty, such as expanding the school lunch program during the summer months, face challenges of transportation and access in rural communities. This means that fewer rural poor are able to participate in these programs. In addition, unique rural priorities, such as access to social services, rural economic development, and agricultural loans, are likely to be overlooked by policymakers (Salerno 2016). In short, the lack of legislative champions from rural districts means that, while the poor overall are underrepresented, the rural poor are particularly neglected.

CONCLUSION

This chapter shifts the focus to individual House members to explain who serves as a champion for the poor. Looking at their activity over their careers results in a more positive, albeit surrogate-based, portrayal of the congressional representation of the poor. There are thirty-five "consistent champions," and an additional forty-five "occasional champions" who offer more than just the sporadic piece of poverty-related legislation. Moreover, most of these champions do not come from districts with

---

[29] The US Census Bureau reports that non-metro areas had a poverty rate of 17.7 percent, and metro areas had a poverty rate of 14.5 percent (2012 Census CPS).

[30] See Farrigan 2017. From 1983 to 2014, 56 percent of rural districts were represented by Republicans, and this increases to 66 percent when looking only at the last twenty years (since the 104th Congress, 1995–1996).

[31] The lone Democratic consistent champion from a rural district with high poverty is Rep. Ronnie Shows (D-MS). The only Democratic occasional champion from a rural district with high poverty is Rep. Carl C. Perkins (D-KY).

high – or often even moderate – levels of district poverty. Instead, the majority of the champions of the poor are surrogate representatives.

Although the evidence of some representation is encouraging, there are two important limitations to consider. First, the extent to which one finds these eighty consistent and occasional champions reassuring depends on whether that number is put in its broader context. In isolation, eighty legislators regularly introducing poverty-related legislation over their careers sounds like quite a lot. However, there are 1399 legislators who served during this period, which means that these champions comprise only 6 percent of House members.

Second, there are limits to surrogate representation that should give one pause. Due to the lack of a district connection, surrogate representatives cannot be held electorally accountable – a point which Mansbridge (1999, 2003, 2011) emphasizes. In the absence of an electoral connection, she argues that monetary support can provide a means of holding the surrogate accountable (Mansbridge 2003; see also Gimpel, Lee, and Pearson-Merkowitz 2008). However, surrogate representation of the poor is not supported by financial contributions, because the poor do not have the resources to make campaign contributions. Instead, the poor receive "pure" surrogate representation wherein they depend on the legislator's sense of responsibility as a surrogate (Mansbridge 2003). As shown in this chapter, for some legislators, a sense of group experience as women or minorities does foster increased activity on behalf of the poor. However, given that hardly any members of Congress are themselves working class or poor (e.g., Carnes 2012, 2013; Grumbach 2015), it is unlikely that legislators – even those identified as champions – have a sense of shared experience to strengthen their sense of responsibility to the poor.

Therefore, without an electoral connection to the poor, and without financial ties or shared identity to provide a stronger sense of responsibility, heavy reliance on surrogate representation carries risks for the poor. It is at best a tenuous representative relationship. This is important because accountability both allows constituents to remove a legislator, and also provides incentives for legislators to listen to the voices of their constituents. Without it, surrogate representation works only as long as the well-meaning legislators who are active on poverty-relevant issues decide to be active, and as long as these legislators "get it right."

Despite these limitations, however, surrogate representation of the poor is preferable to no representation at all. This is particularly true, in light of the very limited dyadic representation afforded the poor. The efforts of legislative champions are critically important in compelling the House to acknowledge the interests of the poor. In the next chapter, then, I examine whether the efforts of these legislative champions translate into successful legislation, and whether surrogate representation is also the means by which poverty legislation is passed.

7

Positioned for Legislative Success

The previous two chapters focused primarily on whether members of Congress represent the poor through the legislation they introduce. Chapter 5 uncovered little evidence of dyadic representation of the poor when looking at the bills legislators author, but, as Chapter 6 detailed, there are certain legislators who call congressional attention to the interests of the poor. Most of these legislative champions are surrogate representatives with a sense of purpose driven by race, gender, and party identification that is not rooted in a district connection. The story of who represents the poor could end here, and indeed, doing so would end the story on a relatively high note. To do so, however, would be to neglect the fact that representation of the poor in Congress is not only about calling attention to the interests of the poor, but also about passing policies that address their interests. It is to this aspect of representation that I now turn.

Passing poverty-related legislation is quite different from introducing or even voting on a bill, most notably because it requires a majority of House members to vote in favor of the legislation. To pass a bill, a legislator must shepherd his bill through the committee and floor stages, and must win the votes of a majority of House members. This takes considerable effort in terms of time, staff, and political capital, and ultimately the legislator does not control the outcome. As a result, the factors that influence whether a legislator's bill is likely to pass the House may differ from the factors that determine who offers poverty-related legislation.

I argue that the rules and structures of the House advantage some legislators over others when it comes to navigating the lawmaking process. Put simply, legislators' institutional position is central to understanding who represents the poor when representation is defined as the passage of poverty-related legislation. Those who occupy prime positions, whether in leadership or on a relevant committee, are most likely to successfully shepherd the occasional poverty-related bill through Congress. In contrast, those surrogate champions for the poor who introduce poverty legislation regularly are not necessarily likely to see their bills pass. Although certain legislators may be a voice for the poor in Congress, their passion and efforts may not lead to legislative success if they are not in an institutionally advantageous position.

The empirical tests in this chapter reveal that a legislator's institutional position is the primary determinant of getting poverty-related legislation passed. In particular, whether a legislator is in the majority party in the House, is on a poverty-relevant committee, holds a leadership position, or has served many years in the House are all factors that increase the chances a bill will be successful. These findings are equally true for both Democrats and Republicans. Another key finding is that legislators from poorer districts, as well as African Americans, women, and Democrats, are no more likely to pass poverty-related legislation than their colleagues. Therefore, despite their active role in bringing issues to the congressional agenda, these champions for the poor nevertheless run into the reality of the institutional structure of the House.

PASSING POVERTY-RELATED LEGISLATION

Compared to introducing legislation, passing a poverty-related bill is a very different way that legislators can represent their poor constituents. Only about 13 percent of all bills introduced in the House pass the chamber (Ornstein et al. 2014), so bill passage is a significant accomplishment in terms of the policymaking process. It is also important to examine successful legislation because different conceptualizations of representation can reveal different stories about who represents the poor. In particular, the importance of factors such as race, constituency, party, and institutional position may depend on whether representation takes the form of introducing legislation or authoring successful legislation.

The Importance of Institutional Position

The rules and hierarchical structure of the House matter for successful passage in a way that they do not for sponsoring legislation. Whereas a sponsored bill reflects an individual legislator's discretionary choice to call attention to poverty-related issues, a successful bill reflects the cumulative decision of party and committee leaders to advance the bill and secure support of a majority of House members. The rules of Congress present hurdles to the passage of poverty-related legislation that simply do not exist when examining who introduces legislation. As a result, we should look to legislators' institutional position in the party system and the committee system as much more important indicators of which bills will be successful than is appropriate when looking at proposals.

Perhaps the most obvious distinction within the House of Representatives is whether a legislator's party is in the majority or minority. This one difference has significant implications because of the strongly majoritarian nature of the institution. As congressional scholars have noted, the rules of the House give considerable advantages to the majority party (e.g., Cox and McCubbins 1993; Rohde 1991; Sinclair 1995), most notably the fact that normal order for the House requires majority support for the passage of legislation.[1] This means that it is possible for legislation sponsored by a majority party member to pass with support only from co-partisans – a luxury not available to members of the minority party.

Additionally, majority status confers advantages well before the final vote is taken. This is because majority party leaders dominate the House Rules Committee, which determines the rules of floor debate, including how long the bill will be discussed and whether (and what types of) amendments will be allowed. As a result, the majority party can grant bills offered by majority party legislators more favorable rules on the House floor. Given the myriad of institutional advantages enjoyed by the majority party, I expect that poverty-related legislation offered by majority party members will be more likely to pass the House than bills authored by minority party members.

In addition, legislators who hold positions of leadership in their party enjoy additional advantages when it comes to moving their own bills through the House. In particular, party leaders benefit from strong connections to their copartisans that they have developed while moving up through the party leadership. Party leaders also have a number of carrots and sticks they can use to help build support for their legislation, such as more (or less) favorable scheduling of a legislator's bill and assistance

---

[1] Although there are special rules that can require a supermajority of support (e.g., passage of legislation under suspension of the rules), the default mode of operation in the House is to use majority rule.

with campaign events or fundraising. Thus, I incorporate a variable that indicates whether the sponsoring member holds any of the top three party positions in a given congress: Speaker of the House, House Majority Leader, or House Minority Leader.[2]

A second important organizational framework in the House is the committee system, which divides the lawmaking duties of Congress by issue area and designates groups of legislators as primarily responsible for consideration of relevant legislation (e.g., Cox and McCubbins 1993; Fenno 1973; Krehbiel 1991; Mayhew 1974; Shepsle 1978). As with the majority party, being on a committee with jurisdiction for poverty-related issues increases the likelihood that a member's poverty-focused bill will pass the House. One reason for this improved chance of passage is that the committee process is where hearings, mark-up, and amending activity takes place. As a result, when a legislator authors legislation that is referred to a committee on which he serves, he is in the position to advocate for his own legislation at critical junctures in the legislative process.

Another reason bills authored by committee members may be advantaged is because of the information advantages associated with committees (e.g., Krehbiel 1991). Committee members are likely to be more familiar with and informed about the substantive issues (in this case, poverty-related issues), and, therefore, better able to craft legislation that builds a winning coalition. Therefore, whether due to the procedural or information advantages (or both), the clear expectation is that legislators who serve on committees relevant to poverty issues are more likely to author successful bills than legislators who are not on these relevant committees.

In addition to membership on poverty-relevant committees, some legislators also hold committee leadership positions, which afford greater impact on legislative outcomes. Committee leaders have gatekeeping power at the committee stage, including deciding whether bills receive a hearing or a committee vote. Committee leaders can also can advocate for their own bill during this stage and help to determine key procedural details, such as subcommittee referral and who will be invited to testify before the committee. In addition, their dual position as the bill's sponsor and a relevant committee leader gives them a higher profile on the House floor and when approaching party leaders for support. Thus, I include an

---

[2] Additionally, the results are robust if the definition of party leader is expanded to include party whips.

additional variable indicating whether a member is either the chairperson or ranking minority member of a poverty relevant committee.

I define relevant committees based on patterns of committee referral. Using data from the Congressional Bills Project (Adler and Wilkerson 1960–2014) for every poverty-related bill introduced in the House from 1983 to 2014, I generate a list of every committee that the bills were referred to, including cases where a bill was referred to multiple committees. A clear pattern emerges of the committees to which poverty focused legislation were most likely be referred: Ways and Means, Education and Labor, Financial Services, and Agriculture. Together, these four committees account for more than 77 percent of the nearly 3,000 committee referrals.[3] I, thus, identify the members of each of these four committees for all sixteen congresses, and create a summary dichotomous measure of poverty-relevant committee membership. I expect that, when these committee members introduce poverty-relevant legislation, their bills will be more likely to successfully pass the House.

The House is also structured by seniority, such that legislators who have served longer are advantaged. Traditionally, seniority confers a higher official ranking on committees, as well as a certain degree of deference (e.g., Davidson 1969; Kingdon 1989; Oleszek et al. 2016; Polsby 1968). Previous scholars have also argued that more senior legislators are more effective (e.g., Fiorina 1977; Mayhew 1974; Volden and Wiseman 2014), which should extend to their ability to pass their legislation. Here, I argue that seniority affords legislators two advantages when it comes to the success of their proposed legislation. First, some senior legislators may develop a reputation as an authority on a policy issue, in this case poverty-related policy, which increases the likelihood that their bills will be received favorably in the chamber and win sufficient support to pass. Second, legislators who have been in the House longer are likely to enjoy greater familiarity with the lawmaking process in general, including the rules of the chamber and how to navigate the procedural hurdles. As before, a legislator's seniority is measured by the number of terms previously served in the House.

---

[3] In total, there were 2,417 bills that received 2,979 referrals. The most common referral for poverty-focused legislation was to the House Ways and Means Committee (30%), followed by the Education and Labor Committee (27%), Financial Services Committee (13%), and Agriculture Committee (8%).

Legislators' Characteristics

Although the institutional considerations above are expected to be the primary predictors of whose poverty-related bills are successful, an alternate perspective is that certain types of legislators, namely those who were shown in Chapters 5 and 6 to be more likely to bring poverty issues to the congressional agenda in the first place, might also be more successful in seeing bills through to passage. Indeed, recent work by Volden and Wiseman (2014) demonstrates that some legislators are more effective than others in getting their bills passed. Previous scholars have also shown that, when legislators expend extra effort on behalf of legislation, it increases the likelihood of legislative success (see Anderson et al. 2003; Krutz 2005; Wawro 2000). Here, I posit that legislators who typically sponsor legislation addressing the interests of the poor, such as minority and female legislators, might also be more willing to put in the extra work necessary to advance a bill through to passage. The question is whether their efforts are enough.

Of particular interest is whether African American legislators are able to follow through and convert their legislative proposals into policy outcomes. African American legislators are not only more likely to sponsor legislation and vote in favor of anti-poverty policies (see Chapter 5), but they also make up quite a few of the champions of the poor profiled in Chapter 6, including the Urban Black Democrats and some of the Democratic Women. Given their demonstrated willingness to advocate for the poor, I expect that they are also more likely to make the extra effort to try to pass their bills. In short, the cumulative evidence that African American legislators are more likely to care about poverty issues suggests that they will want to follow their proposed policies through to legislative success.

Similarly, the previous two chapters revealed that women are more likely to be surrogate representatives of the poor when it comes to offering legislation. Some of the most vocal champions for the poor are women like Representatives Patsy Mink (D-HI), who was profiled in the previous chapter, and Barbara Lee (D-CA). The analyses in Chapter 5 likewise showed that female legislators are systematically more likely to cast votes in support of poverty-related bills. As a result, I expect that female legislators may be more successful in passing poverty-focused legislation because of their expressed interest in these issues.

Success passing poverty legislation is also likely to vary by party. The evidence thus far suggests that Democratic legislators will be more likely than Republican legislators to prioritize spending their limited resources and political capital to advance poverty-related proposals. As discussed in Chapters 5 and 6, the public sees the Democratic Party as better able to address poverty-related and social welfare policy, which gives Democratic members an additional incentive to be active on poverty-related issues (e.g., Petrocik 1996; Stonecash 2000). This reputation may also encourage Democrats to put in the extra effort necessary to pass these proposals, since there is potential electoral reward if voters are more likely to give credit to the Democrats for any legislative success.

In addition to the above surrogate-type representatives, another type of legislator who should be more likely to devote the effort necessary to shepherd their legislation through the House are legislators who represent the very poorest districts in the country. Although Chapter 5 uncovered no systematic evidence that district-level poverty predicts whether legislators sponsor poverty-focused legislation, there is some evidence that members of Congress from the very poorest districts, including some of the Urban Black Democrat champions in Chapter 6, are more active on issues affecting the poor. Thus, legislators from districts with significant poverty might be more likely to work to push their poverty-related proposals through to successful passage because it will help so many of their constituents and carries potential electoral benefits. I include an indicator variable denoting whether a legislator's district has a poverty rate of 25 percent or more during the specified congress.

The previous chapters also offer some evidence that members of Congress from urban districts are more likely to introduce poverty-related legislation and more likely to vote for bills aimed at helping the poor. In fact, Chapter 6 revealed that many of the champions of the poor come from urban districts in cities such as Los Angeles, Oakland, Houston, and New York. In light of these findings, I consider whether urban legislators' bills might also be more likely to succeed. Once again, their demonstrated interest in poverty-related issues is expected to extend to a greater willingness to work for the passage of their proposed legislation. I, therefore, include in the models a measure of the percentage of the district classified as urban by the US Census Bureau, which ranges from zero (no urban areas) to 100 (district is entirely urban).

Expectations of success for poverty-related bills authored by Latino legislators are also heightened, albeit more modestly, based on their demonstrated support for poverty legislation. Chapter 5 reveals that Latino legislators are more likely to vote for anti-poverty legislation, even though the relationship in the case of bill sponsorship does not always attain standard levels of statistical significance. In addition, Latino legislators are well-represented among the occasional champions for the poor discussed in Chapter 6. Drawing on this previous evidence of their expressed support for policies that address poverty, I include in the subsequent models an indicator variable denoting whether the legislator is Latino.

Political and Economic Context

Lastly, I take into account two broader considerations that may affect which poverty-related bills are successful: party control of Congress and national economic conditions. The weight of the literature on divided party control of Congress indicates that it hinders the passage of major legislation (e.g., Binder 1999, 2003; Howell et al., 2000; Lapinski 2008, but see Mayhew 1991). With this in mind, a measure of divided Congress is included to account for the possibility that all bills, regardless of topic or sponsor, are simply less likely to pass in the House when the Senate is controlled by the other party. I posit that such a negative relationship reflects the fact that House members anticipate that a bill is not likely to advance in the Senate, and, therefore, House members make the rational decision not to devote their limited time and resources to pushing a bill through the House that will be dead on arrival in the Senate.

The second indicator of the broader context focuses on national economic conditions. Specifically, I expect that, when unemployment levels are higher, it is more likely that poverty-related legislation will pass the House, all else equal. This is because poverty-related issues should be more salient to the public during periods of high unemployment, which should increase the pressure on all legislators to pass relevant legislation. Although the previous chapters have not found that poor economic conditions increase representation of the poor, the shift in focus from bill sponsorship to bill passage warrants further examination of this potential relationship.

EMPIRICAL TESTS AND FINDINGS

The dependent variable here is whether a legislator sponsors a successful poverty-related bill in a given congress. In order to predict which legislators provide representation of the poor by authoring successful legislation, I employ the same type of multi-level mixed effects model used in Chapter 5. The data includes 435 House members for each of the sixteen congresses (the 98th Congress through the 113th Congress), resulting in 6,960 legislator–congress observations. Because two important features of

TABLE 7.1 *Poverty-related bill passage, 1983–2014*

	Legislator passes poverty-related bill
Institutional position	
Majority party	2.410 (0.331)*
Relevant committee member	1.340 (0.198)*
Relevant committee leader	0.996 (0.300)*
Party leader	1.670 (0.760)*
Seniority	0.052 (0.014)*
Legislator characteristics	
African American	−0.160 (0.557)
Latino	0.209 (0.595)
Female	0.455 (0.372)
Democratic	−0.892 (0.364)*
District and national context	
Very high poverty district	0.490 (0.577)
Percentage urban district	0.013 (0.005)*
National unemployment rate	−0.236 (0.340)
Divided congress	−1.050 (0.834)
Constant	−6.460 (3.290)*
Random effects (legislator)	1.490 (0.216)*
N	6,960
Wald Chi^2 (26)	130.78

Mixed-effects multilevel logit model with random-effects estimated for legislators and fixed congress effects.
* Denotes significance at $p < 0.05$ level.

the data potentially violate textbook assumptions about the independence of observations, I again use the multi-level mixed effects model. This hierarchical model incorporates fixed effects and random effects that account for differences by legislator, and includes dummy variables for each congress, except one, to take into account congress-specific variation.

Table 7.1 presents the estimated results for the core model, predicting whether a legislator authors at least one successful poverty-related bill during a given congress. The results are consistent across a number of alternate model specifications presented later in the chapter. The most important finding in Table 7.1 is that legislators' institutional position is the dominant explanation for who represents the poor by means of passing legislation addressing poverty. The specified ways in which the institution advantages some legislators over others are all positively signed and statistically significant at conventional levels. In short, the rules of both the party system and the committee system have real implications for whose poverty-relevant legislation is more likely to pass the House.

Furthermore, members of Congress who are more active in bringing forth issues relevant to the poor are not more likely to see their bills pass the House. As Table 7.1 illustrates, there is no evidence that legislators' race or gender, or even the degree of poverty in their district, increases the likelihood that they will author successful poverty-related legislation. Put simply, the champions of the poor from Chapter 6 hit an institutional wall. Thus, the tension between who is most active in raising poverty-related issues and who is most successful in advancing poverty-related bills to passage provides new insight into the way the institution shapes how the poor are represented.

Looking at the findings reported in Table 7.1, members who belong to the majority party are more likely to author successful legislation addressing poverty than their colleagues, as expected. The estimated coefficient for majority party status is positive at conventional levels of statistical significance (see Table 7.1). In contrast, a minority party legislator's bill is far less likely to pass, due to the numerous procedural hurdles in the legislative process. Notably, this is true, regardless of whether the majority party is the Democrats or the Republicans. In short, the results presented in Table 7.1 indicate that the increased probability of passing poverty-focused legislation is not rooted in the policy preferences or ideological position of the two major parties, but rather in the procedural advantages enjoyed by whichever party controls the House of Representatives.

The importance of majority party status can also be seen in a simple comparison between who sponsors legislation and whose bills pass. When looking at who sponsors poverty-related legislation, the breakdown between majority party and minority party legislators mirrors the composition of the House during this period. From 1983 to 2014, 56 percent of all House members are from the majority party, and 57 percent of legislators who sponsored poverty-relevant legislation are from the majority party. However, when focusing on who sponsors poverty-focused legislation that ultimately passes, the advantages of party status are strikingly clear: 88 percent of legislators who sponsor successful poverty-relevant legislation are from the majority party. Moreover, this strong bias in favor of the passage of majority-legislator-sponsored bills holds when the Democrats control the House (85 percent of successful poverty bills were authored by majority party legislators during the eight congresses under Democratic control), as well as when Republicans are the majority party (92 percent of successful poverty bills were authored by majority party legislators during the eight congresses under

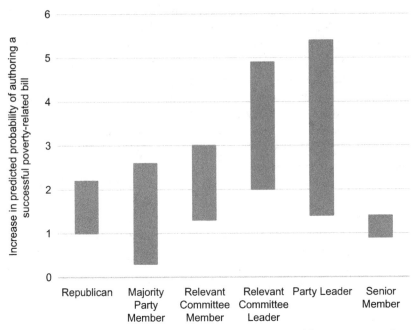

FIGURE 7.1 Predicted effects of institutional position variables on passage of poverty-related legislation

Republican control). This balance between the two parties underscores the importance of party status (as compared to the parties themselves) for bill passage, and the ways in which the rules of the House tip the law-making scales in favor of the majority party, even on an issue like poverty.

To estimate the effects of the estimated model, I calculated the predicted probability that a legislator authors a poverty-related bill that passes the House, and found that it increases more than eight-fold if the member is in the majority party.[4] Although the relative change is quite large, Chapters 3 and 4 show that poverty-related legislation passes the House at very low rates. As a result, the magnitude of the effect must be considered in context: the predicted probability that any minority party legislator passes a poverty-related bill in a given congress is near zero (0.3 percent), but this increases to 2.6 percent for any majority party legislator (see Figure 7.1).

---

[4] All predicted probabilities presented here are calculated with both fixed and random effects, as specified by the mixed multilevel model presented in Table 7.1. The predicted probabilities are presented for change in a specified variable, while all other variables are held at their observed values.

Another way in which the rules and structure of the House advantage some legislators over others is rooted in the committee system. Table 7.1 reveals that legislators who serve on a committee relevant to poverty-related issues are more successful than their colleagues when it comes to passing legislation. This result confirms the expectation that committee members benefit from the information and experience gained in committee, as well as the opportunity to participate in this important stage in the legislative process. The substantive effect of this positive relationship is that a legislator who is a member of one of the four committees relevant to poverty legislation is more than twice as likely to represent the poor through successful policy passage, as compared to legislators who do not serve on one of the relevant committees (see Figure 7.1). Again, given the overall low rate of successful passage, this means that the predicted probability that a committee member's poverty-focused bill passes the House is 3 percent, as compared to only 1.3 percent for colleagues not on a relevant committee.

While majority party legislators and relevant committee members enjoy certain institutional advantages, there is a subset of legislators who enjoy even greater procedural prerogatives. Party and committee leaders benefit from additional advantages when it comes to guiding their poverty-focused legislation through the House and on to successful passage. The findings presented in Table 7.1 reveal the positive and statistically significant relationship between holding either type of leadership position (committee or party) and the chances that a legislator's bill passes the House.[5] The predicted probability that poverty-related legislation proposed by a committee leader passes the House is more than double the likelihood of passage of legislation sponsored by a rank and file member of the committee. Once again, the overall likelihood of poverty-related legislation passing the House is low, but, as Figure 7.1 illustrates, the predicted probability that a relevant committee leader sponsors a successful bill is 4.9 percent, as compared to 2 percent for a committee member who does not hold a leadership position.

The rate of successful passage is even more dramatically affected by whether the bill's sponsor is a top party leader. Party leaders are three times more likely to pass poverty-related legislation than other members of the House, *ceteris paribus*. Whereas a non-party leader is predicted to pass poverty-related legislation in the House about 1.4 percent of the

---

[5] The results are robust if the variables for relevant committee leader and party leader are combined into a single leadership variable.

time, for a top party leader, the predicted probability of passage increases to 5.4 percent (see Figure 7.1). This expected difference in absolute terms is greater than any other marginal impact, and reflects the weight that the highest party leaders carry in the legislative process.

A final way in which legislators' institutional position affects the passage of successful poverty legislation is that more senior House members are systematically more likely to author successful poverty-focused bills (see Table 7.1). The hypothesized benefits of seniority include greater familiarity with legislative procedures and rules, and a potential reputation as an authority on poverty-related issues. Although more senior legislators are indeed more likely to pass poverty-related legislation, the magnitude of this relationship is modest compared to the impact of other institutional factors. A very senior legislator (e.g., in their tenth term in the House) is 50 percent more likely to pass poverty legislation than freshman legislators, which may suggest that some of the advantages of seniority take longer to attain (see Figure 7.1).

In sharp contrast to the widespread, positive relationship between legislators' institutional position and their passage of legislation, there is scant evidence that the personal factors that led legislators to sponsor more poverty-focused legislation also predict successful legislation. Whereas African-Americans, women, and Democrats were more likely to sponsor bills, often as surrogates, these champion legislators are no more likely to produce successful legislation than their white, Republican, male colleagues. The coefficient estimates for African American, Latino, and female legislators in Table 7.1 fail to achieve conventional levels of statistical significance. Only in the case of legislators from more urban districts is there any suggestion that these legislators may also be success-ful in passing their bills, but the evidence is weak, and the coefficient estimate achieves standard levels of statistical significance in only one of four estimated models (see Tables 7.1 and 7.2). In sum, the champions for the poor put poverty issues on the agenda, but they cannot pass them.

The finding that Democratic legislators are actually less likely to pass poverty legislation than their Republican colleagues, however, is striking. In this case, Table 7.1 reveals a negatively signed coefficient that achieves statistical significance, and the predicted probability of a Democrat pass-ing poverty legislation is half that of their Republican colleague.[6] This finding not only runs counter to expectations based on Democratic

---

[6] The predicted probabilities using both fixed and random effects are 1.0 and 2.2 for Democrats and Republicans, respectively.

TABLE 7.2 *Alternate approaches to estimating poverty-related bill passage,*
1983–2014

	Mixed-effects multilevel logit (1)	Mixed-effects multilevel logit (2)	Heckman selection probit (3)
Institutional position			
Majority party	02.18 (0.348)*	2.360 (0.357)*	0.118 (0.016)*
Relevant committee member	0.952 (0.219)*	0.850 (0.239)*	0.058 (0.016)*
Relevant committee leader	0.655 (0.337)*	0.701 (0.353)*	0.088 (0.038)*
Party leader	01.83 (0.794)*	3.050 (1.27)*	0.292 (0.203)
Seniority	0.052 (0.015)*	0.052 (0.017)*	0.002 (0.001)*
Legislator characteristics			
African American	−1.130 (0.694)	−0.773 (0.664)	−0.032 (0.023)
Latino	−0.160 (0.695)	0.259 (0.692)	0.047 (0.048)
Female	−0.081 (0.421)	0.146 (0.427)	−0.003 (0.020)
Democratic	−1.020 (0.383)*	−1.160 (0.394)*	−0.053 (0.017)*
District and national context			
Very high poverty district	0.417 (0.695)	0.741 (0.716)	0.029 (0.039)
Percentage urban district	0.002 (0.007)	0.006 (0.006)	0.0002 (0.0004)
National unemployment rate	−0.201 (0.363)	−0.020 (0.391)	0.001 (0.017)
Divided congress	−1.180 (0.898)	0.572 (0.958)	0.012 (0.041)
Number of poverty bills sponsored	1.120 (0.102)*	—	—
Constant	−6.330 (3.500)	−5.730 (3.770)	−0.050 (0.162)
Random effects (legislator)	1.480 (0.273)*	1.510 (0.307)*	—
N	6,960	1,601	6,960
Wald Chi^2 (26)	187.48	79.87	98.10

(1) and (2): Mixed-effects multilevel logit model with random-effects for legislators and fixed congress effects.

(3): Heckman selection model with logit estimator (selection stage not shown).

* Denotes significance at $p < 0.05$ level.

legislators' greater propensity to sponsor legislation, but also to the conventional wisdom that Democrats care more about the poor, and so will put forth the effort to shepherd bills to passage (see Krutz 2005). Recall that the model already considers the role of majority party status, so this finding speaks to the impact of legislators' specific identity as Democrats or Republicans.

Another way to think about this is that when Republican legislators sponsor poverty-focused legislation, which as discussed in previous chapters is somewhat rare, they are more likely to be successful. One explanation for this counterintuitive finding focuses on the coalition dynamics when Democrats are in the minority, and contends that legislation from Democrats may be less likely to pass the House because it is discounted as being a predictable offering, and may have difficulty attracting Republican supporters (hence, reducing the chances of passage). In contrast, when a Republican legislator in the minority offers legislation addressing poverty-issues, he is cutting against expectations, and may be more likely to attract some Democratic votes to win passage, despite not controlling the chamber.

In addition to the absence of surrogate representation, when it comes to whose bills successfully pass the House, there also is no evidence of dyadic representation of the poor. Legislators who come from extremely poor districts are not more likely to pass successful poverty-related legislation. As shown in Table 7.1., the coefficient estimate for legislators who come from high poverty districts fails to achieve statistical significance. This null finding is consistent with the general lack of evidence of dyadic representation of the poor, but contrasts with the finding in Chapter 5 that these legislators are more likely to introduce poverty-related bills. In short, without the advantages of institutional position to facilitate passing legislation, even those few motivated legislators from the poorest districts, along with the champions from Chapter 6, are not more likely to see their proposed poverty-related legislation pass the House.

More broadly, these data reveal that who represents the poor in the US House of Representatives depends on how representation is measured. When representation of the poor is measured by sponsoring legislation (as in Chapters 5 and 6), one group of sympathetic, surrogate legislators acts in the interest of the poor by proposing poverty-relevant legislation and carrying the voice of the poor to Congress. However, if representation is defined as successfully passing legislation, it is quite a different set of legislators, those who are institutionally privileged, who are able to pass poverty-related bills into law. Nevertheless, the passage of poverty-related legislation is quite rare overall, even when offered by institutionally advantaged legislators.

Alternate Estimations

As noted earlier, I also estimate the model using a number of alternate approaches, as presented in Table 7.2, and the results are robust. The three additional models reflect different approaches to thinking about bill passage as part of the broader legislative process. The first column in Table 7.2 is identical to the core specification (i.e., Table 7.1), except that it adds a control variable to indicate how many poverty-related bills the legislator sponsored that congress. The inclusion of this variable explicitly takes into account the variation in legislators' opportunity to author successful legislation based on their sponsorship activity. As expected, sponsoring more poverty-related bills increases the probability of passing a piece of poverty-related legislation, and, notably, none of the other relationships are affected by the inclusion of this measure (see Table 7.2, column 1).

The second column of Table 7.2 estimates the original model (as specified in Table 7.1), but only for those legislators who sponsored at least one poverty-related bill in that congress. By selecting only those legislators who introduced poverty legislation, this specification draws comparisons among legislators who were active on poverty focused issues rather than among all legislators. Put differently, why do some of the members of Congress who are active on poverty issues succeed in passing their bills? Once again, the results are robust in terms of their statistical and substantive significance (see Table 7.2, column 2). Even when looking only at legislators who sponsored one or more poverty-related bills, those who hold positions of institutional advantage are much more likely to pass legislation, while the personal characteristics that mark the champions of the poor are not associated with the passage of legislation.

The final alternate estimation presented in Table 7.2 (column 3) approaches the question of which legislators sponsor successful poverty-related bills as a selection model, where the likelihood that legislators offer a poverty-related bill, as well as the likelihood that legislators' bills will pass the House, are estimated as part of a single, two-stage process. Using a Heckman selection model, the first (selection) stage, which is not reported, estimates whether a legislator sponsors a bill as a function of the explanatory variables that were shown to be statistically significant predictors of bill sponsorship in Chapter 5.[7] Then the second (outcome) stage, which is presented in the third column of Table 7.2, estimates the likelihood of a legislator passing poverty-related legislation using the core model presented in Table 7.1. These findings are once again consistent with the previous models, with the only notable difference being that the positive relationship between party leadership and poverty-related bill passage falls below conventional levels of statistical significance.[8]

Across all alternate estimations, then, the findings are consistent. Legislators in advantageous institutional positions are more likely to successfully pass their poverty-focused bills, while the legislators who actively introduce poverty legislation are unable to follow through when it comes to passage. The stability of these core relationships increases our confidence that the models accurately capture the realities of the representation of the poor. Taken together with Chapters 5 and 6, this chapter reveals how dyadic representation unfolds on issues of interest to the poor. In sum, who acts on behalf of the poor varies by how representation is defined, but it remains disconnected from the poverty in the district.

CONCLUSION

One obvious conclusion to be drawn by looking at the poverty-related legislation that passes the House is that there is very little of it. Whereas Chapter 5 already showed that a small portion of the congressional agenda addresses poverty-related issues, this chapter reveals that only a very small percentage of those bills are passed. Given this type of "winnowing" (Krutz 2005) and the low odds of success, one might have expected that the legislators willing to put in the work would be those few legislators who are active champions of the poor. This would seem to make sense: the costs of ushering a legislative proposal through the House are significant, and legislators who have demonstrated their interest and commitment to poverty-related issues should be most willing to bear these costs. However, this is not what happens.

Rather, whether a legislator's poverty-related bill passes depends heavily on whether that legislator holds positions in the institution that give

---

[7] These variables are the percentage urban in the district, whether the legislator is a Democrat, whether the legislator is in the majority party, whether the legislator is African American, and the number of years the legislator has served in the House.

[8] It is worth noting that, although the estimated coefficient on party leaders falls short of statistical significance, it is still positively signed. This sensitivity of this estimate likely reflects the fact that there are fewer party leaders than other specified types of legislators.

him an institutional advantage in the lawmaking process. In many ways, it is not surprising that the institution matters when looking at the passage of poverty-related legislation. Congressional scholars have produced a rich literature that shows that institutional structure, including the committee system and the majoritarian rules of the House, shape legislative output (e.g., Cox and McCubbins 1993; Sinclair 1995). Thus, even if it is quite rare for poverty bills to pass the House in general, institutional position plays a significant role when it does.

One silver lining of this power of institutional position is that the passage of poverty legislation appears to be a less partisan undertaking than one might otherwise expect. Unlike bill introductions and votes on anti-poverty legislation, where Democrats dominate the activity (see Chapter 5), Democratic legislators are not the only ones who get their legislation passed. The fact that Republican legislators are occasionally able to pass legislation addressing poverty issues means there is the promise that Republican members of the House could do more to address the interests of the poor. This is especially true because the findings presented here also indicate that just a few legislators in advantaged positions like relevant committees or leadership positions can make a difference. One must guard, however, against making too much of this potential for seeming nonpartisanship. The fact remains that Democratic legislators are much more active on poverty-related issues in Congress, which is illustrated by the mismatch between bill introductions (in Chapter 5) and bill passage.

The contrast in outcomes for legislators with an expressed interest in poverty issues is sharpened by the fact that some of the types of legislators most likely to give voice to poverty issues are African Americans and women, who are also the types of legislators less likely to hold institutionally advantaged positions (e.g., Haynie 2005; Swers 2002a). Taken together, this has the potential effect of limiting the impact of black and female legislators in representing the poor through legislating, despite their interest in serving as surrogate representatives of the poor.

An important conclusion, then, is that there are limits on the surrogate representation provided by the legislative champions in Chapter 6. These legislators can be a voice for the poor, and can work to lay the foundations for policy, but they are not necessarily able to translate these efforts into policy outcomes. In contrast, those members of the House best positioned to pass legislation that addresses the interests of the poor due to their institutional position are not necessarily focused on poverty. This somewhat mismatched result provides the poor with neither adequate dyadic nor surrogate representation.

8

Achieving Better Representation

The phrase "poor representation" has two very different, and somewhat opposing, meanings. The first is a straightforward and literal one, which tells us that representation of the poor is lacking, which is now clear. The second meaning conveys that there is a unique way that the poor are represented, which is via surrogate representation that exists without the usual district connection to the poor. This concluding chapter draws upon both of these meanings to consider why the representation of poor Americans is both unconventional, as well as inadequate, and what might be done to improve it. In other words, how can we achieve less-poor representation?

Perhaps the most obvious conclusion one draws from the book is that the poor are woefully underrepresented. Put simply, members of Congress, whether individually or collectively, are not responsive to the poor they are charged with representing. This is revealed in several ways. Most generally, Congress devotes only a small fraction of its legislative effort to issues directly relevant to the poor. This is true, despite a wide-ranging conceptualization of poverty-related legislation and regardless of whether one examines bills introduced, hearings held, or legislation passed. Also dispiriting is the fact that congressional activity on such issues does not pick up during periods of economic downturn or as poverty affects more parts of the country. Most notably, at the individual level, House members with the greatest numbers of poor in their districts are not more active than their counterparts with few poor constituents. Overall, Congress and its members are largely inactive and unresponsive to the needs of the poor. This leaves the task of representing the poor to a handful of surrogate champions.

Before trying to answer the question of why the poor are so poorly represented, it is important to engage some of the more common retorts that might be offered. The first is the "benign neglect" defense: legislators are simply unaware of the poor, which is why the poor are unrepresented. Quite simply, this is not the case. Recall that Chapter 2 demonstrated that the poor are politically salient – perhaps surprisingly so. In both party platforms, as well as State of the Union addresses, the poor are singled out more than twice as frequently as the middle class. The reality is that Members are aware of the poor, and choose not to prioritize poverty-related issues. An illustration of this dynamic is the recent decision by Congress to let the funding for the Children's Health Insurance Program (CHIP) expire in September 2017. CHIP provided health care for nine million low-income children, and has generally received widespread bipartisan support in Congress. In fact, public opinion polling reveals that 76 percent of Americans said that reauthorizing CHIP is either very or extremely important (Kirzinger et al. 2017). Yet, despite the salience of the program, Congress chose to let the funds run out, which forced states to begin to terminate coverage for low-income children.[1]

Another retort that can be rejected is that the Republican Party does not believe in legislative action to help the poor; thus, the lack of activity is a philosophical statement by half of the membership in Congress. One piece of evidence to the contrary is that the Republican Party platform mentions the poor almost as much as the Democratic one. The same is true of Republican presidents in their State of the Union addresses.[2] In addition, nationally prominent Republicans regularly call for action to alleviate poverty. For instance, former Representative Jack Kemp (R-NY) fought for a "conservative War on Poverty" in Congress and as part of the Bush Administration (DeParle 1993). Another example is former Senate Majority Leader Bob Dole (R-KS), who was a staunch supporter of food stamps and led reforms of the program in the late 1970s, along with Senator George McGovern (D-SD) (Henneberger 2013). Similarly, House Speaker Paul Ryan (R-WI) has a reputation for prioritizing the fight against poverty, as evidenced by his 2016 poverty plan entitled "A Better Way." In sum, Republicans engage the issue of poverty, and believe they have legislative solutions that can help the poor.

---

[1] Congress eventually extended the CHIP program in late January 2018 as part of a larger continuing resolution to fund the government.

[2] Republican presidents devote nearly 10 percent of their State of the Union speech to poverty-related topics, as compared to 11 percent for Democratic presidents.

One might insist that Republicans want to reform and replace current poverty programs, but I would suggest that this too should lead to legislative effort. If Republicans were working to bring about a more conservative approach to reducing poverty, they would be introducing legislation that would be captured by the inclusive, non-partisan coding for "poverty-relevant" issues used throughout the book. As is evident from discussions in previous chapters, I incorporate Republican approaches to addressing poverty, including reforms to existing programs, providing flexibility to states through block grants, and using the tax code to promote work and offer incentives to the private sector. Thus, the evidence that Republican House members are largely inactive on poverty-related issues is not a reflection of coding decisions, but rather reflects the important reality that Republicans in the House have largely failed to represent poor Americans.

A third response that can be dismissed is that representing the poor would be irrational because the poor do not matter electorally. The "poor don't vote" myth was debunked in Chapter 2, and has been challenged by previous scholars who find that class-based differences in responsiveness to public opinion are not determined by variation in turnout rates by class (e.g., Bartels 2008; Butler 2014; Flavin 2012b; Gilens 2012). Although the poor vote at lower rates than high income groups, they still vote in substantial numbers. Turnout rates for individuals who made less than $30,000 a year exceeded 50 percent in both 2008 and 2012, and nearly half of individuals with incomes under $20,000 turned out to vote in 2012 (Malter 2015). While these rates are lower than those of wealthy Americans, it would be irrational for a reelection-minded member of Congress to neglect tens of thousands of poor constituents (or more) in their district, about half of whom may turn out to vote. This is particularly true in districts with high poverty rates, where basic math dictates that legislators have strong electoral incentives to be attentive to the poor in their district.

In sum, Democrats and Republicans may have different policy approaches to combatting poverty, but both parties engage the poor in their platforms, and prominent Republican members of Congress have made fighting poverty a central political message. Therefore, I argue that these three initial explanations – visibility, partisan beliefs about the role of government, and electoral rationality – cannot answer the question of why the poor are under-represented in Congress. Next I identify three factors that can help to explain why Congress does so little to represent the poor before then identifying ways that representation of the poor can be improved as it relates to these factors.

THE INTEREST GROUP PROBLEM

The poor have an interest group problem. That is to say, there are relatively few organized groups working on their behalf in Washington DC. Moreover, this has been true for decades. Schattschneider (1960) famously found that there is a bias in favor of upper-class interests in the group system. Remarkably, this upper-class bias has not really changed despite the exponential growth in the number of interest groups in Washington (e.g., Imig 1996; Schlozman 1984, 2010; Schlozman et al. 2012). The 1970s brought about a large increase in the number of interest groups, including "citizen groups" that advocate for the environment, consumers, and women's rights, among other causes (Schlozman 2010). However, the poor were not a part of this boom in citizen groups. Schlozman found that less than 1 percent of contemporary advocacy organizations are focused on social welfare issues, while the majority of organizations can be classified as corporations, business and trade associations, and non-union occupational organizations (Schlozman 2010).

Even if one concentrates only on citizen organizations, the interests of the poor remain woefully underrepresented. Berry's (1999) influential study of citizen interest groups reveals that they primarily emphasize the interests of the middle class, not the poor. He notes "the agenda of citizen groups has focused largely on issues unconnected to the problems of the poor, the disadvantaged, or even the working class" (Berry 1999, 57). Likewise, Strolovitch (2006, 2007) shows that disadvantaged subgroups within organizations that advocate for traditionally underrepresented constituents are actually the least likely to have their interests advanced. Within women's groups, for instance, she finds that issues that affect poor women (e.g., welfare) are less likely to be the focus of the organization's efforts, as compared to issues like gender equality in higher education. The problem of interest groups, then, is that few groups exist to advocate for the poor, and those that do often focus their efforts elsewhere.

Another aspect of the interest group problem is that the poor have few natural allies in the interest group arena. For one, the relatively small number of groups working on poverty issues means that there are fewer similar groups with whom to partner. This is important because working in a coalition with like-minded interest groups is one way that smaller organizations can pool their resources and be more effective as a group than as single organizations (e.g., Baumgartner et al. 2009; Gray and

Lowery 1998; Hojnacki 1997; Hula 1999; Schlozman and Tierney 1986). Similarly, the decline of organized labor since the 1970s has diminished the role of unions as an important partner for anti-poverty advocacy (e.g., Baumgartner et al. 2009). Without these natural collaborators, existing poverty organizations have fewer opportunities to form coalitions and magnify their voice. Gilens (2012) notes that there may still be times when coalition politics can help the poor, as long as the interests of the poor coincide with the interests of large, resource-rich organizations. Policy, therefore, occasionally reflects the preferences of the poor, but only because of the "happy coincidence" that large, resource-rich interest groups (e.g., AARP, PhARMA, etc.) have the same policy preferences (Gilens 2009).

Although some organizations are working on poverty-related issues, there are few of them, and they tend to have only modest resources (e.g., Baumgartner and Leech 2001; Baumgartner et al. 2009). Consequently, one obvious remedy to the underrepresentation of the poor in Congress is to increase the number of interest groups devoted to poverty issues. More and better-resourced poverty advocacy groups could engage in more activity on behalf of the poor. However, adding or enhancing such groups is easier said than done, and thus reshaping the balance of the interest group community is a desirable but unlikely solution.

A less ambitious, but perhaps more practical, approach is to consider what can be done within the current framework to help existing poverty-focused interest groups. One of the primary ways that interest groups can influence the policymaking process is through direct lobbying of members of Congress. Particularly relevant here is Hall and Deardorff's (2006) theory of lobbying as legislative subsidy, wherein interest groups lobby legislators who are sympathetic to their cause. Given limited resources, it is valuable for poverty-related groups to concentrate their lobbying on their strongest allies, who are most likely to allocate their time and resources to advance their shared goals of reducing poverty. The challenge for anti-poverty interest groups is that it may be unclear who the friends of the poor are. This book demonstrates that congressional friends of the poor are not always the usual suspects. Instead, they include one or more types of surrogates, which were the focus of Chapter 6. Identifying the champions of the poor provides valuable guidance as to which legislators have demonstrated their commitment to working on poverty-relevant issues, and, hence, who should be targeted by interest groups seeking to increase legislative activity on poverty-related issues.

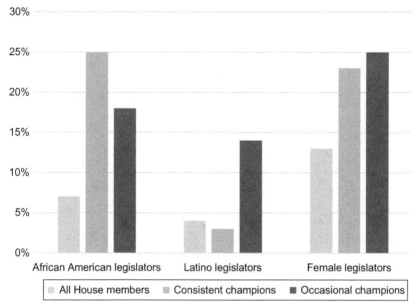

FIGURE 8.1 Diversity among champions in the House of Representatives

THE DIVERSITY PROBLEM

Surrogate champions, most of whom come from districts without high poverty rates, provide much of the representation for the poor. As Figure 8.1 illustrates, legislators from traditionally disadvantaged groups, such as women, African Americans, and to a lesser extent Latinos, comprise a larger portion of both the consistent and occasional champions than they do of the overall House membership. The challenge associated with this dynamic is that women and minorities are themselves underrepresented among members of the House of Representatives. This places a ceiling on the amount of representation they can provide. Therefore, the poor's overreliance on female and minority legislators to make their voice heard in the House, coupled with the still-lagging diversity among members of Congress, is part of the reason why the poor are underrepresented.

In order to better understand how diversity in Congress might enhance the representation of the poor moving forward, it is helpful to review how the number of women and minorities in the House of Representative has changed over time. Historically, there were few women and minorities in

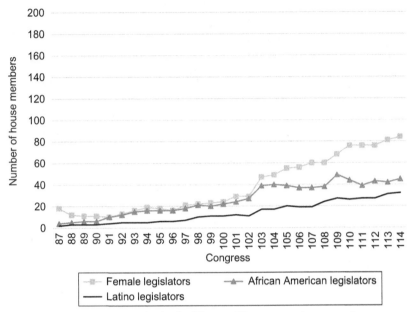

FIGURE 8.2 Diversity in the House of Representatives over time

the House, and, thus, few potential surrogate representatives for the poor. During the 87th Congress (1961–1962), for instance, only twenty-four of 435 House members were not white males. Figure 8.2 illustrates this low starting point, but also shows the eventual, if uneven, increases among each group. Twenty years later (1981–1982) that number had climbed to forty-four women and minority members, which is still only 10 percent of the House. For female legislators, the so-called Year of the Women in 1992 resulted in a substantial increase of eighteen House members in a single election, and, since then, the number of women has increased to eighty-four in the 114th Congress (2015–2016). African American members displayed the largest jump in the early 1990s, and, although this has tapered off, the number of black members of the House is now approaching fifty. Latinos have been among the slowest to be elected to the House, with only a dozen members in 1990. However, their numbers are increasing steadily, too, and, by the 114th Congress, there were thirty-two Latino House members serving in the body. Today, 19 percent of House members are women, 10 percent are African American, and 7 percent are Latino. These percentages may lag the diversity in the population, but this also indicates room for further diversification in the future, particularly in light of the clear upward trajectory depicted in Figure 8.2.

Increasing diversity in the House should also broaden the scope of anti-poverty efforts. As shown in Chapter 6, women and minorities place unique types of poverty-related issues on the congressional agenda. For instance, female champions of the poor tend to sponsor legislation that addresses gendered poverty issues, such as the costs of childcare, and the implications of work requirements for workplace sexual harassment victims. Likewise, Latino champions propose funding for bilingual education in poor schools, and target jobs programs to border communities. A more diverse Congress, then, will address a wider range of issues associated with poverty and, in doing so, may identify policy innovations that could help people break out of persistent poverty.

Some of the optimism generated by the diversification of Congress, however, is tempered by the shortage of female and minority legislators in positions of institutional power. Recall from Chapter 7, the disconnect between the legislators who take the initiative to put poverty-related legislation on the congressional agenda, and those who are best able to pass poverty-relevant legislation, namely party leadership and committee leadership. The challenge is that few women and minorities hold leadership positions. In the history of the House of Representatives, only four individuals who were not white, male legislators have held top party leadership positions such as the Speaker, majority leader, minority leader, or the party whips: Rep. Jim Clyburn (D-SC), Rep. Tony Coelho (D-CA), Rep. William Gray (D-PA), and Rep. Nancy Pelosi (D-CA). If one also considers the chairs of the Democratic Caucus and Republican Caucus, there are five additional minority or female legislators who have held a leadership post: Rep. Xavier Becerra (D-CA), Rep. Robert Menendez (D-NJ), Rep. Cathy McMorris-Rogers (R-WA), Rep. Deborah Pryce (R-OH), and Rep. J.C. Watts (R-OK). Notably, none of these legislators is a consistent or occasional champion of the poor. Similarly, there is little diversity in the House committee leadership. Since 1877, only fifty-five members who are not white, male legislators have chaired a standing committee in the House, despite the fact that, over this period, there have been more than 1,400 committee chairs.[3] Thus, resolving the diversity problem requires increasing diversity in the House leadership as well.

---

[3] The number of women and minority committee chairs is taken from the Biographical Directory of the United States Congress, and made available online through the website of the Clerk of the House. The estimated number of committee chair positions is based on

THE REPUBLICAN PARTY PROBLEM

Another reason why Congress does so little to represent the poor is that Republican legislators, even those who represent districts with high poverty rates, rarely take-up poverty-related issues. A general illustration of this Republican problem is that 55 percent (383 of 691) of Republican House members who served from 1983 to 2014 did not sponsor a single bill addressing a poverty-related issue. This lack of activity by Republicans is especially striking given the wide-ranging definition of poverty-related legislation used to generate these numbers. It also drives down the overall amount of representation afforded the poor in Congress. Clearly, more legislators from both parties could be doing more to represent the poor, but it would be disingenuous to ignore the clear partisan gap. Moreover, while 9 percent of Democratic legislators are either consistent or occasional champions for the poor, only 3 percent of Republican legislators are. The crux of the Republican problem, then, is that there are many Republican legislators who could be doing more – indeed, doing anything – to address poverty.

When looking only at legislators from high poverty districts, the absence of Republican legislators willing to engage issues related to poverty is glaring. There are forty-four Republican House members who represent a high poverty district, and not a single one is a consistent or occasional champion. Furthermore, almost three-quarters of Republicans in this group never sponsor a single poverty-related bill.[4] These two eye-popping details direct us to the heart of the poor representation problem – the growing number of inactive Republicans from high-poverty districts, which are heavily rural and concentrated in the South.

Republicans' non-representation of the poor is all the more interesting in light of the fact that Republican House members often highlight, in prominent ways, the problem of poverty. For instance, in June 2016, House Speaker Paul Ryan (R-WI) invited the press to a low-income neighborhood in Washington DC to launch "A Better Way," his policy

---

twenty standing committees per congress for the seventy congresses from 1877 to 2017. However, it is important to note that this calculation underestimates the number of committee chair positions, since there were nearly sixty standing committees in the post-Civil War House. The Legislative Reorganization Act of 1946 reduced the number of committees from forty-eight to nineteen (see Smith and Deering 1990; Welsh 2008). Today, the House has twenty-one standing committees.

[4] In comparison, only 38 percent of Democrats from high poverty districts are completely inactive.

proposal to fight poverty (Snell and DeBonis 2016). Flanked by several House Republicans, Ryan lauded a local nonprofit organization saying, "These are the people who are fighting poverty on the front lines ... If there is anyone we should listen to, it is them – the people here in our communities who are actually successful in fighting, and winning, and beating back poverty." However, more than a year later, there has been little legislative follow-up to this high profile campaign to fight poverty. More generally, Speaker Ryan has taken multiple opportunities to call attention to a conservative plan to fight poverty, including moderating the 2016 Jack Kemp Foundation presidential candidate forum on poverty (which the eventual Republican nominee, Donald Trump, did not attend) and forming a Speaker's Task Force on Poverty, Opportunity, and Upward Mobility. However, all of this political rhetoric about embracing people in poor communities is not followed by tangible legislative action from Republicans, either individually or collectively.

This gulf between congressional Republicans' promises to pursue a conservative anti-poverty policy and the reality of very little legislative action suggests that many Republicans realize that poverty is a problem, but they do not care very much about it and are primarily motivated by other issues. The risk for Republicans is that this may create unmet expectations among voters. It is yet unclear whether the result would be merely disillusionment or whether there could be significant electoral consequences. However, at a minimum, the absence of action on poverty-related issues is a missed opportunity for the Republican Party to expand its electoral coalition.

If Republicans' inactivity on poverty-relevant issues helps to explain why Congress does so little to address poverty, what are the prospects that this may improve in the future? One force working against more activity by Republicans in the future is the strong tide of polarization in Washington, which pushes the parties further away from one another, as well as from compromise and more moderate policy solutions. One feature of heightened polarization is that much of congressional politics focuses on national political issues rather than local concerns. Whereas Tip O'Neill quipped that "all politics is local," (1993, xv) today it seems that all politics is partisan. Indeed, Lee (2009, 2016) shows that even procedural votes and other non-ideological votes have become highly partisan, and partisan messaging is often prioritized over substantive policymaking. These trends suggest that it may be unlikely for Republicans, including those from high poverty districts, to focus on the interests of the poor. If the first year of unified Republican control of government is indicative, it appears that Republicans are not only unlikely to champion the poor, but may pursue policies antithetical to the interests of the poor. Indeed, the much anticipated tax overhaul is projected to help upper-income Americans much more than lower-income Americans, leading to the American Enterprise Institute, a right-leaning thinktank, to call for the House bill to "do more to fight poverty and advance opportunity."[5]

MOVING TOWARD LESS-POOR REPRESENTATION

The above discussion of the representation of the poor in Congress presents a somewhat skeptical view of the current state of affairs. However, in light of recent political developments, there is also some room for optimism. Having examined some of the reasons why the poor are not better represented, the question shifts to whether and how this is likely to change. I already discussed how interest groups might be able to tailor their lobbying strategy in light of what we know about who is (and who is not) active on behalf of the poor. I also outlined the ways in which the increasing diversity in Congress is likely to increase the pool of surrogate representatives for the poor. In this concluding section, then, I consider how recent political dynamics have the potential to move Congress towards better representation of the millions of Americans living in poverty. Much of this can be done by creating electoral incentives for both Republicans and Democrats to represent the poor.

Traditionally, the electoral incentives for Democratic legislators to represent poor constituents were stronger than for Republicans, because low-income voters supported the Democratic Party. This has begun to change, and now party differences in legislators' electoral incentives are a matter of degree, not absolutes. Stonecash (2000, 2012) shows that low income voters lean more Democratic than high income groups, but the poor are far from a monolithic voting bloc.[6] Across the 1980s through the 2000s, low income voters chose the Democrats 60 percent of the time in presidential elections and 67 percent of the time in House elections. However, if looking only at low-income white voters (given that African Americans are a strong Democratic voting bloc regardless of class), these figures fall to a more balanced 49 percent in presidential elections and 59 percent in House elections (Stonecash 2012). This means that a

---

[5] Quoted in Kurtzleben 2017.
[6] Stonecash 2000, 2012 defines low-income individuals as those in the bottom third of the income distribution.

majority of low-income white voters now vote for Republican presidential candidates, and over 40 percent vote for Republican House candidates. Consequently, Republican legislators cannot afford to ignore the poor, especially in high poverty districts where low income voters make up a greater portion of a Republican legislator's electoral coalition than at the presidential level. Furthermore, these Republican voters want legislators to take actions to combat poverty; 53 percent of low-income Republicans say that they believe that the federal government "should play a major role in helping people get out of poverty" (Pew Research Center 2015).

A substantial number of poor Americans were already receptive to the Republican message. Then came the historic 2016 election, and the political messaging of Donald Trump, whose rhetoric targeted a range of voters from varying political underclasses, especially low-income, non-urban whites. Populism is not new to American politics, but this iteration has provided signs that the poor may become more of a political consideration for elected officials, both Republican and Democratic.

Initial assessments of the surprising outcome of the presidential election proclaimed that Trump's victory reflected the rise of white working class voters. Although this group is not a perfect stand-in for poor Americans, the issues of concern to each group overlap significantly, and share the sense that many Americans are struggling while politicians do nothing to help. This characterization was amplified by Trump's campaign rhetoric, which was full of references to those being left behind, workers losing out in the global economy, and unemployment ravaging communities. However, as the dust settled and journalists and political scientists engaged in the election postmortem, some have expressed skepticism that the election was driven by the frustrations of the lower class. Carnes and Lupu (2017), for instance, point out that the National Election Study (NES) data shows that only 35 percent of Trump supporters in the general election had household incomes of less than $50,000.

Whether white working class Americans cast the decisive votes in Trump's victory may not actually matter. I argue that this is a case where the perception matters more than the reality. The lesson that politicians, pundits, and citizens took from 2016 is that Donald Trump's campaign woke a sleeping giant of working-class Americans who have been ignored by previous politicians of both parties, and who may be the key to electoral victory in this competitive, partisan era. Perhaps fitting for this political moment, whether this perception comports with reality is almost beside the point. From the perspective of improving the representation of the poor, what matters is that politicians, especially Republicans, think that their voters want them to address issues related to poverty. This may provide incentives to do so, not just on the campaign trail, but through legislative action as well. To the extent that issues related to poverty play a larger role in campaigns, reelection-minded legislators should have strong incentives to keep their promises and take-up poverty-related issues in office (see Sulkin 2011). For their part, poor and working-class constituents, as well as voters more generally, can facilitate increased legislative action on poverty-related issues by holding Republicans accountable to their rhetoric. In short, the key questions are whether Republicans will make the political calculation to focus on these voters, and whether they have the political will to follow-through on the populist promises of a conservative version of the War on Poverty. Early indications are that congressional Republicans have decided not to prioritize a more populist agenda, but whether they will face electoral consequences in the 2018 midterm cycle remains to be seen.

For Democrats, the populist mood of the 2016 election cycle took the form of a rising progressive wing of the party, and the surprise success of self-avowed socialist, Bernie Sanders (D-VT). As embodied by Senator Sanders and Senator Elizabeth Warren (D-MA), populism in the Democratic Party also targets working class Americans struggling to make ends meet. However, it points the finger at the excesses of capitalism on Wall Street and corporations that "put profits before people." Sen. Warren's role in the creation of the Consumer Financial Protection Bureau helped to establish the storyline that hard-working Americans were being taken advantage of by wealthy corporations. Sen. Sanders' attacks on corporations' tax advantages, as well as their campaign contributions, reinforced this populist image.

The rise of this populist strain of liberalism among Democrats was coupled with the denouncement of the New Democrat pragmatism associated with former President Bill Clinton. For two decades, this centrist wing of the Democratic Party has dominated party dynamics. Democrats have pursued more moderate policies, often by coopting the most popular elements of Republican policy and rhetoric. For instance, President Clinton not only collaborated with then-Speaker of the House Newt Gingrich (R-GA) and the Republican House on welfare reform, but also on criminal justice policy that imposed harsher sentencing minimums.

However, in 2016, the pragmatic, centrist New Democrat approach appeared to become a liability. Rising liberal activists saw little merit in the type of compromise and deal-making that marked the 1990s. In fact, the emboldened progressive wing of the party called on Democratic presidential candidate Hillary Clinton to denounce the aforementioned welfare and crime policies of her husband, former President Bill Clinton (e.g., Covert 2016; Stockman 2016).

In the aftermath of Hillary Clinton's general election loss, the Democratic Party continues to debate the direction of the party. The key question is whether to cultivate the power of the rising liberal activist wing or to try to hold the center and seek more moderate common ground. These tensions played out after the 2016 election in a close and contentious battle for leadership of the Democratic Party between Tom Perez and Keith Ellison, who were seen as the establishment and progressive candidates, respectively (e.g., Hamid 2017). In Congress, members of the more progressive wing challenged the existing congressional leadership, and argued that the election served as a call for Democrats to embrace more liberal policies such as a higher minimum wage and tuition-free higher education (e.g., Kane 2016). In the days after the election, Sen. Sanders argued that Democrats need to pursue progressive policies that would help the poor, "we have got to channel that [voters'] anger against the people who caused the decline of the middle class and so many people living in poverty" (Parks 2016). Although the outcome of the fight over the future direction of the Democratic Party is not yet resolved, it will have consequences for the poor either way. If the party chooses a more progressive identity, it will assume a more extensive set of antipoverty policies, but, even if the establishment faction prevails, the Democrats' election postmortem has shifted the focus of party elites and voters expectations towards issues that affect the working class and poor.

Only time will tell how the representation of the poor will evolve in the future. The 2016 election, coupled with other ongoing trends, has revealed political and electoral dynamics that could compel both Republicans and Democrats to be more attentive to the poor in the years ahead. This could happen if President Trump truly embraces some of the populist promises of his campaign, or if the New Left ascends and becomes the face of the Democratic Party. A year after the election of 2016, there clearly has been change in the political rhetoric and an increased awareness of inequality. However, the reality is that there has been little tangible change from either party.

Shifting back to the present, what this book shows is that poverty has been, and continues to be, a major policy problem. It is one that our leaders are keenly aware of, but also one that nearly all of them are hesitant to engage with. In a notable 2013 speech on the House floor, Democratic Leader Nancy Pelosi (D-CA) acknowledged as much:

"Poverty in America, poverty. I'm saying the word on the floor of the House: poverty, poverty, poverty, poverty. Poverty in America seems to be a word that people get nervous about" (2013). Regardless of whether Members of Congress feel ill at ease talking about poverty, there is a clear need among their poor constituents for issues related to poverty to be addressed. The question moving forward is whether members of Congress will overcome their past hesitations and begin to engage in greater representation of the poor.

Bibliography

Adler, E. Scott. 2002. *Why Congressional Reforms Fail: Reelection and the House Committee System*. Chicago, IL: University of Chicago Press.
    2000. "Constituency Characteristics and the 'Guardian' Model of Appropriations Subcommittees, 1959–1998." *American Journal of Political Science* 44(1): 104–14.
Adler, E. Scott and John S. Lapinski. 1997. "Demand-side Theory and Congressional Committee Composition: A Constituency Characteristics Approach." *American Journal of Political Science* 41(3): 895–918.
Adler, E. Scott and John S. Lapinski, eds. 2006. *The Macropolitics of Congress*. Princeton, NJ: Princeton University Press.
Adler, E. Scott and John D. Wilkerson. 2012. *Congress and the Politics of Problem Solving*. New York, NY: Cambridge University Press.
Adler, E. Scott and John D. Wilkerson. Congressional Bills Project: 1960–2014. NSF 00880066 and 00880061. The views expressed are those of the authors and not the National Science Foundation.
Ainsworth, Scott and Thad E. Hall. 2010. *Abortion Politics in Congress: Strategic Incrementalism and Policy Change*. New York, NY: Cambridge University Press.
Aldrich, John and David Rohde. 1998. "The Transition to Republican Rule in the House: Implications for Theories of Congressional Politics." *Political Science Quarterly* 112(4): 541–67.
Allard, Scott W. 2017. *Places in Need: The Changing Geography of Poverty*. New York, NY: Russell Sage Foundation.
    2009. *Out of Reach: Place, Poverty, and the New American Welfare State*. New Haven, CT: Yale University Press.
    2008. "Place, Race, and Access to the Safety Net." In *Colors of Poverty*. eds. Ann Chih Lin and David Harris. New York, NY: Russell Sage Foundation, 232–60.
Alter, Johnathan. 1984. "Homeless in America." *Newsweek*. January 2, 1984. Pages 20–3.

American Political Science Association. 1950. "Toward a More Responsible Two-Party System: A Report of the Committee on Political Parties." *American Political Science Review* 3(2): xi–99.

Anderson, William D., Janet Box-Steffensmeier, and Valeria Sinclair-Chapman. 2003. "The Keys to Legislative Success in the U.S. House of Representatives." *Legislative Studies Quarterly* 28(3): 357–86.

Ansolabehere, Stephen and Philip Edward Jones. 2011. "Dyadic Representation." In *The Oxford Handbook of the American Congress*, eds. George C. Edwards III, Frances E. Lee, and Eric Schickler. New York, NY: Oxford University Press, 293–314.

Ansolabehere, Stephen, James Snyder, and Charles Stewart. 2001. "Candidate Positioning in U.S. House Elections." *American Journal of Political Science* 45(1): 136–59.

Applebaum, Binyamin. 2016. "The Millions of Americans Donald Trump and Hillary Clinton Barely Mention: The Poor." *New York Times*. August 11, 2016.

Arceneaux, Kevin. 2003. "The Conditional Impact of Blame Attribution on the Relationship between Economic Adversity and Turnout." *Political Research Quarterly* 56(1): 63–71.

Ardoin, Phillip and James Garand. 2003. "Measuring Constituency Ideology in U.S. House Districts: A Top-Down Simulation Approach." *Journal of Politics* 65(4): 1165–89.

Arnold, R. Douglas. 1990. *The Logic of Congressional Action*. New Haven, CT: Yale University Press.

Avery, James M. and Mark Peffley. 2003. "Race Matters: The Impact of News Coverage of Welfare Reform on Public Opinion." In *Race and the Politics of Welfare Reform*. eds. Sanford S. Schram, Joe Soss and Richard C. Fording. Ann Arbor, MI: University of Michigan Press, 131–50.

Azari, Julia and Stephen Engel. 2007. "Do the Words Matter? Party Platforms and Ideological Change in Republican Politics." Paper presented at the Annual Meeting of the Midwest Political Science Association, Chicago, IL.

Bachrach, Peter, and Morton S. Baratz. 1963. "Decisions and Nondecisions: An Analytical Framework." *American Political Science Review* 57(3): 632–42.

1962. "Two Faces of Power." *American Political Science Review* 56(4): 947–52.

Bafumi, Joseph and Michael Herron. 2010. "Leapfrog Representation and Extremism: A Study of American Voters and Their Members in Congress." *American Political Science Review* 104(3): 519–42.

Bailey, Michael. 2001. "Quiet Influence: The Representation of Diffuse Interests on Postwar Trade Policy." *Legislative Studies Quarterly* 26(1): 45–80.

Barnello, Michelle and Kathleen A. Bratton. 2007. "Bridging the Gender Gap in Bill Sponsorship." *Legislative Studies Quarterly* 32(3): 449–74.

Barrett, Edith and Fay Lomax-Cook. 1991. "Congressional Attitudes and Voting Behavior: An Examination of Support for Social Welfare." *Legislative Studies Quarterly* 16(3): 375–92.

Bartels, Larry. 2008. *Unequal Democracy: The Political Economy of the New Gilded Age*. Princeton, NJ: Princeton University Press.

1998. "Where the Ducks Are: Voting Power in a Party System." In *Politicians and Party Politics*, ed. John Geer. Baltimore, MD: Johns Hopkins University Press, 43–79.

1991. "Constituency Opinion and Congressional Policy Making: The Reagan Defense Build Up." *American Political Science Review* 85(2): 457–74.

Baumgartner, Frank R., Jeffrey M. Berry, Marie Hojnacki, David C. Kimball and Beth L. Leech. 2009. *Lobbying and Policy Change: Who Wins, Who Loses, and Why*. Chicago, IL: University of Chicago Press.

Baumgartner, Frank R., Suzanna DeBoeuf, and Amber Boydstun. 2008. *The Decline of the Death Penalty and the Discovery of Innocence*. New York, NY: Cambridge University Press.

Baumgartner, Frank R. and Bryan D. Jones. 2015. *The Politics of Information: Problem Definition and the Course of Public Policy in America*. Chicago, IL: University of Chicago Press.

2004. "Representation and Agenda Setting." *Policy Studies Journal* 32(1): 1–24.

1993. *Agendas and Instability in American Politics*. Chicago: University of Chicago Press.

Policy Agendas Project: 1960–2014. NSF SBR 9320922 and 0111611.

Baumgartner, Frank R. and Beth L. Leech. 2001. "Interest Niches and Policy Bandwagons: Patterns of Interest Group Involvement in National Politics." *Journal of Politics* 63(4): 1191–213.

1998. *Basic Interests: The Importance of Groups in Politics and Political Science*. Princeton, NJ: Princeton University Press.

Bawn, Kathleen, Martin Cohen, David Karol, Seth Masket, Hans Noel, and John Zaller. 2012. "A Theory of Political Parties: Groups, Policy Demands and Nominations in American Politics." *Perspectives in Politics* 10(3): 571–97.

Berinsky, Adam. 2004. *Silent Voices: Public Opinion and Political Participation in America*. Princeton, NJ: Princeton University Press.

Berman, Ari. 2011. "Obama: Triangulation 2.0?" *The Nation*. February 7, 2011.

Berry, Jeffrey M. 1999. *The New Liberalism: The Rising Power of Citizen Groups*. Washington, DC: Brookings Institution Press.

Bhatti, Yosef and Robert Erikson. 2011. "How Poorly Are the Poor Represented in the U.S. Senate?" In *Who Gets Represented?*, eds. Peter Enns and Christopher Wlezien. New York, NY: Russell Sage Foundation, 223–46.

Binder, Sarah. 2003. *Stalemate: Causes and Consequences of Legislative Gridlock*. Washington, DC: Brookings Institution Press.

1999. "The Dynamics of Legislative Gridlock, 1947–96." *American Political Science Review* 93(3): 519–33.

Bishin, Benjamin. 2009. *Tyranny of the Minority: The Subconstituency Politics Theory of Representation*. Philadelphia, PA: Temple University Press.

2000. "Constituency Influence in Congress: Does Subconstituency Matter?" *Legislative Studies Quarterly* 25(3): 389–415.

Bishin, Benjamin and Charles A. Smith. 2013. "When do legislators defy popular sovereignty? Testing theories of minority representation using DOMA." *Political Research Quarterly* 66(4): 794–803.

Black Americans in Congress, 1870–2007. 2008. Prepared under the direction of The Committee on House Administration of the US House of Representatives. The Office of History and Preservation, Office of the Clerk, US House of Representatives. Washington, DC: US Government Printing Office.

Blidook, Kelly and Matthew Kerby. 2011. "Constituency Influence on 'Constituency Members': The Adaptability of Roles to Electoral Realities in the Canadian Case." *The Journal of Legislative Studies* 17(3): 327–39.

Bobo, Lawrence and Ryan A. Smith. 1994. "Antipoverty policy, affirmative action, and racial attitudes." In *Confronting Poverty: Prescriptions for Change.* eds. Sheldon Danzinger, Gary Sandefur, and Daniel H. Weinberg. Cambridge, MA: Harvard University Press, 365–95.

Brady, David and Edward Schwartz. 1995. "Ideology and interests in congressional voting: The politics of abortion in the U.S. Senate." *Public Choice* 84(1): 25–48.

Bratton, Kathleen A. 2006. "The Behavior and Success of Latino Legislators: Evidence from the States." *Social Science Quarterly* 87(5): 1136–57.

Bratton, Kathleen A. and Kerry L. Haynie. 1999. "Agenda Setting and Legislative Success in State Legislatures: The Effects of Gender and Race." *Journal of Politics* 61(3): 658–79.

Bricker, Jesse, Alice Henriques, Jacob Krimmel, and John Sabelhaus. 2016. "Measuring income and wealth at the top using administrative and survey data." *Brookings Papers on Economic Activity.* Washington, DC: Brookings Institution.

Broockman, David. 2016. "Approaches to Studying Policy Representation." *Legislative Studies Quarterly* 41(1): 181–215.

Bruni, Frank. 2000. "The 2000 Campaign: The Texas Governor. Bush Campaign Turns Attention to Middle Class." *New York Times.* September 18, 2000.

Burden, Barry C. 2007. *Personal Roots of Representation.* Princeton, NJ: Princeton University Press.

Burke, Edmund. 2009 (1790). *Reflections on the Revolution in France.* ed. Leslie G. Mitchell. Series *Oxford World's Classics.* New York: Oxford University Press.

    1949. "Letter to Langriche." In *Burke's Politics, Selected Writings and Speeches of Edmund Burke on Reform, Revolution and War,* eds. Ross J. S. Hoffman and Paul Levack. New York, NY: Alfred Knopf, 495.

Busch, Marc and Eric Reinhardt. 1999. "Industrial Location and Protection: The Political and Economic Geography of U.S. Nontariff Barriers." *American Journal of Political Science* 43(4): 1028–50.

Butler, Daniel M. 2014. *Representing the Advantaged: How Politicians Reinforce Inequality.* New York, NY: Cambridge University Press.

Cain, Bruce, John Ferejohn, and Morris Fiorina. 1987. *The Personal Vote: Constituency Service and Electoral Independence.* Cambridge, MA: Harvard University Press.

Campbell, Andrea Louise. 2003. *How Policies Make Citizens: Senior Political Activism and the American Welfare State.* Princeton, NJ: Princeton University Press.

Campbell, Karlyn Kohrs and Kathleen Hall Jamieson. 2000. *Presidents Creating the Presidency: Deeds Done in Words*. Chicago, IL: University of Chicago Press.

Cameron, Charles, David Epstein, and Sharyn O'Halloran. 1996. "Do Majority-Minority Districts Maximize Substantive Black Representation in Congress?" *American Political Science Review* 90(4): 794–812.

Cameron, David R. 1988. "Politics, Public Policy, and Distributional Inequality: A Comparative Analysis." In *Power, Inequality, and Democratic Politics: Essays in Honor of Robert A. Dahl*, eds. Ian Shapiro and Grant Reeher. Boulder, CO: Westview Press, 219–59.

Canes-Wrone, Brandice, David Brady, and John Cogan. 2002. "Out of Step, Out of Office: Electoral Accountability and House Members' Voting." *American Political Science Review* 96(1): 127–40.

Canon, David. 1999. *Race, Redistricting, and Representation: The Unintended Consequences of Black Majority Districts*. Chicago, IL: University of Chicago Press.

Carnes, Nicholas. 2013. *White-Collar Government: The Hidden Role of Class in Economic Policy Making*. Chicago, IL: University of Chicago Press.

2012. "Does the Numerical Underrepresentation of the Working Class in Congress Matter?" *Legislative Studies Quarterly* 37(1): 5–34.

Carnes, Nicholas and Meredith L. Sadin. 2015. "The 'Mill Worker's Son' Heuristic: How Voters Perceive Politicians from Working-class Families – And How They Really Behave in Office." *Journal of Politics* 77(1): 285–98.

Carnes, Nicholas and Noam Lupu. 2017. "It's time to bust the myth: Most Trump voters were not working class." *Washington Post*. June 5, 2017.

Carpenter, Daniel P., Kevin M. Esterling, and David M. Lazer. 2004. "Friends, Brokers and Transitivity: Who Talks with Whom in Washington Lobbying?" *Journal of Politics* 66(1): 224–46.

Carroll, Susan J. 2002. "Representing Women: Congresswomen's Perceptions of Their Representational Roles." In *Women Transforming Congress*, ed. Cindy Simon Rosenthal. Norman, OK: University of Oklahoma Press, 50–68.

Carson, Jamie, Charles Finocchiaro, and David Rohde. 2002. "Partisanship, Consensus, and Committee-Floor Divergence: A Comparison of Member Behavior in the 96th and 104th Congresses." *American Politics Research* 30(1): 3–33.

Casellas, Jason P. 2011. *Latino Representation in State Houses and Congress*. New York, NY: Cambridge University Press.

Caughey, Devin and Christopher Warshaw. 2016. "The Dynamics of State Policy Liberalism, 1936–2014." *American Journal of Political Science* 60(4): 899–913.

Caves, Richard. 1976. "Economic Models of Political Choice: Canada's Tariff Structure." *Canadian Journal of Economics* 9: 278–300.

Chase, Kerry. 2015. "Domestic Geography and Policy Pressures." In *The Oxford Handbook of the Political Economy of International Trade*, ed. Lisa Martin. New York, NY: Oxford University Press, 316–35.

Clemens, Austin, Michael Crespin, and Charles Finocchiaro. 2015. "The Political Geography of Distributive Politics." *Legislative Studies Quarterly* 40(1): 111–36.

Clinton, Joshua. 2006. "Representation in Congress: Constituents and Roll Calls in the 106th House." *Journal of Politics* 68: 397–409.

Cobb, Michael and Jeffrey Jenkins. 2001. "Race and Representation of Blacks' Interests During Reconstruction." *Political Research Quarterly* 54(1): 181–204.

Cohen, Cathy J. and Michael C. Dawson. 1993. "Neighborhood Poverty and African American Politics." *American Political Science Review* 87(2): 286–302.

Cohen, Jeffrey E. 1995. "Presidential Rhetoric and the Public Agenda." *American Journal of Political Science* 39(1): 87–107.

Collins, Chuck and Josh Hoxie. 2015. "Billionaire Bonanza: The Forbes 400 and the Rest of Us." *Institute for Policy Studies.* December 1, 2015.

Converse, Phillip. 1964. "The Nature of Belief Systems in Mass Publics." In *Ideology and Discontent,* ed. David Apter. Ann Arbor, MI: University of Michigan Press, 206–61.

Covert, Bryce. 2016. "Why Hillary Has Never Apologized for Welfare Reform." *The Atlantic.* June 14, 2016.

Cox, Gary and Mathew McCubbins. 2005. *Setting the Agenda: Responsible Party Government in the U.S. House of Representatives.* New York, NY: Cambridge University Press.

    1993. *Legislative Leviathan: Party Government in the House.* Berkeley, CA: University of California Press.

Cramer, Katherine J. 2012. *The Politics of Resentment: Rural Consciousness in Wisconsin and the Rise of Scott Walker.* Chicago, IL: University of Chicago Press.

Dahl, Robert. 1971. *Polyarchy: Participation and Opposition.* New Haven, CT: Yale University Press.

Dao, James. 1992. "Rep. Ted Weiss, 64, Dies; Liberal Stalwart in House." *New York Times.* September 15, 1992.

Davidson, Roger H. 1969. *The Role of the Congressman.* New York, NY: Pegasus.

Davidson, Sue. 1994. *A Heart in Politics: Jeannette Rankin and Patsy Mink.* Seattle, WA: Seal Press.

Dawson, Michael C. 2003. *Black Visions: The Roots of Contemporary African-American Political Ideologies.* Chicago, IL: University of Chicago Press.

    1995. *Behind the Mule: Race and Class in African-American Politics.* Princeton, NJ: Princeton University Press.

Delli Carpini, Michael X. and Scott Keeter. 1997. *What Americans Know About Politics and Why it Matters.* New Haven, CT: Yale University Press.

DeParle, Jason. 1993. "How Jack Kemp Lost the War on Poverty." *New York Times.* February 28, 1993.

DeSante, Christopher D. 2013. "Working Twice as Hard to Get Half as Far: Race, Work Ethic, and America's Deserving Poor." *American Journal of Political Science* 57(2): 342–56.

Dexter, Lewis. 1957. "The Representative and His District." *Human Organization* 16(1): 2–13.

Dodson, Debra. 2006. *The Impact of Women in Congress.* New York, NY: Oxford University Press.

1991. *Reshaping the Agenda: Women in State Legislatures.* New Brunswick, NJ: Rutgers University.

Downs, Anthony. 1957. *An Economic Theory of Democracy.* New York, NY: Harper.

Dreier, Peter. 2012. "Poverty in America 50 Years After Michael Harrington's The Other America." *Huffington Post.* May 25, 2012.

Duncan, Cynthia M. 1999. *Worlds Apart: Why Poverty Persists in Rural America.* New Haven, CT: Yale University Press.

ed. 1992. *Rural Poverty in America.* Westport, CT: Auburn House.

Eaton, William J. 1990. "Hawkins Retiring – but Not Quitting." *Los Angeles Times.* December 23, 1990.

Edmiston, Kelly D. 2013. "The Low- and Moderate-Income Population in Recession and Recovery: Results From a New Survey." Federal Reserve Bank of Kansas City, *Economic Review*, First Quarter.

Edwards, George C. III and Dan B. Wood. 1999. "Who Influences Whom? The President and the Public Agenda." *American Political Science Review* 93(2): 327–44.

Ellis, Christopher. 2013. "Social Context and Economic Biases in Representation." *Journal of Politics* 75(3): 773–86.

2012. "Understanding Economic Biases in Representation." *Political Research Quarterly* 65(4): 938–51.

Ellis, Christopher and Christopher Faricy. 2011. "Social Policy and Public Opinion: How the Ideological Direction of Spending Influences Public Mood." *Journal of Politics* 73(4): 1095–110.

Ellis, Christopher and James Stimson. 2012. *Ideology in America.* New York, NY: Cambridge University Press.

Enns, Peter. 2014. "The Public's Increasing Punitiveness and its Influence on Mass Incarceration in the United States." *American Journal of Political Science* 58(4): 857–72.

Enns, Peter, Nathan Kelly, Jana Morgan, Thomas Volscho, and Christopher Witko. 2014. "Conditional Status Quo Bias and Top Income Shares: How U.S. Political Institutions Have Benefitted the Rich." *Journal of Politics* 76(2): 289–303.

Enns, Peter and Christopher Wlezien, eds. 2011. *Who Gets Represented?* New York, NY: Russell Sage Foundation.

Ensley, Michael, Michael Tofias, and Scott De Marchi. 2009. "District Complexity as an Advantage in Congressional Elections." *American Journal of Political Science* 53(4): 990–1005.

Erikson, Robert. 2015. "Income Inequality and Policy Responsiveness." *Annual Review of Political Science* 18: 11–29.

1990. "Economic Conditions and the Congressional Vote: A Review of the Macrolevel Evidence." *American Journal of Political Science* 34(2): 373–99.

Erikson, Robert, Michael MacKuen and James Stimson. 2006. "Public Opinion and Congressional Policy: A Macro-Level Perspective." In *The Macropolitics of Congress*, eds. E. Scott Adler and John S. Lapinski. Princeton, NJ: Princeton University Press, 79–95.

Erikson, Robert, Michael MacKuen, and James Stimson. 2002. *The Macro Polity*. New York, NY: Cambridge University Press.

Erikson, Robert and Gerald Wright. 1980. "Policy representation of constituency interests." *Political Behavior* 2(1): 91–106.

Esterling, Kevin M. 2007. "Buying Expertise: Campaign Contributions and Attention to Policy Analysis in Congressional Committees." *American Political Science Review* 101(1): 93–109.

Evans, C. Lawrence. 2001. "Committees, Leaders, and Message Politics." In *Congress Reconsidered (7th Edition)*, eds. Lawrence Dodd and Bruce Oppenheimer. Washington, DC: Congressional Quarterly Press, 217–43.

Fallows, James. 2000. "The Invisible Poor." *New York Times Magazine*. March 19, 2000.

Faricy, Christopher. 2016. "The Politics of Income Inequality in the United States." *Oxford Bibliographies*. DOI: 10.1093/obo/9780199756223–0147.

2015. *Welfare for the Wealthy: Parties, Social Spending, and Inequality in the United States*. New York, NY: Cambridge University Press.

Farrigan, Tracey. 2017. *Rural Poverty & Well-Being: Geography of Poverty*. Washington, DC: U.S. Department of Agriculture, Economic Research Service.

Farrington, Dana. 2012. "Stuck in the Middle (Class) With You." *National Public Radio (online)*. November 4, 2012.

Fenno, Richard F., Jr. 2013. *The Challenges of Congressional Representation*. Cambridge, MA: Harvard University Press.

2006. *Congressional Travels: Places, Connections, and Authenticity*. New York, NY: Routledge Press.

2003. *Going Home: Black Representatives and Their Constituents*. Chicago, IL: University of Chicago Press.

2000. *Congress at the Grassroots: Representational Change in the South, 1970–1998*. Chapel Hill, NC: University of North Carolina Press.

1996. *Senators on the Campaign Trail: The Politics of Representation*. Norman, OK: University of Oklahoma Press.

1978. *Homestyle: House Members in Their Districts*. New York, NY: Harper Collins.

1973. *Congressmen in Committees*. Boston, MA: Little, Brown, ad Co.

File, Thom. 2015. "Who Votes? Congressional Elections and the American Electorate: 1978–2014." *Population Characteristics, P20–577*. Washington, DC: U.S. Census Bureau.

Fiorina, Morris. 1981. *Retrospective Voting in American National Elections*. New Haven, CT: Yale University Press.

1978. "Economic Retrospective Voting in American National Elections: A Micro-Analysis." *American Journal of Political Science* 22(2): 426–43.

1977. *Congress: Keystone of the Washington Establishment*. New Haven, CT: Yale University Press.

1974. *Representatives, Roll Calls, and Constituencies*. Lexington, MA: Lexington Books.

Flavin, Patrick. 2015. "Lobbying Regulations and Political Equality in the American States." *American Politics Research* 43(2): 304–26.

2012a. "Income Inequality and Policy Representation in the American States." *American Politics Research* 40(1): 29–59.

2012b. "Does Higher Voter Turnout among the Poor Lead to More Equal Policy Representation?" *Social Science Journal* 49(4): 405–12.

Fogel, Richard L. 1985. "Homelessness: A Complex Problem and the Federal Response." *The American Journal of Economics and Sociology* 44(4): 3859.

Frazer, Phillip. 1992. "Obituary: Ted Weiss." *The Independent* (UK). September 23, 1992.

Frederick, Brian. 2009. "Are Female House Members Still More Liberal in a Polarized Era? The Conditional Nature of the Relationship Between Descriptive and Substantive Representation." *Congress and the Presidency* 36: 181–202.

Frisch, Scott A. and Sean Q. Kelly. 2006. *Committee Assignment Politics in the U.S. House of Representatives*. Norman, OK: University of Oklahoma Press.

Frizell, Sam. 2016. "Why Bernie Sanders is Talking About Poverty." *Time Magazine*. April 12, 2016.

Gamble, Katrina. 2007. "Black Political Representation: An Examination of Legislative Activity within US House Committees." *Legislative Studies Quarterly* 32: 421–46.

Gaventa, John. 1980. *Power and Powerlessness: Quiescence and Rebellion in an Appalachian Valley*. Urbana, IL: University of Illinois Press.

Gelman, Andrew, Boris Shor, David Park, and Joseph Bafumi. 2007. "Rich State, Poor State, Red State, Blue State: What's the Matter with Connecticut?" *Quarterly Journal of Political Science* 2: 345–67.

Gelman, Andrew, David Park, Boris Shor, and Jeronimo Cortina. 2008. *Red State, Blue State, Rich State, Poor State: Why Americans Vote the Way They Do*. Princeton, NJ: Princeton University Press.

Gerring, John. 2001. *Party Ideologies in America, 1828–1996*. New York, NY: Cambridge University Press.

Gerrity, Jessica, Tracy Osborn, and Jeanette Mendez. 2007. "Women and Representation: A Different View of the District." *Politics & Gender* 3: 179–200.

Gilens, Martin. 2012. *Affluence & Influence: Economic Inequality and Political Power in America*. Princeton, NJ: Princeton University Press.

2011. "Policy Consequences of Representational Inequality." In *Who Gets Represented?*, eds. Peter Enns and Christopher Wlezien. New York, NY: Russell Sage Foundation, 247–84.

2009. "Preference Gaps and Inequality in Representation." *PS: Political Science and Politics* 42(3): 335–41.

2005. "Inequality and Democratic Responsiveness." *Public Opinion Quarterly* 69(5): 778–96.

2003. "How the Poor Became Black: The Racialization of American Poverty in the Mass Media." In *Race and the Politics of Welfare Reform*, eds. Sanford F.

Schram, Joe Soss, and Richard C. Fording. Ann Arbor, MI: University of Michigan Press, 101–30.

1999. *Why Americans Hate Welfare: Race, Media, and the Politics of Anti-Poverty Policy.* Chicago, IL: University of Chicago Press.

Gilens, Martin and Benjamin Page. 2014. "Testing Theories of American Politics: Elites, Interest Groups, and Average Citizens." *Perspectives on Politics* 12(3): 564–81.

Gimpel, James G., Frances E. Lee, and Shanna Pearson-Merkowitz. 2008. "The Check is in the Mail: Interdistrict Funding Flows in Congressional Elections." *American Journal of Political Science* 52(2): 373–94.

Glickman, Dan. 2013. "America's Invisible Poor." *US News and World Report.* May 1, 2013.

Gray, Virginia and David Lowery. 1998. "To Lobby Alone or in a Flock: Foraging Behavior Among Organized Interests." *American Politics Research* 26(1): 5–34.

Griffin, John and Brian Newman. 2013. "Voting Power, Policy Representation, and Disparities in Voting's Rewards." *Journal of Politics* 75(1): 52–64.

2008. *Minority Report: Evaluating Political Inequality in America.* Chicago, IL: University of Chicago Press.

2005. "Are Voters Better Represented?" *Journal of Politics* 67(4): 1206–27.

Griffin, John, Brian Newman, and Christina Wolbrecht. 2012. "A Gender Gap in Policy Representation in the U.S. Congress?" *Legislative Studies Quarterly* 37(1): 35–66.

Grose, Christian R. 2011. *Congress in Black and White: Race and Representation in Congress and at Home.* New York, NY: Cambridge University Press.

Grumbach, Jacob. 2015. "Does the American Dream Matter for Members of Congress? Social-Class Backgrounds and Roll-Call Votes." *Political Research Quarterly* 68(2): 306–23.

Gurley, Lauren. 2016. "Who's Afraid of Rural Poverty? The Story Behind America's Invisible Poor." *American Journal of Economics and Sociology* 75(3): 589–604.

Hacker, Jacob. 2004. "Privatizing Risk Without Privatizing the Welfare State: The Hidden Politics of Social Policy Retrenchment." *American Political Science Review* 98(2): 243–60.

Hacker, Jacob S. and Paul Pierson. 2016. *American Amnesia: How the War on Government Led Us to Forget What Made America Prosper.* New York: Simon & Schuster.

2010. *Winner Take All Politics.* New York, NY: Simon & Schuster.

Hacker, Jacob, Suzanne Mettler, and Joe Soss. 2007. "The New Politics of Inequality: A Policy-Centered Perspective." In *Remaking America: Democracy and Public Policy in an Age of Inequality*, eds. Joe Soss, Jacob Hacker, and Suzanne Mettler. New York: Russell Sage Foundation, 3–24.

Haider-Markel, Don. 2010. *Out and Running: Gay and Lesbian Candidates, Elections, and Policy Representation.* Washington, DC: Georgetown University Press.

Hall, Richard L. 1996. *Participation in Congress*. New Haven, CT: Yale University Press.

1987. "Participation and Purpose in Committee Decision Making." *American Political Science Review* 87: 105–27.

Hall, Richard L. and Alan V. Deardorff. 2006. "Lobbying as Legislative Subsidy." *American Political Science Review* 100(1): 69–84.

Hall, Richard L. and Bernard Grofman. 1990. "The Committee Assignment Process and the Conditional Nature of Committee Bias." *American Political Science Review* 84(3): 797–820.

Hall, Richard L. and Colleen Heflin. 1994. "The Importance of Color in Congress: Minority Members, Minority Constituents, and the Representation of Race in the U.S. House." Paper presented at the Annual Meeting of the Midwest Political Science Association, Chicago, IL. April 14–16, 1994.

Hamid, Shadi. 2017. "Why the Battle for Leadership of the Democratic Party Mattered." *The Atlantic*. February 27, 2017.

Hansen, Eric and Sarah Truel. 2015. "The Symbolic and Substantive Representation of LGB Americans in the US House." *Journal of Politics* 77(4): 955–67.

Harrington, Michael. 1962. *The Other America: Poverty in the United States*. New York, NY: Simon & Schuster.

"Hawai'i, nation lose 'a powerful voice'." *Honolulu Observer*. September 29, 2002.

Hawkesworth, Mary. 2003. "Congressional Enactments of Race-Gender: Toward a Theory of Race-Gendered Institutions." *American Political Science Review* 97: 529–50.

Hayes, Thomas. 2012. "Responsiveness in an Era of Inequality: The Case of the U.S. Senate." *Political Research Quarterly* 66(3): 585–99.

Haynie, Kerry. 2005. "African Americans and the New Politics of Inclusion: A Representational Dilemma?" In *Congress Reconsidered*, eds. Lawrence Dodd and Bruce Oppenheimer. Washington, DC: CQ Press, 395–410.

2001. *African American Legislators in the American States*. New York, NY: Columbia University Press.

Henneberger, Melinda. 2013. "Bob Dole honored for work in helping to feed the poor." *Washington Post*. December 12, 2013.

Herszenhorn, David M. 2007. "A.F. Hawkins, Civil Rights Lawmaker, Dies at 100." *New York Times*. November 14, 2007.

Hibbing, John and David Marsh. 1987. "Accounting for the Voting Patterns of British MPs on Free Votes." *Legislative Studies Quarterly* 12: 275–97.

Highton, Benjamin and Michael Rocca. 2005. "Beyond the Roll-Call Arena: The Determinants of Position Taking in Congress." *Political Research Quarterly* 58(2): 303–16.

Hill, Kim Quaile and Patricia Hurley. 2003. "Beyond the Demand-Input Model: A Theory of Representational Linkages." *Journal of Politics* 65(2): 304–26.

Hill, Kim Quaile, Soren Jordan, and Patricia Hurley. 2015. *Representation in Congress: A Unified Theory*. New York, NY: Cambridge University Press.

Hochschild, Jennifer. 1995. *Facing Up to the American Dream: Race, Class, and the Soul of the Nation*. Princeton, NJ: Princeton University Press.

1981. *What's Fair? American Beliefs about Distributive Justice.* Cambridge, MA: Harvard University Press.

Hoffman, Donna and Alison Howard. 2006. *Addressing the State of the Union: The Evolution and Impact of the President's Big Speech.* Boulder, CO: Lynne Rienner Publishers.

Hojnacki, Marie. 1997. "Interest Groups' Decisions to Join Alliances or Work Alone." *American Journal of Political Science* 41(1): 61–87.

Hokayem, Charles, and Misty L. Heggeness. 2014. "Living in Near Poverty in the United States: 1966–2012." *Current Population Reports* (May). Washington, DC: US Census Bureau.

Holian, David, Timothy Krebs, and Michael Walsh. 1997. "Constituency Opinion, Ross Perot, and Roll-Call Behavior in the U.S. House: The Case of the NAFTA." *Legislative Studies Quarterly* 22(3): 369–92.

Howell, William, Scott Adler, Charles Cameron, and Charles Riemann. 2000. "Divided Government and the Legislative Productivity of Congress, 1945–1994." *Legislative Studies Quarterly* 25: 285–312.

Hula, Kevin W. 1999. *Lobbying Together: Interest Group Coalitions in Legislative Politics.* Washington, DC: Georgetown University Press.

Hussey, Wesley and John Zaller. 2011. "Who Do Parties Represent?" In *Who Gets Represented?*, eds. Peter Enns and Christopher Wlezien. New York, NY: Russell Sage Foundation, 311–44.

Hutchings, Vincent. 1998. "Issue Salience and Support for Civil Rights Legislation Among Southern Democrats." *Legislative Studies Quarterly* 23(4): 521–44.

Hutchings, Vincent, Harwood McClerking, and Guy Uriel Charles. 2004. "Congressional Representation of Black Interests: Recognizing the Importance of Stability." *Journal of Politics* 66: 450–68.

Iceland, John. 2006. *Poverty in America: A Handbook (2nd Edition).* Berkeley, CA: University of California Press.

Imig, Douglas. 1996. *Poverty and Power: The Political Representation of Poor Americans.* Lincoln, NE: University of Nebraska Press.

Jacobs, Lawrence and Benjamin Page. 2005. "Who Influences Foreign Policy?" *American Political Science Review* 99(1): 107–23.

Jacobs, Lawrence and Joe Soss. 2010. "The Politics of Inequality in America: A Political Economy Framework." *Annual Review of Political Science* 13: 341–64.

Jacobs, Lawrence and Robert Y. Shapiro. 2005. "Polling Politics, Media, and Election Campaigns." *Public Opinion Quarterly* 69(5): 635–41.

Jacobs, Lawrence and Theda Skocpol. 2005. *Inequality and American Democracy: What We Know and What We Need to Learn.* New York, NY: Russell Sage.

Jacobson, Gary. 2004. *The Politics of Congressional Elections (6th Edition).* New York, NY: Longman.

1987. *The Politics of Congressional Elections (2nd Edition).* Boston, MA: Little, Brown and Company.

Jargowsky, Paul. 1997. *Poverty and Place: Ghettos, Barrios, and the American City.* New York, NY: Russell Sage Foundation.

Jennings, James. 1994. *Understanding the Nature of Poverty in Urban America.* Westport, CT: Praeger Publishers.

Jones, Bryan D. 2001. *Politics and the Architecture of Choice: Bounded Rationality and Governance.* Chicago, IL: University of Chicago Press.

Jones, Bryan D. and Frank R. Baumgartner. 2005. *The Politics of Attention: How Government Prioritizes Problems.* Chicago, IL: University of Chicago Press.

Kane, Paul. 2016. "Rep. Tim Ryan launches long-shot challenge to Pelosi as Democrats struggle with postelection strategy." *Washington Post.* November 17, 2016.

Karol, David. 2009. *Party Position Change in American Politics: Coalition Management.* New York, NY: Cambridge University Press.

Kastellac, John, Jeffrey Lax, and Justin Phillips. 2010. "Public Opinion and Senate Confirmation of Supreme Court Nominees." *Journal of Politics* 72(2): 767–84.

Kathlene, Lyn. 1994. "Power and Influence in State Legislative Policymaking: The Interaction of Gender and Position in Committee Hearing Debates." *American Political Science Association* 88(3): 560–76.

Katznelson, Ira. 2006. *When Affirmative Action Was White: An Untold History of Racial Inequality in Twentieth-Century America.* New York, NY: W.W. Norton.

Katznelson, Ira and Margaret Weir. 1988. *Schooling for All: Class, Race, and the Decline of the Democratic Ideal.* Berkeley, CA: University of California Press.

Keefe, Linda. 2010. "Dwight MacDonald and Poverty Discourse, 1960–1965: The Art and Power of a Seminal Book Review." *Poverty and Public Policy* 2(2): 145–88.

Kelly, Nathan. 2009. *The Politics of Income Inequality in the United States.* New York, NY: Cambridge University Press.

Kelly, Nathan and Christopher Witko. 2012. "Federalism and American Inequality." *Journal of Politics* 74(2): 414–26.

Key, V.O. 1966. *The Responsible Electorate: Rationality in Presidential Voting 1936–1960.* Cambridge, MA: Harvard University Press.

Killian, Mitchell, Ryan Schoen, and Aaron Dusso. 2008. "Keeping Up with the Joneses: The Interplay of Personal and Collective Evaluations in Voter Turnout." *Political Behavior* 30(3): 323–40.

Kinder, Donald R. and Lynn M. Sanders. 1996. *Divided by Color: Racial Politics and Democratic Ideals.* Chicago, IL: University of Chicago Press.

Kinder, Donald R. and Nicholas Winter. 2001. "Exploring the Racial Divide: Blacks, Whites, and Opinion on National Policy." *American Journal of Political Science* 45(2): 439–56.

Kinder, Donald R. and D. Roderick Kiewiet. 1981. "Sociotropic Politics: The American Case." *British Journal of Political Science* 11(2): 129–61.

1979. "Economic Discontent and Political Behavior: The Role of Personal Grievances and Collective Economic Judgments in Congressional Voting." *American Journal of Political Science* 23(3): 495–527.

Kingdon, John W. 1989. *Congressmen's Voting Decisions (3rd Edition).* Ann Arbor, MI: University of Michigan Press.

1984. *Agendas, Alternatives, and Public Policies.* New York, NY: Longman.

1973. *Congressmen's Voting Decisions*. New York, NY: Harper & Row.

Kirzinger, Ashley, Bianca DiJulio, Liz Hamel, Bryan Wu, and Mollyann Brodie. 2017. "Kaiser Health Tracking Poll – September 2017: What's Next for Health Care?" *The Henry J. Kaiser Family Foundation*. September 22, 2017.

Kneebone, Elizabeth. 2014. "The Growth and Spread of Concentrated Poverty, 2000 to 2008–2012." *Metropolitan Opportunity Series*. Washington, DC: The Brookings Institution. July 31, 2014.

Kneebone, Elizabeth and Alan Berube. 2013. *Confronting Suburban Poverty in America*. Washington, DC: Brookings Institution.

Kneebone, Elizabeth and Emily Garr. 2010. *The Suburbanization of Poverty: Trends in Metropolitan America, 2000 to 2008*. Washington, DC: Brookings Institution.

Koger, Gregory. 2003. "Position Taking and Cosponsorship in the U.S. House." *Legislative Studies Quarterly* 28(2): 225–46.

Krehbiel, Keith. 1991. *Information and Legislative Organization*. Ann Arbor, MI: University of Michigan Press.

1990. "Are Congressional Committees Composed of Preference Outliers?" *American Political Science Review* 84(1): 149–63.

Krimmel, Katherine, Jeffrey Lax, and Justin Phillips. 2016. "Gay Rights in Congress: Public Opinion and (Mis)representation." *Public Opinion Quarterly* 80(4): 888–913.

Krutz, Glen S. 2005. "Issues and Institutions: "Winnowing" in the U.S. Congress." *American Journal of Political Science* 49(2): 313–26.

Kurtzleben, Danielle. 2017. "Here's How GOP's Tax Breaks Would Shift Money to Rich, Poor Americans." *National Public Radio (online)*. November 14, 2017.

Lapinski, John. 2008. "Policy Substance and Performance in American Lawmaking, 1877–1994." *American Journal of Political Science* 52(2): 235–51.

Lax, Jeffrey and Justin Phillips. 2009. "How Should We Estimate Public Opinion in the States?" *American Journal of Political Science* 53(1): 107–21.

Lazarus, Jeffrey. 2013. "Issue Salience and Bill Introduction in the House and Senate." *Congress and the Presidency* 40(3): 215–29.

Lee, Frances E. 2016. *Insecure Majorities: Congress and the Perpetual Campaign*. Chicago, IL: University of Chicago Press.

2009. *Beyond Ideology*. Chicago, IL: University of Chicago Press.

2004. "Bicameral Institutions and Geographic Politics: Allocating Federal Funds for Transportation in the House and Senate." *Legislative Studies Quarterly* 24(2): 185–214.

2003. "Geographic Politics in the U.S. House of Representatives: Coalition Building and Distribution of Benefits." *American Journal of Political Science* 47(4): 713–27.

1998. "Representation and Public Policy: The Consequences of Senate Apportionment for the Geographic Distribution of Federal Funds." *Journal of Politics* 60(1): 34–62.

Lepore, Jill. 2012. "How a New Yorker Article Launched the First Shot in the War Against Poverty." *Smithsonian Magazine*. September 2012.

Lin, Ann Chih and David Harris, eds. 2008. *The Colors of Poverty: Why Racial and Ethnic Disparities Persist*. New York, NY: Russell Sage Foundation.

Lindblom, Charles E. and Edward J. Woodhouse. 1993. *The Policy Making Process (3rd Edition)*. Upper Saddle Hill, NJ: Prentice Hall.

Lomax-Cook, Fay and Edith Barrett. 1992. *Support for the American Welfare State*. New York, NY: Columbia University Press.

Long, Heather. 2016. "U.S. inequality keeps getting uglier." *CNN/Money* (online). December 22, 2016.

Lovett, John, Shaun Bevan, and Frank R. Baumgartner. 2014. "Popular Presidents Can Affect Congressional Attention, for a Little While." *Policy Studies Journal* 43(1): 22–43.

Lublin, David. 1997a. *The Paradox of Representation: Racial Gerrymandering and Minority Interests in Congress*. Princeton, NJ: Princeton University Press.

 1997b. "Congressional District Demographic and Political Data, 1972–1994." American University, Washington DC.

Macartney, Suzanne, Alemayehu Bishaw, and Kayla Fontenot. 2013. *Poverty Rates for Selected Detailed Race and Hispanic Groups by State and Place, 2007–2011*. Washington, DC: U.S. Census Bureau.

MacDonald, Dwight. 1963. "Our Invisible Poor." *The New Yorker*. January 19, 1963.

MacDonald, Jason and Robert McGrath. 2016. "Retrospective Congressional Oversight and the Dynamics of Legislative Influence Over the Bureaucracy." *Legislative Studies Quarterly* 41(4): 899–934.

Maisel, L. Sandy. 1993. "The Platform-Writing Process: Candidate-Centered Platforms in 1992." *Political Science Quarterly* 108(4): 671–98.

Malter, Jordan. 2015. "Why poor people still aren't voting." *CNN (online)*. August 5, 2015.

Mansbridge, Jane. 2011. "Clarifying the Concept of Representation." *American Political Science Review* 105(3): 621–30.

 2003. "Rethinking Representation." *American Political Science Review* 97(4): 515–28.

 1999. "Should Blacks Represent Blacks and Women Represent Women? A Contingent 'Yes'." *Journal of Politics* 61(3): 627–57.

Massey, Douglas S. and Nancy A. Denton. 1993. *American Apartheid: Segregation and the Making of the Underclass*. Cambridge, MA: Harvard University Press.

Mayhew, David. 1991. *Divided We Govern*. New Haven, CT: Yale University Press.

 1974. *Congress: The Electoral Connection*. New Haven, CT: Yale University Press.

McCall, Leslie. 2013. *The Undeserving Rich: American Beliefs about Inequality, Opportunity, and Redistribution*. Cambridge, UK: Cambridge University Press.

McCarty, Nolan, Keith Poole, and Howard Rosenthal. 2013. *Political Bubbles: Financial Crises and the Failure of American Democracy*. Princeton, NJ: Princeton University Press.

2006. *Polarized America: The Dance of Political Ideology and Unequal Riches.* Cambridge, MA: MIT Press.

McGillivray, Fiona. 2004. *Privileging Industry: The Comparative Politics of Trade and Industrial Policy.* Princeton, NJ: Princeton University Press.

1997. "Party Discipline as a Determinant of the Endogenous Formation of Tariffs." *American Journal of Political Science* 41(2): 584–607.

Mettler, Suzanne. 2014. *Degrees of Inequality: How the Politics of Higher Education Sabotaged the American Dream.* New York, NY: Basic Books.

2011. *The Submerged State: How Invisible Government Policies Undermine American Democracy.* Chicago, IL: University of Chicago Press.

2005. *Soldiers to Citizens: The G.I. Bill and the Making of the Greatest Generation.* New York, NY: Oxford University Press.

1998. *Dividing Citizens: Gender and Federalism in New Deal Public Policy.* Ithaca, NY: Cornell University Press.

Mian, Atif and Amir Sufi. 2015. *House of Debt.* Chicago, IL: University of Chicago Press.

Miler, Kristina C. 2016. "Legislative Responsiveness to Constituency Change." *American Politics Research* 44: 794–815.

2011. "The Constituency Motivations of Caucus Membership." *American Politics Research* 39: 859–84.

2010. *Constituency Representation in Congress: The View from Capitol Hill.* New York, NY: Cambridge University Press.

2007. "The View from the Hill: Legislative Perceptions of Constituents." *Legislative Studies Quarterly* 33(4): 597–628.

Miler, Kristina C. and Katti McNally. 2016. "Whose Issues? Congressional Representation of the Poor vs. the Rich." Paper presented at the Annual Meeting of the Midwest Political Science Association, Chicago, IL, April 7–10, 2016.

Mill, John Stuart. 1861. Considerations on Representative Government.

Miller, Warren and Donald Stokes. 1963. "Constituency Influence in Congress." *American Political Science Review* 57(1): 45–56.

Minta, Michael. 2011. *Oversight: Representing the Interests of Blacks and Latinos in Congress.* Princeton, NJ: Princeton University Press.

2009. "Legislative Oversight and the Substantive Representation of Black and Latino Interests in Congress." *Legislative Studies Quarterly* 34(2): 193–218.

Morgen, Sandra and Jeff Maskovsky. 2003. "The Anthropology of Welfare 'Reform': New Perspectives on U.S. Urban Poverty in the Post-Welfare Era." *Annual Review of Anthropology* 32 (October): 315–38.

Mutz, Diana and Jeffrey Mondak. 1997. "Dimensions of Sociotropic Behavior: Group-Based Judgments of Fairness and Well-Being." *American Journal of Political Science* 41(1): 284–308.

New York Times. 2014. "Exit Polls." November 4, 2014. https://www.nytimes .com/interactive/2014/11/04/us/politics/2014-exit-polls.html?_r=1

Norton, Noelle. 2002. "Transforming Policy from the Inside: Participation in Committee." In *Women Transforming Congress,* ed. Cindy Simon Rosenthal. Norman, OK: University of Oklahoma Press, 316–40.

O'Neill, Tip (with Gary Hymel). 1993. *All Politics is Local and Other Rules of the Game*. Holbrook, MA: Bob Adams, Inc.

Oleszek, Walter J., Mark J. Oleszek, Elizabeth Rybicki, and Bill Heniff Jr. 2016. *Congressional Procedures and the Policy Process*. Washington, DC: CQ Press.

Ornstein, Norman J., Thomas E. Mann, Michael J. Malbin, Andrew Rugg, and Raffaela Wakeman. 2014. *Vital Statistics on Congress*. Washington, DC: Brookings Institution.

Overby, Marvin and Kenneth M. Cosgrove. 1996. "Unintended Consequences? Racial Redistricting and the Representation of Minority Interests." *Journal of Politics* 58(2): 540–50.

Page, Benjamin. 1978. *Choices and Echoes in Presidential Elections: Rational Man and Electoral Democracy*. Chicago, IL: University of Chicago Press.

Page, Benjamin and Lawrence Jacobs. 2009. *Class War*. Chicago, IL: University of Chicago Press.

Page, Benjamin and Robert Y. Shapiro. 1992. *The Rational Public: Fifty Years of Trends in Americans' Policy Preferences*. Chicago, IL: University of Chicago Press.

1983. "Effects of Public Opinion on Policy." *American Political Science Review* 77(1): 175–90.

1982. "Changes in Americans' Policy Preferences, 1935–1979." *Public Opinion Quarterly* 46: 24–42.

Park, David, Andrew Gelman, and Joseph Bafumi. 2004. "Bayesian Multilevel Estimation with Poststratification: State-Level Estimates from National Polls." *Political Analysis* 12(4): 375–85.

Parks, MaryAlice. 2016. "Top Democrats Line up Behind Progressive Keith Ellison for Party Chair." *ABC News (online)*. November 11, 2016.

Pattillo, Mary. 2007. *Black on the Block: The Politics of Race and Class in the City*. Chicago, IL: University of Chicago Press.

Pearson, Kathryn and Eric Schickler. 2009. "Agenda Control, Majority Party Power, and the House Committee on Rules, 1937–52." *Legislative Studies Quarterly* 34(4): 455–91.

Pearson, Kathryn and Logan Dancey. 2011. "Elevating Women's Voices in Congress: Speech Participation in the House of Representatives." *Political Research Quarterly* 64(4): 910–23.

Pelosi, Nancy. 2013. "Providing for Consideration of H.R. 2642, Federal Agriculture Reform and Risk Management Act of 2013." *Congressional Record* 159: 99. (July 11, 2013) p. H4385.

Petrocik, John. 1996. "Issue Ownership in Presidential Elections, with a 1980 Case Study." *American Journal of Political Science* 40(3): 825–50.

Pew Research Center. 2017. "Government Gets Lower Ratings for Handling Health Care, Environment, Disaster Response." December 14, 2017.

2016. "Household Expenditures and Income." March 30, 2016.

2015. "Most Say Government Policies Since Recession Have Done Little to Help Middle Class, Poor." March 4, 2015.

2014. "Most See Inequality Growing, but Partisans Differ over Solutions." January 2014.

212 *Bibliography*

2012. "Fewer, Poorer, Gloomier: The Lost Decade of the Middle Class." August 2012.

Piketty, Thomas. 2014. *Capital in the 21st Century*. Cambridge, MA: Harvard University Press.

Pincus, J.J. 1975. "Pressure Groups and the Pattern of Tariffs." *Journal of Political Economy* 83(4): 757–78.

Pitkin, Hanna F. 1967. *The Concept of Representation*. Berkeley, CA: University of California Press.

Policy Agendas Project at the University of Texas at Austin. 2017. www.comparativeagendas.net.

Polsby, Nelson W. 1968. "The Institutionalization of the U.S. House of Representatives." *American Political Science Review* 62(1): 144–68.

Poulton, E.C. 1989. *Bias in Quantifying Judgments*. New York, NY: Taylor & Francis.

Ranney, Austin. 1954. *The Doctrine of Responsible Party Government: Its Origins and the Present State*. Urbana, IL: University of Illinois Press.

Ray, Edward J. 1981. "The Determinants of Tariff and Nontariff Trade Restrictions in the United States." *Journal of Political Economy* 89(1): 105–21.

Reckhow, Sarah and Margaret Weir. 2011. "Building a Stronger Regional Safety Net." *Metropolitan Opportunity Series*. Washington, DC: Brookings Institution.

Reed, Stephen. 2014. "One hundred years of price change: the Consumer Price Index and the American inflation experience." *Monthly Labor Review* (April). U.S. Bureau of Labor Statistics.

Reid, Carolina. 2009. "Addressing the Challenges of Unemployment in Low-Income Communities." *Community Investments* 21(1): 3–7.

Reingold, Beth. 2008. "Women as Office Holders: Linking Descriptive and Substantive Representation." In *Political Women and American Democracy*, eds. Christina Wolbrecht, Karen Beckwith, and Lisa Baldez. New York, NY: Cambridge University Press, 128–47.

2000. *Representing Women: Sex, Gender, and Legislative Behavior in Arizona and California*. Chapel Hill, NC: University of North Carolina Press.

1992. "Concepts of Representation among Female and Male State Legislators." *Legislative Studies Quarterly* 17(4): 509–37.

Rickard, Stephanie J. 2012. "A Non-Tariff Protectionist Bias in Majoritarian Politics: Government Subsidies and Electoral Institutions." *International Studies Quarterly* 56(4): 777–85.

Rigby, Elizabeth and Gerald C. Wright. 2011. "Whose Statehouse Democracy? Policy Responsiveness to Poor Versus Rich Constituents in Poor Versus Rich States." *In Who Gets Represented?*, eds. Peter Enns and Christopher Wlezien. New York, NY: Russell Sage Foundation, 189–222.

Rocca, Michael, Gabriel Sanchez, and Joseph Uscinski. 2008. "Personal Attributes and Latino Voting Behavior in Congress." *Social Science Quarterly* 89(2): 392–405.

Rogers, David. 2012. "Farm bills follow different paths." *Politico*. July 8, 2012.

Rogowski, Ronald. 2002. "Trade and Representation: How Diminishing Geographic Concentration Augments Protectionist Pressures in the US House of

Representatives." In *Shaped by War and Trade: International Influences on American Political Development*, eds Ira Katznelson and Martin Shefter. Princeton, NJ: Princeton University Press, 181–210.

Rohde, David. 1991. *Parties and Leaders in the Post-Reform House*. Chicago, IL: University of Chicago Press.

Rouse, Stella M. 2013. *Latinos in the Legislative Process: Interests and Influence*. New York, NY: Cambridge University Press.

Ryan, Paul. 2016. "Press Release: Ryan Discusses a #BetterWay to Fight Poverty." *Official website of Representative Paul Ryan*. September 7, 2016. https://paulryan.house.gov/news/documentsingle.aspx?DocumentID=398560

Saez, Emmanuel and Gabriel Zucman. 2016. "Wealthy Inequality in the United States since 1913: Evidence from Capitalized Income Tax Data." *Quarterly Journal of Economics* 131(2): 519–78.

Salerno, Lillian. 2016. FY *16–17: Agency Priority Goal, Increasing Assistance for Rural, Persistent Poverty Communities*. Washington, DC: United States Department of Agriculture.

Sanchez, Gabriel R. 2006. "The Role of Group Consciousness in Latino Public Opinion." *Political Research Quarterly* 59(3): 435–46.

Sanchez, Ray. 2016. "Occupy Wall Street: 5 years later." *CNN* online. September 16, 2016. https://www.cnn.com/2016/09/16/us/occupy-wall-street-protest-movements/index.html

Sard, Barbara. 2009. *Number of Homeless Families Climbing Due to Recession*. Washington, DC: Center on Budget and Policy Priorities, January 8, 2009.

Sargent Shriver National Center on Poverty Law. 2007–2014. "Poverty Scorecards."

Saward, Michael. 2010. *The Representative Claim*. New York, NY: Oxford University Press.

Schattschneider, E. E. 1960: *The Semisovereign People*. Hinsdale, IL: Dryden.

Schiller, Wendy. 1999. "Trade Politics in the American Congress: A Study of the Interaction of Political Geography and Interest Group Behavior." *Political Geography* 18(7): 769–89.

1995. "Senators as Political Entrepreneurs: Using Bill Sponsorship to Shape Legislative Agendas." *American Journal of Political Science* 39: 186–203.

Schlozman, Kay Lehman. 2010. "Who Sings in the Heavenly Chorus?: The Shape of the Organized Interest System." In *The Oxford Handbook of American Political Parties and Interest Groups*, eds. L. Sandy Maisel, Jeffrey M. Berry, and George C. Edwards III. New York, NY: Oxford University Press, 425–50.

1984. "What Accent the Heavenly Chorus? Political Equality and the American Pressure System." *Journal of Politics* 46(4): 1006–32.

Schlozman, Kay Lehman and John T. Tierney. 1986. *Organized Interests and American Democracy*. New York, NY: Harper Collins Publishers.

Schlozman, Kay Lehman, Sidney Verba, and Henry Brady. 2012. *The Unheavenly Chorus: Unequal Political Voice and the Broken Promise of American Democracy*. Princeton, NJ: Princeton University Press.

Schwarzer, Marie-Sophie. 2012. "10 Magazine Articles That Shook the World." *The New York Review of Magazines*. May 10, 2012.

Shapiro, Ian and Grant Reeher, eds. 1988. *Power, Inequality, and Democratic Politics: Essays in Honor of Robert A. Dahl*. Boulder, CO: Westview Press.

Shapiro, Robert Y. 2011. "Public Opinion and American Democracy." *Public Opinion Quarterly* 75(5): 982–1017.

Shapiro, Robert Y. and Benjamin I. Page. 1994. "Foreign Policy and Public Opinion." In *The Politics of American Foreign Policy*, ed. David A. Deese. New York, NY: St. Martins, 216–35.

Sharkey, Patrick. 2013. *Stuck in Place: Urban Neighborhoods and the End of Progress Toward Racial Equality*. Chicago, IL: University of Chicago Press.

Shenker-Osorio, Anat. 2013. "Why Americans All Believe They Are 'Middle Class'." *The Atlantic*. August 1, 2013.

Shepsle, Kenneth A. 1978. *The Giant Jigsaw Puzzle: Democratic Committee Assignments in the Modern House*. Chicago, IL: University of Chicago Press.

Sherman, Jennifer. 2009. *Those Who Work, Those Who Don't: Poverty, Morality and Family in Rural America*. Minneapolis, MN: University of Minnesota Press.

Shogan, Colleen. 2001. "Speaking Out: An Analysis of Democratic and Republican Women-Invoked Rhetoric of the 105th Congress." *Women and Politics* 23: 129–46.

Sinclair, Barbara. 2014. *Party Wars: Polarization and the Politics of National Policy Making*. Norman, OK: University of Oklahoma Press.

1995. *Legislators, Leaders, and Lawmaking: The U.S. House of Representatives*. Baltimore, MD: The Johns Hopkins University Press.

1989. *The Transformation of the U.S. Senate*. Baltimore, MD: The Johns Hopkins University Press.

1983. *Majority Leadership in the U.S. House*. Baltimore, MD: The Johns Hopkins University Press.

Skocpol, Theda. 2004. "Voice and Inequality: The Transformation of American Civic Democracy." *Perspectives on Politics* 2(1): 1–18.

1997. "The G.I. Bill and U.S. Social Policy, Past and Future." *Social Philosophy and Policy* 14(2): 95–115.

1995. *Social Policy in the United States: Future Possibilities in Historical Perspective*. Princeton, NJ: Princeton University Press.

1992. *Protecting Soldiers and Mothers: The Political Origins of Social Policy in the United States*. Cambridge, MA: Harvard University Press.

1991. "Targeting within Universalism: Politically Viable Policies to Combat Poverty in the United States." In *The Urban Underclass*, eds. Christopher Jencks and Paul E. Peterson. Washington, DC: Brookings Institution Press, 411–36.

Smith, Steven S. and Christopher J. Deering. 1990. *Committees in Congress (2nd Edition)*. Washington, DC: CQ Press.

Snell, Kelsey and Mike DeBonis. 2016. "Ryan unveils anti-poverty proposal as part of election-year policy agenda." *Washington Post*. June 7, 2016.

Sniderman, Paul M. and Thomas Piazza. 1993. *The Scar of Race*. Cambridge, MA: Harvard University Press.

Soergel, Andrew. 2016. "Long Live the Middle Class." *US News and World Report*. May 20, 2016.

Soroka, Stuart, Erin Penner, and Kelly Blidook. 2009. "Constituency Influence in Parliament." *Canadian Journal of Political Science* 42(3): 563–91.

Soroka, Stuart and Christopher Wlezien. 2010. *Degrees of Democracy*. Cambridge, MA: Cambridge University Press.

2008. "On the Limits to Inequality in Representation." *PS: Political Science and Politics* 41(April): 219–327.

Stimson, James A. 2004. *Tides of Consent: How Public Opinion Shapes American Politics*. New York, NY: Cambridge University Press.

1999. *Public Opinion in America: Moods, Cycles, and Swings (2nd Edition)*. Boulder, CO: Westview Press.

Stimson, James A., Michael B. MacKuen, and Robert S. Erikson. 1995. "Dynamic Representation." *American Political Science Review* 89(3): 543–65.

Stockman, Farrah. 2016. "On Crime Bill and the Clintons, Young Blacks Clash With Their Parents." *New York Times*. April 18, 2016.

Stoll, Michael A. 2008. "Race, Place, and Poverty Revisited." In *The Colors of Poverty: Why Racial and Ethnic Disparities Persist*, eds. Ann Chih Lin and David R. Harris. New York, NY: Russell Sage Foundation, 201–31.

Stonecash, Jeffrey. 2012. "Does Class Matter When Americans Vote?" *Scholars Strategy Network*. January 2012.

2000. *Class and Party in American Politics*. Boulder, CO: Westview Press.

Strolovitch, Dara Z. 2007. *Affirmative Advocacy: Race, Class, and Gender in Interest Group Politics*. Chicago, IL: University of Chicago Press.

2006. "Do Interest Groups Represent the Disadvantaged? Advocacy at the Intersection of Race, Class, and Gender." *Journal of Politics* 68(4): 894–910.

Sulkin, Tracy. 2011. *The Legislative Legacy of Congressional Campaigns*. New York, NY: Cambridge University Press.

2005. *Issue Politics in Congress*. New York, NY: Cambridge University Press.

Swain, Carol. 1993. *Black Faces, Black Interests: The Representation of African Americans in Congress*. Cambridge, MA: Harvard University Press.

Swers, Michele. 2013. *Women in the Club: Gender and Policy Making in the Senate*. Chicago, IL: University of Chicago Press.

2002a. *The Difference Women Make: The Policy Impact of Women in Congress*. Chicago, IL: University of Chicago Press.

2002b. "Transforming the Agenda: Analyzing Gender Differences in Women's Issue Bill Sponsorship." In *Women Transforming Congress*, ed. Cindy Simon Rosenthal. Norman, OK: University of Oklahoma Press, 260–83.

1998. "Are Women More Likely to Vote for Women's Issue Bills Than Their Male Colleagues?" *Legislative Studies Quarterly* 23(3): 435–48.

Swers Michele and Stella Rouse. 2011. "Descriptive Representation: Understanding the Impact of Identity on Substantive Representation of Group Interests." In *The Oxford Handbook of the American Congress*, eds. George C. Edwards III, Frances Lee, and Eric Schickler. New York, NY: Oxford University Press, 241–71.

Tate, Katherine. 2003. *Black Faces in the Mirror: African Americans and Their Representatives in the U.S. Congress*. Princeton, NJ: Princeton University Press.

Tausanovitch, Christopher and Christopher Warshaw. 2013. "Measuring Constituent Policy Preferences in Congress, State Legislatures, and Cities." *Journal of Politics* 75(2): 330–42.

Tavernise, Sabrina. 2012. "Education Gap Grows Between Rich and Poor, Studies Say." *New York Times*. February 9, 2012.

Tetlock, Philip E. 2005. *Expert Political Judgement: How Good is it? How Can We Know?* Princeton, NJ: Princeton University Press.

Theriault, Sean. 2005. *The Power of the People: Congressional Competition, Public Attention, and Voter Retribution*. Columbus, OH: Ohio State University Press.

Thomas, Sue. 1994. *How Women Legislate*. New York, NY: Oxford University Press.

Trefler, Daniel. 1993. "Trade Liberalization and the Theory of Endogenous Protection: An Econometric Study of US Import Policy." *Journal of Political Economy* 101(1): 138–60.

Trescott, Jacqueline. 1990. "The Long Haul of Rep. Gus Hawkins." *Washington Post*. October 24, 1990.

Tversky, Amos and Daniel Kahneman. 1982. "Availability: A Heuristic for Judging Frequency and Probability." In *Judgement Under Uncertainty: Heuristics and Biases*, eds. Daniel Kahneman, Paul Slovic, and Amos Tversky. Cambridge, UK: Cambridge University Press, 163–78.

Ura, Joseph and Christopher Ellis. 2008. "Income, Preferences, and the Dynamics of Policy Responsiveness." *PS: Political Science and Politics* (October): 785–94.

US Census Bureau. 2016. "The Majority of Children Live with Two Parents, Census Bureau Reports." Release Number CB16-192. November 17, 2016. Washington, DC.

US Department of Education, National Center for Education Statistics. 2016. "Digest of Education Statistics (Table 219.75)." Washington, DC.

US Government Printing Office Serial 105–82, Hearings before the Subcommittee on Oversight of the Committee on Ways and Means, House of Representatives, April 23 and May 1, 1997.

"U.S. Rep. Ted Weiss, 64, Dies." *Washington Post*. September 15, 1992.

Volden, Craig and Alan E. Wiseman. 2014. *Legislative Effectiveness in the United States Congress: The Lawmakers*. New York, NY: Cambridge University Press.

Walsh, Katherine Cramer. 2002. "Enlarging Representation: Women Bringing Marginalized Perspectives to Floor Debate in the House of Representatives." In *Women Transforming Congress*, ed. Cindy Simon Rosenthal. Norman, OK: University of Oklahoma Press, 370–98.

Warshaw, Christopher and Jonathan Rodden. 2012. "How Should We Measure District-Level Opinion on Individual Issues?" *Journal of Politics* 74(1): 203–19.

Wawro, Gregory. 2000. *Legislative Entrepreneurship in the U.S. House of Representatives*. Ann Arbor, MI: University of Michigan Press.

Weir, Margaret. 2011. "Creating Justice for the Poor in the New Metropolis." In *Justice and the American Metropolis*, eds. Clarissa Rile Hayward and Todd Swanstrom. Minneapolis, MN: University of Minnesota Press. 237–56.

Weissberg, Robert. 1978. "Collective vs. Dyadic Representation in Congress." *American Political Science Review* 72(June): 535–47.

Welch, Susan and John R. Hibbing. 1984. "Hispanic Representation in the U.S. Congress." *Social Science Quarterly* 65(2): 328–35.

Welsh, Michael. 2008. "An Overview of the Development of U.S. Congressional Committees." Law Librarians; Society of Washington, DC.

Whitby, Kenny. 1997. *The Color of Representation: Congressional Behavior and Black Interests*. Ann Arbor, MI: University of Michigan Press.

   1989. "Measuring Congressional Responsiveness to the Policy Interests of Black Constituents." *Social Science Quarterly* 68: 367–77.

Williams, Melissa S. 1998. *Voice, Trust, and Memory: Marginalized Groups and the Failing of Liberal Representation*. Princeton, NJ: Princeton University Press.

Wilson, William Julius. 1996. *When Work Disappears: The World of the New Urban Poor*. New York, NY: Alfred A. Knopf.

   1987. *The Truly Disadvantaged: The Inner-City, the Underclass, and Public Policy*. Chicago, IL: University of Chicago Press.

Wlezien, Christopher. 1995. "The Public as Thermostat: Dynamics of Preferences for Spending." *American Journal of Political Science* 39(4): 981–1000.

Wlezien, Christopher and Stuart Soroka. 2011. "Inequality in Policy Responsiveness?" In *Who Gets Represented?*, eds. Peter Enns and Christopher Wlezien. New York, NY: Russell Sage Foundation, 285–310.

Wolbrecht, Christina. "American Political Party Platforms: 1948–2008." Policy Agendas Project at the University of Texas at Austin. 2017. www.comparativeagendas.net.

Woolley, John T. and Gerhard Peters. 2017. *The American Presidency Project*. Santa Barbara, CA: University of California.

Woon, Jonathan. 2009. "Issue Attention in the U.S. Senate." *Legislative Studies Quarterly* 34(1): 29–54.

Young, Iris Marion. 2002. *Inclusion and Democracy*. New York, NY: Oxford University Press.

Younge, Gary. 2008. "The Invisible Poor." *The Guardian (online)*. January 23, 2008.

Index